TELLING STORIES OUT OF COURT

Telling Stories out of Court

Narratives about Women and Workplace Discrimination

Edited by Ruth O'Brien
Foreword by Liza Featherstone

ILR Press

AN IMPRINT OF
CORNELL UNIVERSITY PRESS
ITHACA AND LONDON

First published 2008 by Cornell University Press
First printing, Cornell Paperbacks, 2008

Printed in the United States of America

Library of Congress Cataloging-in-Publication Data

Telling stories out of court : narratives about women and workplace discrimination /
edited by Ruth O'Brien ; foreword by Liza Featherstone.
       p.   cm.
   Fictional short stories illustrating the experiences of women who have faced
sexism and discrimination at work, grouped into thematic clusters with interpretive commentary and legal analysis.
   Includes bibliographical references and index.
   ISBN 978-0-8014-4530-9 (cloth : alk. paper)—ISBN 978-0-8014-7357-9 (pbk. :
alk. paper)
   1. Sex discrimination against women—United States.   2. Sex discrimination in
employment—United States.   3. Sexual harassment of women—United
States.   I. O'Brien, Ruth, 1960–   II. Title.

   HD6060.5.U5T45 2008
   331.4'1330973--dc22
                                                                      2008012058

Cornell University Press strives to use environmentally responsible suppliers and
materials to the fullest extent possible in the publishing of its books. Such materials
include vegetable-based, low-VOC inks and acid-free papers that are recycled, totally
chlorine-free, or partly composed of nonwood fibers. For further information, visit
our website at www.cornellpress.cornell.edu.

Cloth printing   10   9   8   7   6   5   4   3   2   1
Paperback printing 10   9   8   7   6   5   4   3   2   1

For Max and Theo for being brave, liberated boys
and for my mother

Contents

FOREWORD

By Liza Featherstone

Law is fundamentally about storytelling. While the narrative delights
of criminal law are prominently featured in television courtroom dramas
(and for *Law and Order* fans, available almost any time of day!) stories
about workplace law are far less celebrated. Yet they are equally compel-
ling and, sadly, relevant to most people's everyday lives. Forty percent of
women say they have faced workplace sex discrimination, and the rate is
much higher for mothers of young children. A survey of blacks and His-
panics in the Boston area found that one in five had experienced racial
discrimination on the job *within the past year.*[1] One of the most deeply felt
motives for bringing a discrimination complaint against an employer—in
addition, of course, to wanting justice, monetary payment, a long-deserved
promotion, or systemic reform—is the desire to be heard, to tell one's story
at last.

Legal scholars agree that while discrimination lawsuits often yield disap-
pointingly little change, one of their greatest potential benefits is the possibility for public storytelling. That is, even when they fail to achieve concrete
institutional change, they get the public to talk about the company's practices, compare notes, and perhaps even discuss their own experiences. A
large-scale lawsuit attracts media attention; the story is told in many different ways. Some versions will be more favorable to one party, others biased
toward another, while some will aspire to journalistic or scholarly neutral-
ity. One thing is certain, though: The employer would prefer silence. And

employers have, over the years, tried hard to stop workers from telling stories—in or out of court.

That silence begins on the job, where most employees do not know that the right to discuss—and compare—wages is legally protected. Many supervisors exploit that ignorance, telling them that discussing wages is "against company rules." That's one reason workers can go for years not knowing that white or male colleagues are getting paid more for doing the same work. Employees also decide, often, that speaking up is simply worth neither the risk of losing their jobs nor the hassle and humiliation. There is also a social taboo in the workplace against complaining too much about unfair treatment; while gossip about a manager's unreasonable demands, annoying personality quirks, or favoritism is nearly always acceptable watercooler chitchat, discussion of discrimination can be seen as divisive and whiny, often threatening. Workers may be silenced by the sense that by invoking discrimination, they are making excuses for their own imperfections as workers, passing the blame for their personal failure to get ahead. Workers also—very often—don't know that organizing, a powerful form of storytelling, is legally protected (indeed, the law is flimsy protection given that one in three employers admits firing people for union activity). Most often, when workers speak out about unfair practices, whether on websites, blogs, or to a member of the news media, they do so anonymously.

One way that companies seek to stop storytelling about discrimination is through legislation aimed at curbing class action lawsuits. But even when workers bring suit, the forum, and listeners, for the story are not assured. Betty Dukes, the lead plaintiff in *Betty Dukes v. Wal-Mart Stores*, the largest sex discrimination class action suit in history, will almost certainly walk away from her case with some money in her pocket.[2] But she longs for, as she puts it, her "day in court," the chance to tell her tale publicly, with a judge and jury to weigh, and finally affirm, its rightness. If her suit ends in a settlement, negotiated dryly by lawyers on BlackBerries and speakerphones, she will probably always feel cheated of that public narrative—and audience. Of course, Wal-Mart—where Betty still works as a greeter—would prefer it that way, as would most companies, and that is why most significant lawsuits end with settlements. These can be deeply emotionally unsatisfying for plaintiffs. One woman who was awarded such a settlement against a health food retailer told me that she still resents not being able to tell her story in a courtroom. She walked away a little bit richer but with her tale untold.

Perhaps one of the most egregious ways in which stories about discrimination are silenced is through settlements with gag orders, in which employees agree not to publicly tell their stories. This has happened in several recent settlements in the financial industry. The women suing Wal-Mart fervently hope they are not asked to stop telling their stories: They know that their stories are all they really have, their most powerful weapons in the battle for real change.

Few of the countless real-life stories of workplace discrimination suffered by men and women everyday are ever told publicly. This book boldly and eloquently rights that wrong, going where no plaintiff testimony could ever dare because these stories are often too raw, honest, ambiguous, and nuanced to be told in court or reported in a newspaper. Consider a high school girl's genuine passion for her much older boss, for example, or a middle-class black woman's ambivalence about hiring a younger black woman coming off of welfare—just a couple of the riveting situations portrayed in this book. Most real-life stories, of course, are also too complex to be fully rendered in a court case or human resource department memo. Fiction is less instrumental than nonfiction. Sometimes, because it does not have to persuade, outrage, or inspire a remedy—though it can do any of those things—fiction can afford to be more truthful. In the past, authors such as David Mamet, purportedly striving for complexity on workplace discrimination, have simply served up backlash and stereotype. The stories in this book do something far more provocative; some inspire us to anger on the workers' behalf, others to uncomfortable, unwelcome feelings. All of them leave us thinking hard.

Acknowledgments

Sharing stories about office politics took a turn when I started attending professional conferences. Around a hotel lobby table, often over a glass of wine, I quickly realized how easily my female colleagues and I fell into swapping stories about a different kind of office politics. We told stories about discrimination that we had experienced or our friends had faced. They shared their stories, and I shared mine. Nodding our heads as we compared events and made observations helped fortify us, giving us stamina and strength. I found these gatherings emotionally energizing. Both the listening and the telling constituted a constructive way of channeling my frustration. It transformed a solitary situation into a shared experience, with the bonus of often forging new friendships. Our stories brought us together.

In this book I invited a whole table of wonderful writers to tell their discrimination stories. These writers, however, do not relay their own stories. Nor do they present stories about the academy. Rather, they write fiction. The fictional stories in *Telling Stories out of Court* directly *and* indirectly reveal what goes into workplace discrimination. I was delighted that Susan Oard Warner, Ellen Dannin, Harriet Kriegel, Aurelie Sheehan, Eileen Pollack, Catherine Lewis, Kristen Iversen, and Alice Elliott Dark contributed provocative and moving pieces of fiction to that end. Calling them up out of the blue, I had no connection to them other than being fans of their fiction. I was also happy that several contributors to *Voices from the Edge: Narratives about the Americans with Disabilities Act*—Chloë

Atkins, Stephen Kuusisto, and Achim Nowak—brought their talents to this project too. All of them offer us the vivid short stories that compose *Telling Stories out of Court*. Being a political scientist, it's a treat to work with "real" writers, or to be generous to my own discipline, I should say those who reach readers outside the academy walls. And of course I extend thanks to Risa Lieberwitz for her four pieces of astute commentary that place the fiction in legal context. Finally, Liza Featherstone graces the book with a foreword.

Had I not met Jim Phelan at a critical juncture *Telling Stories out of Court* might have remained unfinished. Jim gave me that extra intellectual push I needed by putting the project's goal in literary context. Jill Norgren, Nan Marglin-Bauer, and David Schlesinger provided insightful criticism about the introduction. The reviewers for Cornell University Press provided constructive criticism about the project in its entirety. I greatly appreciate how Judith Baer, Amy Bridges, Joyce Gelb, Judith Grant, Eileen McDonagh, Karen Orren, Frances Fox Piven, and Gretchen Ritter have been wonderful mentors and/or role models, some of whom have been encouraging me for some time to get more involved in gender issues. Martha Fineman and Brigitta van Rheinberg remain great sources of inspiration and support.

Thanks is also extended to my supportive friends and colleagues at the City University of New York Graduate Center, including Tom Halper, Jack Jacobs, Jessica Landis, Tom Weiss, and Richard Wolin. Bill Kelly generously afforded me the time and a new position at the Graduate Center, without which it would have been difficult to complete the project in a timely fashion.

Fran Benson of Cornell University Press was the kind of editor every academic dreams about. From the beginning her enthusiasm and encouragement as well as her critical insight made this a better book.

Lastly I owe great thanks to the following friends who regularly heard about the project's different stages: Martha Campbell, Mark Juarez, Susan Martin-Marquez, and Marta Lauritsen. Cate Du Pron, Linda Findley, Virginia Haufler, Mark Hillary, Carol Hutchins, Corey Lin, Brad MacDonald, Patricia Mainardi, Jeanette Money, Barbara Pfetsch, Rouba Abel Malek Rached, Nancy Solomon, Arlene Stein, Lisa and Slawek Wojotowicz, and Shona Wray. Tara Auciello should also be thanked for making my family life work without too much interference.

Editing the project in a difficult but very poignant and productive year made me realize how precious and precarious the work/family balance can be. It helped me cope with the death of my mother the year I faced the same circumstances that shaped her rich and full life. It is to my mother and my two sons that I dedicate this book.

TELLING STORIES OUT OF COURT

Women's Work

Writing Politics, Sharing Stories

Ruth O'Brien

It is the aim of *Telling Stories out of Court* to reach readers on both an intellectual and an emotional level, helping them think, feel, and share the experiences of women who have faced sexism and discrimination at work. It focuses on how the federal courts interpreted Title VII—the seventh chapter—of the Civil Rights Act of 1964.[1] To do so, this book uses fiction. Short stories offer readers insights that pedantic law texts cannot. These stories help us concentrate on the emotional content of the experience with less emphasis on the particulars of the law. But this is not to say the fiction is free-floating. Grouped into thematic clusters, the narratives are combined with interpretive commentary and legal analysis that anchors the book. It is the commentary and legal analysis that reveals the impact this revolutionary law had on women in the workplace.

In 1963, a year before Congress passed the Civil Rights Act, Betty Friedan published *The Feminine Mystique,* emboldening American middle-class women by chasing away their malaise and raising their consciousness. Describing "the problem that has no name," Friedan captured the cultural and economic traps middle-class women encountered.[2] This volume drew attention to the discrimination women experienced in all facets of their lives and helped initiate the second wave of the women's movement. Friedan, along with other feminists, changed women's outlook about sexism, whereas Title VII of the Civil Rights Act changed the law. Women could now address and redress sex discrimination that occurred at work. Under Title VII, women could marry their new feminist aspirations to the realization of a freer and less discriminatory workplace.

The successes of the women's movement and the protection afforded by this civil rights law freed women of my generation from worry about discrimination in college, graduate school, and the workplace. Taking my first job in 1991, I did not doubt that a career commensurate with my talent could be within my grasp. But this did not mean that I had read *The Feminine Mystique*. Nor did it mean that I had followed the many developmental twists in federal civil rights law. To the rightful consternation of some of my senior female colleagues, what the women's movement had accomplished was what I took for granted. Like many women in my generation, I was overconfident, assuming discrimination had been defeated.

The politics, the internal struggles, and the import of the women's movement's successes sadly had been lost on me. Too late, I realized that National Organization of Women (NOW), an organization Friedan founded in 1966, had a platform that was breathtaking in its scope and vision. Demanding that Title VII be fully enforced, NOW also protested the lack of community child care centers, sought a federal tax deduction for the housekeeping and child care expenses of working parents, and advocated for more equitable divorce laws.[3]

Fairly soon into my career, I confronted most of these issues. Indeed, professional women my age and much younger are writing about their daily struggles with day care, the expense of housekeeping, the guilt associated with paying other women less than they deserve for doing what many men still see as "our" jobs, and the consequences of the poorly constructed, albeit well-intended, divorce law reforms.[4] We combat sexism daily. But having not taken the women's movement's efforts and accomplishments for granted I, and probably many women of my generation, might have gotten involved earlier in overcoming these long-lasting hurdles. Just think what our professional and personal lives would look like had more of NOW's initial platform been achieved?

To be sure, the women's movement did make big strides over the last few decades. Reproductive groups maintained their vibrancy.[5] Hard-fought legislation outlawing violence against women passed in 1989.[6] And the 1992 Family Medical Leave Act got many employers to reconsider their pregnancy leave plans, permitting more women to have children or to care for a sick parent without losing their jobs.[7] Despite all these gains, however, the record of what the women's movement fought for and accomplished, particularly given the Republican Party's snowballing strength starting in the 1980s, is checkered.

Hence, the impetus behind *Telling Stories out of Court* is the hope that my generation and the generation coming up behind us share the vision that NOW first articulated. Figuring out how to convey this message about women's experience, moreover, is critical. Given the uneven record, how can we gauge and express whether our private and public life glasses are half-empty or half-full?

Volumes upon volumes have been written about the Civil Rights Act. Lawyers, historians, and political scientists have studied, interpreted, and analyzed ever facet of this momentous piece of legislation, particularly its impact on racism. Yet, reading about someone's experience in narrative form offers a different vantage point than that provided by a social science monograph or data and statistics.[8] Fiction resonates.

Suggesting that we can learn by reading fiction is not to say that real stories about sex discrimination offer little insight.[9] To be sure, they make for good drama. In *Tales from the Boom Boom Room,* journalist Susan Antilla covers women fighting and winning their sexual harassment suit against "Wall Street."[10] Charlize Theron, an Oscar-winning film star, played the Minnesotan miner who led the first class-action sexual harassment suit in the film *North Country*. These "real" stories, however, are bound by their history. Storytellers and critics alike often focus on facts rather than the essence of the story.

This book is different. Not constrained by the facts, it concentrates on the everyday essence of discrimination. *Telling Stories out of Court* gives readers the opportunity to think about discrimination and ponder how it feels to face it.[11] Indeed, scholars in the field of philosophy and literature have long observed that simply having a narrative creates a means of examining philosophical issues. An author can create characters that embody philosophical ideals. Then, when readers imagine these characters, they explore these same ideals, albeit through their own subjective lens.

Some narratives can go so far as to raise thought-experiments; that is, readers explore characters' motives, observe their actions, and then watch how it all unfolds. A thought-experiment is the creation of a "what if" scenario or a hypothetical. But unlike the legal hypothetical that asks students to plug in different facts and circumstances and then determine a new outcome in the courtroom, the narratives in this book make the legal facts constant and ask readers to explore more a thought-experiment based on a "what happens" in the story as a result of discriminating behavior. What compels someone to practice discriminatory behavior? Is it ignorance or fear? Perhaps the behavior is motivated by an employer's desire to maintain power or a colleague's quest for power? Is discrimination induced by society, nature, or a bit of both? Is it part of the human condition?

The hypotheticals in this book also constitute how-does-it-feel-experiments. How would it feel to be discriminated against given the circumstances of the story? Would it limit someone's potential? Would this type of adversity make her stronger? Does someone's discriminating behavior provoke a protagonist's anger? Should it? Or does it deflate, dampen, or limit her energy or the skill she could put into a job? Can discrimination be so subtle that readers wonder if a character understands how debilitating it is? Can a protagonist help engender her own discrimination? Can she participate in her own exploitation? Literature is a branch of aesthetics that provokes philosophical reflection in terms of experiments about thought and feelings.

Fiction captures vivid ideals and images. To place these ideals and images in a wider context, each of the four parts ends with a commentary. Disconnecting the law from the stories not only gives creative writers more room to bring their characters to life but also permits the scholar the means to cover legal questions systematically. The commentary gives readers the chance to explore how the stories mirror typical sex discrimination cases as a means of supplementing the what-happens and how-do-we-feel hypothetical terrain.

The commentary that follows each story cluster pulls out legal themes from the stories and weaves together threads that embody the federal courts' interpretation of Title VII. Each covers a broad range of issues, from an explanation of gender roles to the growth of sexual harassment lawsuits; from the addition in 1991 of punitive damages paid to victims of discrimination to the apparent limits on the law to eliminate the continuing problem of sex discrimination.

While the stories reveal the full gamut of emotions involved in discrimination, the events in themselves may not be enough to prove discrimination. The commentary also points out what is missing from the stories, such as an overt statement from an employer explaining why he discriminated against a female employee. The federal courts created and rely on legal precedents that do not always capture discriminating behavior. Sometimes what is missing, such as employers not stating the intent underlying their discriminatory actions, can be more debilitating than the evidence of discriminatory conduct. As a result, a person faced with discrimination to never seek relief or to drop it because it is too difficult to prove. The absence too is instructive in that it shows how ill-equipped Title VII is to successfully handle discrimination.

Overall, the commentaries use the fiction liberally—exploring the questions raised and not raised by the characters in a specific setting—drawing out and illustrating specific points within the federal courts' interpretation of Title VII. The commentaries often ask—and respond to—questions: Would the women in these stories have a legal claim under Title VII? If so, how would they go about proving that sex discrimination occurred? If not, what is missing: Is there simply a lack of evidence or does the law not remedy the real problems of everyday gender inequality?

While the commentary offers a broad legal perspective, showing how these stories are typical or representative of charges of discrimination in the federal courts, it is the stories themselves that build the book's structure. The stories are the heart of the book, not flesh on the legal commentaries' bones. The commentary is consciously placed behind the narratives to cast these different kinds of hypothetical and legal shadows rather than to set a foreground. Only after readers identify with a protagonist can they understand the what-happens, how-does-it-feel perspectives. Only after identifying with the protagonist should readers know whether her case would be actionable in a court of law or if she would be disappointed by Title VII's reach. The stories can be read as thought and feeling experiments as well as illustrative of the law or illustrative of what is needed to succeed in a case under Title VII law. Fact follows fiction.

What differentiates this book from that of critical race storytellers, such as Derrick Bell and Patricia Williams, is how it separates fact from fiction, leaving room for many different kinds of interpretation.[12] Little discussion, let alone analysis, of the Civil Rights Act appears in the stories. Setting the narratives apart from the commentary gives readers room to relate to the characters without being distracted by the law. This separation affords the storytellers more space or creative license, freeing them from the artifice of the law.[13] What is more, most of the writers are fiction or short story writers and the commentary is drafted by a legal scholar.

Another reason for separating fiction from fact is aesthetic. Message-driven fiction is simply bad fiction. A "good story only rarely sets out to change the world," writes feminist legal theorist Kathryn Abrams. "[W]e are wont to call literature 'didactic' when an author lets his or her normative framework show."[14] Meanwhile, commentary that lacks rigor could make readers feel manipulated or intellectually out of control. Are they getting a full picture about civil rights law? Separating the stories from the commentary ensures that a reader's reaction to the fiction is not confused with her response to the federal courts' interpretation of Title VII. Whereas a story is aesthetic—it either rings true or false or is authentic; legal commentary can be taken apart logically. The commentary constituted one interpretation, not the only interpretation, of the federal courts' development of employment law.

Finally, highlighting fiction can be subversive. Fiction brings "moral conflict to the forefront."[15] Stories, therefore, have the capacity to inspire collective action, whereas legal interpretations of statutes rarely do.[16] As experiential storyteller Nan Bauer-Maglin explains, "in the 1970s, women turned what they did in private (talking to each other) into something political (consciousness-raising): by telling stories, what is private becomes understood in social context."[17]

Similarly, the stories in the book were solicited for the express purpose of "writing politics"; that is, to seek normative change or reform as all legal scholarship is expected to do. As a result, the book's short story authors created scenes that will evoke an emotional response from readers. Only after experiencing this response do readers seek a legal explanation in the commentary. The book therefore replicates the legal process in that women first encounter the discrimination and then second seek legal counsel about whether the discrimination is actionable.

What if a protaganist's emotional needs are greater than the potential legal response? Such a disjunction between the stories and the legal commentary may provoke an even greater response from readers if the protagonist's emotional needs are greater than the potential legal response. The stories recount how women feel facing discrimination, whereas the federal courts' interpretation of the law, which does not necessarily offer them relief, may provoke a reader to feel frustration, anger, or outrage. The injustice of the discrimination coupled with the unfairness of the federal courts' interpretation may raise readers' consciousness about the judiciary's bias against women and people of color. If narratives motivate enough readers to find their voice, these voices could turn into a chorus for legal reform or, at the very least, address the need for it.[18]

Telling Stories out of Court embraces an ethical or moral point of view. Relying on a branch of narrative theory in literature that rejects universal truths, the book embodies an antidiscrimination set of ethics or morals. What is the difference between writing that espouses a moral point of view and message-driven fiction? As novelist Anne Lamott writes,

> The word moral has such bad associations: with fundamentalism, stiff-necked preachers, priggishness. . . . We have to get past that. If your deepest beliefs drive your writing, they will not only keep your work from being contrived but will help you discover what drives your characters. You may find some really good people beneath the packaging and posing—people whom we, your readers, we like, whose company we rejoice in. . . . So a moral position is not a message. A moral position is a passionate caring inside you . . . A moral position is not a slogan, or wishful thinking. It doesn't come from outside or above. It begins inside the heart of a character and grows from there.[19]

The narratives in this book contain an antidiscrimination message—a message that is buried in it like a piece of sand ingested by an oyster that produces a pearl.[20] The pearl's value, its beauty, comes from the fact that it is not just rare but also natural or organic. A story must be authentic to speak to a reader.

The Facts

American women work. Poor and working-class women have always worked. By the 1970s, it was middle-class women who began entering the workforce in large numbers. Today, 72 percent of women work who are raising children under age eighteen. If the children are under six, this number drops to 65 percent; if they are infants, the number falls more, dropping to 57 percent of women working.[21]

As more women entered the workforce in the 1970s, society shifted. Some adjustments were easy, though perhaps bittersweet. Rather than a wife's earnings being compiled to her husband's healthy earnings, the primary reason the per capita medium household income has not dropped and that there has not been more discontent about the U.S. economy since the 1970s, many economists argue, is because most women work.[22] Put differently, the medium family income would have dropped had women not entered the workforce in such large numbers. Indeed, the gender pay gap itself has narrowed from 31 to 12 points because men make less than they did thirty years ago. It's not that women make much more. Sixty percent of this gain is attributed to a real decline in men's earnings rather than to a rise in women's wages.[23] It is family income that is more.

While pay inequity persists, with women making seventy-seven cents to a man's dollar, the educational gap between the sexes does not.[24] The gap has, dramatically, all but closed. Women now make up 60 percent of all college undergraduates, and half of the undergraduate science majors and more than one-third of the engineering majors are women.[25] Ironically, while former Harvard President Larry Summers argued that "intrinsic aptitude" was a factor in the scarcity of women in the highest ranks of science and engineering, the *Wall Street Journal* ran an article showing that girls are closing the gender gap and pulling ahead of boys in math.[26]

Women not only dominate undergraduate programs, but they constitute two-thirds of those in graduate journalism programs and half of those earning degrees in medicine and law. The numbers are similarly rising in traditionally male disciplines such as biology and mathematics.[27] There is "ample evidence that any performance gap between men and women is changeable and is shrinking to the vanishing point."[28] Clearly, women have caught up in education. But promotions still elude many women given the persistence of glass ceilings. Only 17 percent of women in law firms become partners, though they have been receiving law degrees at about the same rate as men for more than twenty years.[29]

Curiously, education no longer matters as much as it once did in narrowing the gender wage gap. In fact, professional women make less than their nonprofessional counterparts vis-à-vis men. The median income for a woman who worked full time in 2004 was 76 percent of their male counterparts, whereas professional women received 3 percent less than this.[30] There are a few exceptions that seem promising, most notably a study revealing a salary gap in favor of young women working in New York City and Dallas.[31]

Women, however, remain burdened with what sociologist Arlie Hochshild calls the "second shift," meaning doing the housework and being the children's primary caregiver. In the late 1990s, women still do the majority of their family's child care and household duties.[32] Meanwhile, in the countries with national child care, more mothers work, the gap between men's and women's wages is smaller, and there are lower poverty rates among single mothers.[33] A World Economic Forum study placed the United States seventeenth out of fifty-eight nations in measuring the gender gap, finding that little economic opportunity exists for U.S. women.[34] None of the countries in similar standing were industrialized. Lesotho, Swaziland, and Papua New Guinea joined the United States in lagging far behind other nations given the wage inequalities in the private sector, the lack of paid childbirth leave, and little state-sponsored child care.

Family life imposes enormous costs on most women, including lower incomes and higher risks of poverty than men or women without children. Even more than sex discrimination, this "mommy tax," as author Ann Crittenden calls it, exposes women to higher risks of poverty in old age or in the event of divorce. But sex discrimination and the mommy tax are one in the same. Some of the women who cannot afford to work and care for children do drop out of the workforce given how little flexibility there is in the workplace.[35]

Rather than making this a personal or individual choice—a battle between husband and wife, or a contest between mother and child—the state needs to step up. As Crittenden argues, "feminism needs a fresh strategy." After thirty years of liberation, most women continue to do nearly all the parenting work. Instead of making change happen on a personal, household-by-household level, structural changes should occur in law and society.

The European nation-states give families more child care services than anywhere else in the world.[36] But laws only go so far. Faced with balancing a career and children, European women are having fewer children. In Italy, where the birth rate is the second lowest in the world, women do not have more children, a professor of statistics found, largely because of how few of their husbands help out with housekeeping and child rearing. Only 6 percent of Italian men "always" or "often" do household chores. "Many women cannot face the dual burden of going out to work," as one article explains, "and looking after an extra child. They have to give up one of those two options: they usually decide to sacrifice the extra child."[37] Italy was no exception. Social science studies reveal the same juggling act in other industrialized European nations.[38]

Meanwhile, U.S. laws have not gone as far as those in the European nation-states.[39] The absence of a strong welfare state makes life harder for all employees, not just women. New public policies and laws protecting women, in particular, and the family, in general, are needed. A 2004 Bureau of Labor report showed that 89 million of the 122 million employees in the private workforce have less than seven days of paid sick leave that they can use to take care of sick children, spouses, or elderly parents.[40] Over 70 percent of the private workforce cannot spend any paid sick leave time taking care of their dependents.

Neofems and "Mommy Myths"

Given how little women's pay inequity has changed and how much home and child care women still do, compounded by the fact that women have more than achieved educational parity, why hasn't the women's movement rebounded? In the 2006 anniversary edition of *Backlash*, Susan Faludi tells us we are living in an era of new traditionalism.[41] Back in the 1980s, the press made statements like "You're more likely to be killed by a terrorist than to kiss a groom!" Or "your biological clock will strike midnight, and you'll turn into a barren pumpkin."[42]

All this changed in 1991 when the Clarence Thomas Supreme Court confirmation hearings contributed to a new sense of urgency about sexual discrimination in the workplace. Anita Hill's testimony emboldened working women, fostering a fresh sense of solidarity among them. Emily's List, a fund-raising organization for Democratic female candidates, raised an unprecedented six million dollars for thirty-nine women. By 1992, dubbed the "Year of the Woman" by Democrats, the Senate tripled its number of women members to six, and the House added nineteen for a total of forty-seven women Representatives, most of whom were Democrats.[43]

But, the Republicans recovered quickly. By 1994, they went on the offensive with a two-punch strategy, visibly supporting women while advocating a return to their traditional roles. First, House Speaker Newt Gingrich gave five of the top seven posts on the National Republican Congressional Committee to women, showing their commitment.[44] Second, vice presidential candidate Dan Quayle, protesting that "[a] feminist army . . . had invaded our culture," tried to appeal to traditionalism.[45] While this symbolic posturing combined with "let's-turn-back-the-clock appeals in the media did not have the adamancy of the backlash 'trend' stories of the 1980s," writes Faludi, the Republicans, and the so-called neofems or women advocating traditionalism helped foster a new cultural climate in the United States.[46]

This change manifested itself in two conflicting messages. Conservative intellectuals of both sexes, the Christian right, and mainstream media championed the traditional nuclear family, particularly motherhood; whereas the Hollywood film and television industry and the Madison Avenue advertising industry recast some of "the fundamentals of feminism in commercial terms."[47] Faludi herself received offers to brand everything from blue jeans to breast implants. And as she quoted Alexis de Tocqueville's statement "I know of no notion more opposed to revolutionary attitudes than commercial ones."[48]

These conflicting messages within popular culture obscured the conservative/progressive political divide about the women's movement. It was by idealizing the American family and turning feminism into a commodity, Faludi maintains, that a supposedly new women's movement became described as an "opt-out revolution." In this movement, women no longer want to "conquer the world."[49] They no longer roar.

The neofems focused on a few women who chose to leave the workplace. "Why don't women run the world?" asked journalist Lisa Belkin. To her it was simple—because "they don't want to."[50] Or as another women explained on a *60 Minutes* television interview, more and more of these liberated women who supposedly "had it all" regret their "choice." Having it all wasn't enough. And as a result "female careerists were forgoing their fat salaries (though not their husbands') in favor of the stroller-pushing suburban life."[51]

But who were the masses behind this revolution? How many women could even afford to opt out? The number is exceedingly small—unrepresentative of the female workforce. In 2001, 36 percent of women with college degrees stayed home with a child under one year old versus 32 percent in 1995.[52] "This hardly amounts to a revolution," as one journalist put it "It's not even necessarily a steady trend."[53]

Given how few women these numbers represent, the question is not how could this happen, but how could the Republicans make believe women wished it had happened to them. Why did the term "opt-out revolution" resonate? Why did this new traditionalism that idealizes those in the upper socioeconomic stratum capture the public imagination? Did this idea reflect the cultural mentality that characterizes a society built on a growing chasm between the rich and the poor, where only the former are credited and applauded for their choices? The journalist Caitlin Flanagan, who turned her own "choice" into a personal opt-out story for the *Atlantic Monthly*, admitted that she had a nanny.[54] Caitlin opted out of the workforce, but she did not make motherhood a full-time job. The opt-out revolution reveals an acceptance of the early twenty-first century income inequality divide.[55]

What makes the stay-at-home mommy bubble burst even louder is that while the educational and economic elite heralds motherhood, the poor, particularly women of color, are criticized for staying home with children. The same decade that witnessed the promotion of traditional families also witnessed the passage of welfare reform.[56] Politicians found that many voters liked the idea that women on welfare be put to work. While some Democrats had reservations about the 1996 Welfare Reform Act, Republicans and Democrats alike overwhelmingly supported its reauthorization in 2005.[57] And when governors across the country implementing this reform tell their voters that women who do not work enough hours will have their benefits cut, there is little to no public outcry. The double standard about motherhood is glaring. Highly educated women should opt out of the workforce, while women on welfare must enter it. Dependency depends on one's socioeconomic status, which is closely correlated with race, though the gendered economic fallout of divorce does not follow race or class lines.

Sex: That "One Word Surprise"

The present political climate blows few winds for change. The existing civil rights structure for women and people of color is not amenable to much of an architectural overhaul. Built on a foundation of negative rights, Title VII of the Civil Rights Act establishes not what the employer can do for you—the employee—but rather what he or she is prohibited from doing to you. An employer, for instance, cannot fire a woman for having a child.[58] But this does not mean that the employer has to consider this child when planning her work schedule.

Women were an afterthought when Title VII of the Civil Rights Act was constructed.[59] How was it that Title VII of the Civil Rights Act of 1964 applied to women? It was Howard K. Smith who sprang the one-word surprise—*sex*—that made Title VII inclusive of women. By the fall of 1963, the John F. Kennedy administration and Congress began drafting Title VII. While many states had what were commonly referred to as Fair

Employment Practice Commissions, this national statute contained a regulatory commission called the Equal Employment Opportunity Commission (EEOC). The EEOC is a five-member commission that has the authority to hear complaints and investigate charges of discrimination in the public and private sectors. It can subpoena witnesses, require companies to keep records, and ask these companies to write reports periodically about their progress in hiring women and people of color.[60]

The EEOC, however, was not given as much power as other quasi-judicial agencies like the National Labor Relations Board (NLRB). A legislative compromise stripped this new agency of its cease-and-desist authority. If the EEOC had cease-and-desist authority, it could have ordered employers to stop certain discriminatory practices immediately as well as preventing them from continuing these practices in the future. It also diminshed much of the EEOC's structural apparatus as a quasi-judicial agency.[61] While the EEOC kept its prosecutorial powers, gaining the authority to file civil suits in federal district court to prevent employers from committing future violations, as well as the power to reinstate an employee and the recovery of back pay for women and people of color who faced discrimination, it could not investigate, try, and punish these employers.[62] The EEOC had less power than all other quasi-judicial agencies.

The Civil Rights Act passed in the spring of 1964. The EEOC opened its doors scarcely a year later on July 2, 1965. Only one of its five commissioners was female, and no women became members of the professional staff. None of this helped make the EEOC any less cautious about its new ban on sex discrimination. The commissioners did not arrive at a new consensus about sex discrimination during this critical precedent-setting time. Racial discrimination topped the EEOC's priority list.[63]

None of the EEOC's ambiguity about sex discrimination stopped women workers from filing complaints. From the beginning the EEOC was "inundated by complaints from sex discrimination that diverted attention and resources from the more serious allegations by members of racial, religious, and ethnic minorities."[64] Between 1970 and 1989, whereas the caseload in all federal courts grew by 125 percent, the employment discrimination caseload grew by twentyfold to 2,166.[65] This figured quadrupled again less than a decade later. In 1989, there were 8,993 employment discrimination matters filed in federal courts, and by 1997 the number jumped almost fourfold to 24,174. By 2004 one in every ten cases on federal court dockets involves a question of employment discrimination.[66] "At the century's end," said law professor Thomas Kohler, "the United States has more formal employment law than ever before."[67]

Further, Title VII discrimination cases affected wrongful discharge actions that benefited all employees. Employment-at-will shields most hiring/

firing decisions from legal challenge. An employer can hire or fire an employee for no reason at all. Before 1980, what were called wrongful discharge actions were almost unknown. But how was it that women and people of color could protest discrimination? How was it that they could challenge an employer's decision not to promote them or to fire them? State courts began to recognize this discrepancy. They began creating common law or judge-made unjust dismissal claims reigning in some employers and reducing the reach of the employment-at-will doctrine. Wrongful discharge actions for all employees were born. Civil rights legislation was not just good for African Americans, Latinos and Latinas, white women, and other women of color, but all employees, particularly older white men in white-collar positions.[68] By 1990, federal laws protected all employees against age and disability discrimination.

Enforcing these rights was a different matter. Under Presidents Ronald Reagan and George W. Bush, senior, the federal bench became more conservative. It became less reluctant to enforce Title VII, particularly if it involved disparate impact and not intentional discrimination. The federal courts were no longer upholding the 1971 landmark decision of *Griggs v. Duke Power Co.,* which created the disparate impact analysis test that measured the discrepancy between how employers treated men and women in or applying for the same positions.[69] Regardless of an employer's motivation, the fact that certain job requirements, such as physical tests for police officer applicants, excluded more women than men was evidence of discrimination.

The Democratic Congress was aware of the federal courts' reluctance. After the Anita Hill debacle, amendments were passed in 1991 that bolstered Title VII. Referred to as the "Anita Hill Bill," these amendments to the Civil Rights Act created jury trials and made compensatory and punitive damages available in cases alleging intentional discrimination. The legislation therefore created an enforcement mechanism, "encourage[ing] citizens to act as private attorney generals."[70]

While the amendments have had mixed success in the federal courts, the post-1991 judicial developments did emit two rays of hope. The Supreme Court held in 2006 that all but trivial actions taken against a worker filing a discrimination claim must be considered illegal forms of retaliation. Workers who file discrimination complaints cannot be shifted to less appealing jobs, nor can they have their work schedule altered or changed.[71]

Meanwhile, two years earlier, a federal district court opened a door of opportunity for women, certifying the largest class-action employment lawsuit in history against the largest retailer in the world—Wal-Mart. Women can form a class, suing a company for discriminatory employment practices even if the EEOC does not prosecute this retailer for a pattern of such practices. Women can band together in legal protest.

Again in 2007 some Democrats in Congress took the defensive, reacting against the Supreme Court's narrow interpretation of Title VII.[72] In *Ledbetter v. Goodyear Rubber Co.*, a five-person majority overturned a pay discrimination case on procedural grounds.[73] Lilly Ledbetter, a supervisor, sued her long-time employer for pay discrimination after discovering that she took home 40 percent less money than even the lowest ranked male in a managerial position. Having worked at the company for over twenty years, Ledbetter found this out in 1998 shortly before her retirement. Justice Samuel Alito, who ironically filled the seat of the first female justice (Sandra Day O'Connor), wrote the opinion. Alito's opinion reinterpreted the EEOC's 180-day statute of limitations, arguing that it began not when Ledbetter learned of the discrimination, but when she received that first discriminatory paycheck. The statutory clock began ticking almost twenty years earlier when unbeknownst to Ledbetter she received a discriminatory salary based on her gender.[74]

Justice Ruth Bader Ginsberg denounced Alito's opinion as a "parsimonious reading" of the statute of limitations in a biting dissent. Most women and people of color, she argued, will not have proof in time to bring to trial under Title VII. After all, it's a rare employer who shares his or her employees' salaries, knowing that they can be used as a means of comparison and a basis for complaints.

What is more, this decision presents women with a catch-22. If a woman suspects pay discrimination and seeks redress *before* finding evidence that the inequity occurred because of her gender, she could face retaliation. Retaliatory action, however damaging and hostile, does not constitute sex discrimination if the employer's initial action was not caused by her gender. If an employer pays a woman less for good reason, in other words, it is not discrimination. And if no discrimination occurred, any retaliatory action is not discriminatory even if this is a result of the woman's gender. Suggesting that she felt "lonely" on the bench, Ginsberg argued that employers could now "grandfather in" inequitable pay structures that harmed women and people of color.

Story Lines

Whether at home, in politics, or in business, women must deal with powerful stereotypes that put them in their "proper place." In Sharon Oard Warner's *Dream Man*, Susanna is the quintessential traditional wife and mother. Warner explores how she handles her husband's reaction to his teenage son's indiscretion with his high school girlfriend. Esther Jackson, in Bebe Moore Campbell's story, "LaKeesha's Job Interview," is a successful manager in a bank, who wonders whether she should hire LaKeesha Jones as a bank teller. Both Jackson and Jones are African American women. What gives Jackson pause is that Jones comes from an entirely different economic stratum. Will she fit into the staid workplace culture of the bank? Women seek the professional help of the "gender coach" in Achim Nowak's "Games Women Play." They believe he will help them learn how to succeed in the world of big business.

The commentary following these stories reveals the continued force of gender stereotypes—often combined with race and class bias. This commentary presents a great challenge to the role of law. Can antidiscrimination statutes like Title VII eliminate the use of such deep-seated socialization?

The women in the next set of stories face unfair treatment in the workplace. But do they face unlawful discrimination? In Harriet Kriegel's "Getting Even," the male hospital head passed Julia Roschak over for promotion and then fired her. C. G. K. Atkins's "Trading Patients," tells the story of Elisa, a Filipina nurse's aide in a New York City hospital, worried about her supervisor's criticisms about her work. She is also afraid that her sexual orientation may lead to negative treatment by supervisors or coworkers. Kiyanna Lock, in Ellen Dannin's "Flint," is a nurse and a woman of color. She is fired after putting herself on the line for a nurse's aide who filed a grievance under the union contract against their employer.

Exploring what constitutes equal treatment, the commentary following these stories reviews the meaning of intentional discrimination under Title VII. What does it take to meet the challenge of proving that an employer was motivated by gender in hiring, firing, or other employment decisions? Is this the same for individual cases as for class actions? The commentary addresses the intersection between Title VII claims of sex and race discrimination, which can be central to the workplace experience of women of color. This discussion brings in the role of affirmative action programs to move women toward substantive equality at the workplace.

The third set of stories deals with sexual harassment. Two of them involve clear cases of offensive sexual conduct. In Stephen Kuusisto's "Plato, Again," Caroline Moore is the target of sexual conduct by her boss, who then demotes her. In Aurelie Sheehan's story, "Be Who You Are," Wendy complies with her supervisor's sexual demands in order to keep her job. The commentary explores the strength of the potential Title VII claims for Caroline and Wendy, who would be faced with the difficult legal standards for proving sexual harassment. The final story in this section raises the question of "welcome" or consensual romance at work. In Eileen Pollack's

"Hwang's Missing Hand," Dianne Rothman chooses to enter a sexual relationship with a summer job supervisor, who had been her high school history teacher. The commentary addresses the sensitive, but important, issue of whether Title VII should respect women's choices to become romantically involved with a supervisor or coworker.

The final cluster of stories goes beyond intentional discrimination and explores substantive equality for women. What sort of fundamental workplace and social changes are needed to achieve genuine gender equality? This question puts a spotlight on "normal" work requirements that create obstacles to women's economic and professional advancement. And it covers the gamut from long work hours to requiring physical strength tests for firefighter applicants—all of which have a stronger negative impact on women than men. As the commentary shows, Title VII may help in eliminating some of these barriers. In Catherine Lewis's "Artifact," the narrator is a woman working in a man's world as an emergency medical technician (EMT). Women seeking to enter such occupations may be able to challenge physical entrance tests under Title VII as unjustified mechanisms that screen women out of the jobs.

The commentary also reviews the limits of Title VII, which does little to help women coordinate their work and family life. Kristen Iversen's "Final Cut" and Alice Elliott Dark's "Vacation Days" both deal with the challenge of combining work and family, although the women in the stories are affected in different ways. Jodie, in "Final Cut," is a single working mother faced with the problem of finding adequate day care for her child. Her situation typifies the burden women face in coordinating work and family needs. Diane, in "Vacation Days," has left her two children in Jamaica to find work in the United States. She does housekeeping and child care for a wealthy suburban woman. The commentary explores this problem of gender, race, and class—where wealthy women are liberated by shifting family responsibilities to poor women of color.

All the commentaries explore how well Title VII works given the realities of women's lives. These discussions go further, as well, to raise doubts about whether Title VII can, alone, eliminate sex discrimination. Are there tools other than Title VII and other antidiscrimination laws that women could use to achieve gender equality? No doubt, legal tools are important, yet women should not overlook collective action as a tool to define their own goals and agendas for equal rights.

What is more, becoming aware of gender roles, and their pervasiveness in our society, can open doors to women and men alike, presenting an alternate view of our everyday reality. The first story, "Dream Man," the only story not about the workplace, illustrates how fiction gives us pause to feel and think about all that is involved in gender discrimination. Seemingly not about discrimination law at all, this story sets the stage by exploring traditional gender roles that bog down society, thereby enabling the federal courts to ineffectively enforce the law. It reveals the persistent limits and restrictions of gender roles—both the roles society imposes and those that women put upon themselves.

In Their Proper Place

Dream Man

Susan Oard Warner

Wallace sleeps naked, and so do our sons, the older one in his cramped and cluttered apartment across town, the younger in a bedroom at the end of the downstairs hallway. This interlude/incident/misunderstanding—whatever you want to call it—won't change my husband's habits. According to him, his nakedness didn't and doesn't pertain. "I was in my own house," he told me, "minding my own business."

. . .

On that night, Dylan managed to get home *before curfew*, which has to qualify as something of a minor miracle. He's a bit of a handful, our Dylan, your classic underachiever. At sixteen, he coasts through life, using his smarts to get himself out of scrapes. Consider this: Dylan can look me straight in the eye and argue that a C is a perfectly decent grade—A is for excellent, B is for good, C is for satisfactory—and what's wrong with satisfactory, for God's sake? He isn't opposed to lectures, as long as he's the one doing the lecturing: "Mothers like you," he's told me, "are responsible for grade inflation. Teachers are *afraid* to give students the grades they deserve for fear of parental flak. No one wants an average kid. Everyone wants a genius or a football player." What am I supposed to say to that? He's right, now isn't he?

These days, his curfew is twelve-thirty, which is way past our bedtime, so we've worked out an arrangement: As soon as Dylan gets home, he comes upstairs and wakes his dad, who checks the clock and punches him in, so to speak. Back when our older son was in high school, we *stayed* up until he *showed* up, but we can't do that anymore. We must be getting old.

Wallace tells me that Dylan was in a good mood when he came up to the bedroom and reported himself home for the night; the two of them even chatted for a minute in the dark. That happens occasionally, a little father/son bantering—did you and Marcie like the movie, that sort of thing. Me, I slept right through it, engrossed in my dreams. Nothing was amiss, nothing we noticed anyway.

Around three a.m., Wallace woke and realized the furnace was roaring. Turns out, he'd forgotten to adjust the thermostat before he went to bed, the sort of thing that torments him. Before, he'd been sleeping fine, but now he was hot; no way he'd be getting back to sleep until he set things right. As he rolled out of bed, he grabbed up the flashlight he keeps on the bedside table.

The first I knew of the hubbub in Dylan's room was when Wallace came up to wake me. He started by flipping the light switch, and I responded by opening my eyes to slits. There was my Wallace in the doorway, dressed in his sweats and tennis shoes and looking distinctly unhappy. I closed my eyes again, determined to ignore him. If something goes bump in the night, Wallace gets up to investigate. I thought if I persisted in sleeping, he might return to prowling around with his flashlight. It had happened before, you see.

But this time I couldn't deter him. He clapped his hands and when that didn't work, he bounded over to my side of the bed and squeezed my shoulder hard. "Get up!" he bellowed. "*Your* son is in bed with his girlfriend." A rude awakening, if ever there was one.

Now, I know that Dylan's girlfriend is *your* daughter and that all of this must be upsetting. I want to reassure you that we think Marcie is a lovely girl. (She has the same honey-colored hair Dylan has, though you wouldn't know that now that he's shaving his head.) We don't know your daughter well, of course, but I've had a few short conversations with her.

One afternoon, for instance, she told me about you. Said you were a lawyer before you were a mother, that now you volunteer for a theater group, not as a lawyer but as a set designer. You paint trees and night skies, street scenes, and mountainous backdrops. She's looked at the sketches on your desk, but she's never seen the finished product. When I asked if she likes to go to plays, she said, "not usually." So I inquired about her dad. Does he go? Dylan was in the bathroom, you see, so I felt I could ask what I pleased.

Marcie and I were at the kitchen table, the late afternoon sunlight streaming through the blinds. She and Dylan had just finished some left-over pizza, and before she answered the question, Marcie reached out and grabbed a paper napkin. While she was talking, she folded it once, twice, three times. Then, when it was as small as she could possibly make it, she smoothed the napkin out on the table and started again. In this pretend task, she showed patience and concentration but also a fair degree of anxiety.

Marcie told me that her father didn't care much for theater and that he pretty much refused to go, no matter how you begged. I told her that such things were disappointing, maybe, but not unusual in the lives of the long married. Take Wallace and me, for instance. He probably wishes I played golf, and I'd love it if he'd take up ballroom dancing. Not going to happen. If I want ballroom dancing, well, I married the wrong man.

Which brings me to that dream of mine, my own private sleepy-time soap opera. I dream about another man, you see, someone who might be a better match for me. Naturally, this someone is married, and, as luck would have it, to a woman who might be a better match for Wallace. Well, that's the way of these things. You turn fifty; you finally know yourself, but all the important decisions are made. Now, at long last, when you've acquired a little wisdom and self-awareness, it's too late to use it, and your children aren't about to learn from your mistakes. They want the freedom to make their own.

Anyway, I'd just gotten around to asking Marcie what her father does for a living when Dylan reappeared, scowling at me. He complains that I'm nosey, that I ask too many questions, that I stare at strangers. He's right on all three counts. I promised to tell you the whole story, "woman to woman," and I'm not planning to leave anything out, not even the parts that don't reflect well on me, such as the dream man and my nosiness.

To make nice, I asked the kids if they wanted ice cream. We had a half gallon of butter pecan, Dylan's favorite. Marcie smiled brightly—she has wonderful manners—but Dylan had suffered my company long enough. "Nah," he said. "We're going out." Then he jerked his head at Marcie, meaning she should follow, and of course she did, jumped right up and trailed him out the door.

· · ·

Back to that night: If I had to guess, I'd say Dylan jerked his head exactly that same way when he came downstairs from chatting up his father. Marcie must have been waiting for him, probably sitting in Wallace's leather recliner, hands folded in her lap. But by the time I made it downstairs, she was at one end of the sofa, shoulders hunched, hands gripping her thighs. Dylan stood on the shadowy edge of the living room, shirtless and bare-foot, dressed only in jeans loose enough to slip down to the bones of his pelvis, where they held, though just barely.

Though it's easy to forget now, Dylan was a jolly baby and a happy child, a grinning little towhead! If I showed you pictures, you'd see what a doll he was. Once a month, Wallace would sit him on a stack of phone books and carefully clip his hair until our son resembled a tiny blonde Moe from the *Three Stooges*. Now, this same child buzzes his head in the bath-room late at night and emerges with a scowl and a "none of your business" if you ask what he has against hair. He's a good three inches taller than his father, with a muscular chest and shoulders from doing pull-ups on the limb of a tree.

Throughout the argument, his body was pitched slightly forward, the stance of a man in a honky-tonk parking lot, someone intent on picking a fight. Marcie, on the other hand, resembled a passenger in a speeding car braced for impact. She was wearing those ripped bell-bottom jeans, and the lovely knob of one exposed knee glowed pink in the lamplight.

To put her at ease, I shuffled over and patted her shoulder and asked the first thing that occurred to me: "Do your parents know where you are?" The air was so dry, so full of static electricity that hairs from the crown of her head floated halo-like in the air. It was all I could do not to touch them, smooth them down.

Marcie swore she didn't have a curfew, and, at the time, it didn't occur to me to disbelieve her. People raise their children differently, and as Wallace will tell you, I'm gullible from first to the last. I can find a way to believe almost anything, whereas Wallace tends to be distrustful and incredulous. He snorted when Marcie claimed that her parents trusted her, that they didn't care what time she came home. "I don't believe that," he said. "Surely they want you home at 3 a.m."

Marcie shrugged and looked away.

Meanwhile, Dylan was rubbing the top of his head with the palm of his hand, back and forth, as though he was trying to create friction, pro-duce sparks. "Everyone's not as uptight as you are, Dad," he said. Wal-lace and I might have been expecting a little contrition from our son, but if so, we were mistaken. Dylan was downright defiant. He acted as though *Wallace* was the one in the wrong. "And what the hell were you doing in my room?"

Me, I rarely enter Dylan's room anymore. It used to be different: I re-member when the boys wore pajamas with feet in them, and I sat next to them in the bed and read them stories before they went to sleep. These days, I only venture into my younger son's room to gather dirty clothes or to wake him for school, in which case I avert my eyes as he leaps out of bed and rushes past, a flurry of long hairy limbs. Most often, I study the posters on Dylan's wall: Bob Marley sucking a doobie, John Lee Hooker cradling a guitar in his lap, and Albert Einstein, sticking out his tongue.

"Entirely outnumbered," I've joked to my friends, but it isn't entirely a joke. Even our dogs are males, neutered males but males nonetheless, and I can tell you this: What they lack in balls, they make up for in bravado. They'll mount other dogs, the legs of strangers, a blanket heaped on the floor. Oh, I'm sorry. That probably wasn't the best thing to say.

Dylan actually called his dad "man." "The door was closed, man," he said. Like one of the hippies from Woodstock or something. He told his father that he closed the door because he didn't want anyone barging in.

Wallace wasn't having any of it. "This is *my* house," he barked, "and I have a right to know what's going on beneath *my* roof."

Dylan smirked. "So if you *knew*," he said, morphing from hippie to lawyer in the blink of an eye, "if I told you I'd brought Marcie home, would it have been *okay*?"

I didn't know it then, but I know it now: On some level, we were all furious with Wallace, who had forced this meeting, and he was livid at each of us, me as much as them. "*Your* son is in bed with his girlfriend."

On some level, he blamed me, though I don't know why. Did he expect that his sons wouldn't be interested in sex? With Wallace as their dad, how could that be? His subscription to *Playboy* dates back to the sixties, and he's kept all of the back issues, storing them in boxes out in the garage. Of course the boys have rifled through them. They're boys. And it doesn't stop at *Playboy*, either.

Me, I rarely ever think of sex except when I'm sleeping. Then, it seems to be very much on my mind. During my waking hours, I am more concerned with what I've left undone—groceries I haven't bought, clothes I haven't folded, accounts I haven't balanced. On this occasion, as my husband and son sparred, as little Marcie wilted on the sofa, I pondered this important question: when did I last change Dylan's sheets? I hoped they were at least reasonably clean. Ridiculous, isn't it? But I was thinking about the sheets and particularly about the dinosaur pillow sham Dylan still used for his extra pillow. It's printed with a yellow brontosaurus, a green stegosaurus, and a red tyrannosaurus rex. It made me cry to think of that pillowcase. I don't know why, but tears began to leak from the corners of my eyes.

"What's wrong?" Wallace asked me. He doesn't miss a thing, Wallace.

I shook my head. I couldn't have said then, and I'm not sure I could say now, but it was all so sad. I missed my little boy, but I couldn't help being proud of this man-child. That night, he was protective of Marcie, defiant to the point of absurdity, downright dashing. I could see how a young girl might be seduced by his solicitude. I would have been. Suddenly, my son was a young man I didn't quite recognize.

When the night's drama was done, he strode across the room, draped his arm around her shoulder, and ushered her to the door. It isn't a word you hear much anymore, but I thought *gallant*.

. . .

We grounded him, of course we did, and when Dylan is punished, he tends to punish us back by going silent and retreating. For the next few days, he carried a plate to his room and glowered at us from behind closed doors. I could feel his fury every time I went to the laundry room. So, I let a few days go by, but one afternoon, I forced myself to knock on his door. I knew my responsibility. If they were having sex, I needed to be certain that they were using protection. At the very least, I needed to assure myself of that. "Can I come in?" I asked from the other side of the door.

"It's unlocked," he called back.

Dylan was sprawled on the floor, two textbooks stacked in front of him, but he wasn't reading them. Dylan do homework? Not in this life. Instead, they served to prop up an open copy of *National Geographic*. He was sketching an old man's face, a fellow with a hooknose and a turban. Dylan is a talented artist—I know, I know—I'm his mother. But you could certainly see the resemblance between the photograph and the sketch. He paused in his work and looked up at me.

"I'm thinking I should have a chat with Marcie or her mother," I told him.

"Why is that?" he asked.

"Birth control," I sputtered. These talks are always so difficult. "Did you use a condom?"

He squinted up at me. "Duh," he said. I realize now that *duh* is not a conclusive answer, but I did ask him if Marcie was taking the pill. He told me that it wasn't any of my business, that I'm too nosey.

I tried to explain to him that it was my business, that I was the responsible older woman and if Marcie's mother didn't know her daughter was sexually active, then I needed to call and tell her.

"Don't bother," he said, and when I asked why not, he told me that Marcie had already talked to you. "Yeah," he drawled, making fun of my accent. "First, she swore her mother to secrecy. Eleanor can't blab it all to Marcie's dad, who would go berserk."

"Eleanor keeps secrets from her husband?" I found this information reassuring. Then, because the trick to learning a new name is to use it, I asked my son what *Eleanor* had said. I thought when I called you, it would be handy to know your name. I was so busy thinking *Eleanor* that I wasn't ready for my son's bombshell. He didn't look up at me; he went right on sketching, so I can't tell you what expression he was wearing, whether he was pleased with himself or a little frightened of what he was about to do.

"*Eleanor* said it sucked that Marcie had to see Dad's ass."

I wasn't sure I'd heard him right. My ears were buzzing, you see, and I think I grabbed hold of the doorsill. "What did you say?" I asked.

"You heard me."

"Wallace was naked?"

"Duh, Mom," Dylan replied. "And leaning over us with a flashlight."

"And Marcie told her mother?" I asked weakly.

Dylan had returned to his drawing. He was shading the man's prominent cheekbones. "Yeah," he said, then added slyly: "Still want to have that chat?"

. . .

Wallace comes home from work weary. He literally trudges up the stairs to change into sweats. When I heard his car pull into the garage, I was in the kitchen, rustling up dinner. Now that our older son has moved into his own apartment, I've lost interest in cooking, or to be more precise, I've lost motivation. Cooking for four was feeding-my-family in a way that cooking for three is not. Once Dylan goes off to college, Wallace predicts that I will stop cooking altogether. He says we'll be eating cheese toast and sliced tomatoes every night, and he may be right. I think of my own mother and her husband, who subsist on Lean Cuisine and ice cream sandwiches. Their freezer is crammed with boxes.

When dinner was almost ready, I climbed the stairs and discovered Wallace sprawled on the bed in his work attire, feet hanging off the end so that his shoes wouldn't dirty the comforter. For a second or two, I considered the utility of my anger and tried to assess whether to act on it. One of the consolations of age is that you aren't ruled so ruthlessly by your emotions. In dreams, it all seems as life and death as it once was, but in waking life, you know that this, too, shall pass.

"Why didn't you tell me you were naked?" I asked Wallace.

He opened his eyes and gazed at the ceiling. "What are you talking about?"

"When you went into Dylan's room the other night you were naked."

He rolled up onto one elbow so that he could get a good look at me. Some part of me regretted interrupting his brief nap. The skin around his eyes sags when he's tired, and on that night he looked like one of those baggy-faced dogs.

Still, he found the energy to snarl his response: "So?"

Me, I was in my shrew stance—hands on hips. "So, you didn't tell me that. What the hell, Wallace?"

He swung his legs over the side of the bed and sat up, the better to glare at me. "What are you getting at, Susanna? I was in my own house checking my own heat."

"Naked!"

"So what?" He stood and stripped off his work clothes, beginning with his trousers and underwear. Within seconds, he was naked.

"And they were naked, too?" I asked, glancing away from him and toward the Wyeth print on the far wall, Christina crawling in the field.

He sighed, one of his long-suffering exhalations, meant to convey both exhaustion and exasperation. "Of course they were."

He stood before me in the altogether, shoulders slumped, stomach distended. Oh dear, Eleanor, what can I say? He looked like an old gray toddler with a mustache, all belly and bravado.

"You don't see the problem?" I asked him.

"I don't," he replied. "Why don't you explain it to me?"

"Marcie told her mother."

He wasn't fazed, not that I could see. "So?" he said again, throwing out his arms in that flustered way of his. Then, whirling round, he marched off toward the bathroom.

· · ·

So, there you have it. That's why I didn't call you, Eleanor. I was embarrassed and ashamed—unsure of who or what to believe. For several nights, I was nearly sleepless, trying to sort it out. What if I called you and made matters worse? I'm entirely capable of that, as you can see. So, in the end, I decided it was best just to let sleeping dogs lie.

How was I to know that Dylan was full of shit? That Marcie didn't tell you about that night? And damn that Dylan! Are you telling me that he wasn't wearing a condom?

LaKeesha's Job Interview

Bebe Moore Campbell

Esther stared at the scrolling figures on her computer screen. It was hard to comprehend that people could be so careless about their finances that they forgot they had money in the bank, but as she reviewed the dormant accounts, a task she undertook every few months, the evidence was indisputable. In the downtown branch alone, there was nearly three million dollars in accounts that hadn't been active in months, sometimes years. Two million, nine hundred thousand and seventy-eight dollars, to be exact. She logged in the account. Of course, some of the holders of the accounts were deceased, but in those cases, she would have thought that relatives would come and claim the cash. All that money going to waste. She shook her head.

Esther heard a soft knock at the door. She looked at her watch: nine-thirty. She had completely forgotten about her appointment. Well, the interview wouldn't take long. She'd already decided that she was going to hire David Weaver. "Come in," she called.

The door opened slowly, and a young, dark-brown skinned woman stood in front of Esther's desk. Their eyes met, and Esther could read in them the girl's uncensored surprise. Esther realized immediately the reason for the started look in the young woman's eyes: she hadn't expected another black person to be interviewing her.

Two months earlier, Angel City had formed a partnership with the city's social service agency. The bank was obligated to interview a certain number of welfare recipients who were involved in a job training program. Office scuttlebutt said the candidates were pretty poorly qualified.

Esther found the girl's astonishment amusing. Why, the child couldn't even speak. "Were you expecting someone else?" Esther said.

"Oh, no. Well, I—" The girl stopped, and they both laughed. "I'm glad it's you," she said, and they chuckled again. "No, I mean, like, it makes me feel good to know that one of us is the boss. You know what I mean?"

"Yes, I know what you mean," Esther said. The girl seemed a little awkward. This was probably her first job interview. Esther felt a twinge of guilt, knowing that her mind was already made up. Thinking, she probably needs a job worse than old Alex Keaton, Esther extended her hand. When the girl shook it, Esther could feel her fingers trembling like a frightened kitten; then she felt something hard and sharp cutting into her palm. She looked down. Good God! Long. Curved. Bright Red with a capital *R*. And rhinestones were embedded in the pinkie nails. Genuine Hootchy-Mama fingernails. I'm Esther Jackson. Thank you for coming. Sit down, La . . . La . . ."

"LaKeesha. LaKeesha Jones." She talks proper, LaKeesha thought. Just like a white woman.

LaKeesha sat down in the chair near the desk. Esther gave her a quick once-over. The dress was too tight and too short, but not awful. The girl's face was pleasant, even though she wore too much makeup. The braids, well, they weren't the proper hairstyle for a black woman who wanted to get ahead in business. "Tell me a little about yourself, LaKeesha," Esther said. "Have you had any teller experience?"

LaKeesha took a breath, trying not to be nervous in spite of the way Esther was looking at her. Her eyes were like fingers lifting her collar to check for dirt. LaKeesha attempted to concentrate. She'd been through a number of practice interviews. She paused, remembering what Mr. Clark had told her. Look the person straight in her eyes, smile a lot; speak clearly, sell yourself; don't be nervous. But Esther's language, each word so precisely enunciated, was erecting a brick wall between them. There was nothing to be nervous about. LaKeesha told herself. She smiled at Esther. "I just, like, finished the South-Central Alternative Education Center's bank teller program. I was, like, like you know, number one in my class. . . ."

An around-the-way girl if I ever I saw one, Esther said to herself as she listened to LaKeesha describe her course work and a month-long internship at one of the city's banks. "The manager wanted to hire me, but they didn't have no openings at the time."

Esther flinched at the double negative. "Well," she said, getting a word in, "it certainly appears that you've been well trained. Tell me about the school you attended."

"See, I dropped out of high school after I had my baby. Then I met this lady named Mrs. Clark; her and her husband ran this school, and so she talked me into going there to get my GED. She has a contract with the city to train people, so after I got my GED, I decided that I wanted to take the bank teller course, because, well I'm on the county and want to get off." LaKeesha sat back in her chair. She hadn't meant to talk so much, to get so personal. Mrs. Clark told her to be professional. Maybe she shouldn't have mentioned being on the county. She looked at Esther's black suit, the shiny low heels, and all that gold jewelry she wore, not the kind that screamed at you but a nice quiet gold. And words came out of her mouth so sharp they could draw blood. She probably thought she was white, sitting up in her own office, being everybody's boss. She shouldn't have said anything about being on the county.

A baby, Esther thought. She could just hear the phone calls, the excuses: the baby is sick; the babysitter can't make it. Hiring a single mother with a baby—because of course she wasn't married—was asking for trouble. She looked at LaKeesha, who was staring at her uneasily. "Do you know TIPS?"

LaKeesha grinned. "That's what we was trained in."

Esther scratched the back of her neck. The child wasn't ready for prime time, and the bad thing about it was that she probably had no idea just how deficient she was. Esther thought fleetingly of what that asshole Fred Gaskins would say if he was listening to her conversation with LaKeesha. He'd say that LaKeesha was another product of a *substandard high school in South-Central*. She could just see the operations manager, his fat little lightbulb head bobbing back and forth, his bantam chest heaving in and out. Fred Gaskins can go to hell, she thought to herself. She glanced at her watch; ten o'clock. "Come with me, LaKeesha. I'd like to see what you can do."

Leading the young woman out the door to the operations area, Esther guided her past the customer reps' desks, around to the back of the tellers' cage. There were five people on duty. Hector Bonilla smiled in his usual polite manner as soon as he saw the two women approaching him. "Hector, I'd like you to meet LaKeesha Jones. Hector, LaKeesha and I have been chatting about the possibility of her becoming a teller here. I'd like for you two to work together for an hour or so, and then I'll come back for you, LaKeesha. Hector, may I see you for a second?"

Esther walked the young man a few feet away from his station. "Listen, I want you to really pay attention to how LaKeesha works. Look at the way she deals with customers, how she handles money, and how well she knows TIPS. I'll talk with you later, all right?"

"Yes, Esther," Hector said, nodding his head so vigorously that his straight black hair rippled over his forehead. In the eighteen months that he had been with the bank, Hector had proved himself to be a good worker, stable and serious. He always came early and stayed late. Esther knew she could depend upon him for a fair assessment. She might not hire LaKeesha this time, but if the girl had decent skills, she might consider her when there was another opening.

One hour later, Esther stepped outside her office, caught Hector's eye, and motioned him over. In a few moments, he appeared at her door, and she ushered him to a seat inside. "How did she do?" Esther asked.

"She is very good worker," Hector said solemnly, his dark, serious eyes looking straight into hers. "She is polite to customers. She is accurate with money. She knows the computer system too. I didn't have to tell her very much at all." His smile was as earnest and diffident as he was.

"Thank you, Hector. Would you tell LaKeesha to come to my office, please."

"Well, Hector told me you did very well," Esther said after LaKeesha settled herself into her chair. The young woman beamed. Esther asked her a few questions about the transactions she'd just made. Finally, she stood up and extended her hand. "I've enjoyed chatting with you, and I'll be in touch."

LaKeesha stood up. "My grandmother, she lives with me and she keeps my baby, even if he's sick, so you don't have to worry about that."

Esther nodded her head. "Well," she said, opening the door just a little wider, "that's just fine."

She felt the girl's eyes on her. "Just fine," Esther repeated, waiting for LaKeesha to leave.

The young woman stepped toward her. "I know I can do a good job for you. I'll come on time. I know how to be a good worker. I can smile at the customers and be polite and hand them their money. I want to work." She knew she was talking too much, that she should just leave, but the words seemed to be bubbling up from some spring. "My whole family's been on the county for as long as I can remember. I didn't tell none of them where I was going, because I didn't want to get their hopes up. I want to be a good example for my younger sisters. They need to see somebody working," she paused and stood up straighter. "If I don't get this job, would you please call me and like, tell me what I did wrong, so I won't make the same mistake on the next interview? Because if I don't get this job, I'm gonna get me a job from somebody."

Esther hesitated a moment, then closed the door. "Sit down," she told LaKeesha.

"First of all, get rid of those fingernails. This is a place of business, not a nightclub. Second, your dress is too tight and too short, and your heels are too high. Third, you're wearing too much makeup. Fourth, your grammar is poor. It's 'I didn't tell *any* of them,' not '*none* of them.' And don't say 'like' so much. And another thing: get rid of those braids. I think they're beautiful, but when you're working for white folks you want to fit in, not stand out." Seeing the distraught look on LaKeesha's face, Esther spoke a little more gently. "Now, everything I'm telling you can be corrected. It's up to you."

"If I change all those things, will you give me a job?" LaKeesha's expression was eager, hungry.

"I can't promise you that," Esther said quickly, "but I believe that if you make those adjustments, somebody will hire you. And don't think in terms of a job. You have to think about a career."

LaKeesha's eyes, which seemed to grow larger and more hopeful every minute, didn't leave Esther's face.

"You need to think: I'll start as a teller, then I'll become an operation assistant, then I'll get in the operations training program, and then I'll become an operations manager. That's the kind of mind-set employers want to see in an employee."

LaKeesha's face brightened, and she stood up. Before she realized what she was doing, she was hugging Esther and mumbling in her ear: "Thank you, sister."

Esther felt the word even more than she heard it. There was obligation in that word. And she didn't want any part of that.

She pulled away. "Don't ever call me that here," she said quickly. Esther watched as LaKeesha passed through the bank and out the door. Even after she left, the musky odor of TLC oil sheen spray clung to the air in the room. Esther knew the odor well; it was her scent too.

Esther closed her eyes. She could see herself making those fast deals. Lending millions just on her say-so. If she played her cards right, maybe she could be the one who'd transcend the glass ceiling. Every once in a while, they let somebody black slip through. Why shouldn't she be the one?

Esther walked around her desk with her hands clasped together in front of her and then behind her. She pictured LaKeesha's face, the yearning in her eyes. No, no, no! She wouldn't sacrifice her career in the name of racial solidarity. Forget it. She was going to pick up the phone and hire an acceptable white boy, with acceptable grammar and short fingernails, because that was the right move to make. The smart move.

Sister.

That and a dollar won't even get you a ride on the bus.

Esther picked up the telephone.

3

Games Women Play

by Achim Nowak

I am a coach.

I am the kind of coach who helps business leaders to speak with purpose and authentic power. Whenever I ponder the fact that this is what I do for a living, I think to myself: That's an odd thing to do, isn't it? I'm not unlike a vastly opinionated therapist who gives you, my client, microscopic feedback on what you project to the world. For a long time, in fact, I found it difficult to describe what I do. It reaches beyond simply fixing a distracting speech pattern or an uncomfortable gesture. It sometimes involves a bit of life coaching, but that does not fully capture it, either. Then it came to me: I am a performance coach. I help you to investigate how you perform in the world.

And I am a man. More about that later.

If you are like my mom, you are reading these words right now and you may be thinking to yourself, I'm still not sure what the heck he does. *Performance* is a word charged with nuance and meaning, isn't it? Am I "myself" when I speak in public, or do I put on a performance every time I show up? What, actually, does it mean to be "myself" in a professional environment? And what are some of the roles that I take on, consciously or not, every time I appear in public?

Welcome to my world. These are the questions I toy with, day in and day out, as I coach my clients. Imagine, for a moment, that you are coming to visit me for a session. Imagine, as well, that this visit takes place in Manhattan. I coach clients all over the world, but when you are in Manhattan you will come to see me in my office, on the thirty-ninth floor of 245 Park Avenue. Like many New Yorkers I still cling to the illusion that midtown Manhattan is the center of the universe.

245 Park is the quintessential American office tower. Lots and lots of glass windows contain this building, lots of shiny chrome trim seals the glass, and thick white marble floors anchor all of this shine. And because this tower rises in midtown Manhattan, the glass is taller, the chrome shinier, the marble more expensive than almost anywhere else in the United States. Every symbol of this place says "Hello, you have entered a world of money and power and lots of important activity." That is the carefully honed performance of this building: Polished. Impenetrable. Quintessentially male.

My office, you may be relieved to know, looks nothing like this lobby. It does not look like a conventional office, at all. It holds a few round tables with plain conference chairs scattered about. A couple of flip-chart stands near the wall. A view of other shiny chrome buildings. But mostly, it has lots of empty space. This is the laboratory where we play and experiment with who we are. It's where we look at how we fill the empty space.

Now, before you get up and present yourself to me, sit back for a moment and contemplate what happens in this room. What I look for when you start to speak is the split. The split is that millisecond when you first stand in front of me, and you slip into another skin. It's usually a subtle, barely perceptible slip. But suddenly, I see the moment when you no longer behave like the person who first walked into this room. You become somebody else without knowing that you have become somebody else. You sneak into the role of the public person, and into all of the mental blueprints and inner conditioning about how this role is lived. The split is the moment when I begin to understand you.

Some leaders make a conscious decision about how they play the public role. Some, but not many. Most slip into the public skin without any thought. They step into it the way you might step into a puddle during heavy rain, when there simply seems no other way to cross the street. You step into it, you make it across, but the effort of the jump and the splash of the step mark you for hours to come. And this step across the public puddle is different for women than it is for men. It always is.

Meet Rita, for example. She walked into my office last Monday, with a group of ten other sales reps, to practice her standard sales presentation. Rita had a bounce in her walk, a quick easy laugh, and her speech riffed with the unexpected syncopation of a master jazz musician. Fluid, spontaneous. Her frizzed hair was pulled back from her face but still leapt from her skull with a defiant energy. Everything about Rita said "I'm a playful, free spirit."

When Rita stood up and began to address her audience of ten, she spoke with a slow, measured pace. The pauses between her words were long, the emphasis on many of the words heavy and hard, and her language seemed drawn-out, as if she were stretching a piece of chewing gum to the snapping point. Her body hunched forward and leaned toward her audience, with a serious, almost threatening intent. Rita's entire presentation looked studied and deliberate. A sentence or two of this delivery went by, and then I watched her audience withdraw into polite silence.

I was puzzled. Why did Rita speak so slowly and deliberately? Why was her bouncy energy suddenly gone? And more important, how did Rita get the idea that this is how you talk to a group of people?

Rita, I realized, reminded me of a kindergarten or preschool teacher during story-time. She spoke as if she were addressing a group of young children who were not very bright and certainly not at all interested in her story. She had slipped into the role of a teacher. An archetypal teacher, and not a good one, at that. Rita clearly had no idea that she had assumed this role. When I inquired about her professional past, Rita reassured me that she had never been a kindergarten teacher. She had no conscious memories of being in kindergarten. Yet, clearly this was the role she was channeling. Rita was caught in a kindergarten split. What impulse, I wondered, beyond any conscious decision in her brain, propelled Rita into this role? Was it a fear of not being understood? A fear of being too smart for the group? A fear of losing control of an attention-challenged audience?

Marcia was in the same group with Rita. Her physical appearance stood in notable contrast to Rita's. Marcia's torso was stocky and squat, her hair dyed Mae-West-blonde and trimmed into a short, devilish spike. And yet, like Rita, she burst into the room with the same sense of palpable, defiant energy. When Marcia entered it was impossible to not immediately be touched by this inner force. Her entire entrance seemed to scream: "Here I am, you all, so you better watch out!"

When Marcia got up and delivered her formal sales pitch, she didn't mute her energy. No, Marcia magnified all that she had brought into the space. Her voice crackled with aggressive diction and volume. The pauses between her words filled with a throaty laugh and sudden giggles. Her arms circled the air with staccato bursts of excitement. And her speech seemed to move at lightning speed, as if the rapidity of the delivery alone might will audience compliance. Marcia was like the Energizer Bunny whose batteries would never run out.

I took one glance at the audience, and I again noticed folks withdraw into the same resignation that Rita had provoked. What had happened?

Why had Marcia, with her marvelous infectious energy, sedated this receptive audience?

Marcia's innate personal energy, it was clear to me, was so strong that it did not warrant the "extra push." The extra push signaled "Well, I'm not sure you will really like me, so let me try a little harder." Just being Marcia wasn't enough, so Marcia slipped into the role of the cheerleader—the überhappy, übereager, überpeppy, überambitious go-getter. Because Marcia had a healthy dose of cheerleader energy in her anyway, she morphed into a suddenly desperate cheerleader. "Like me, like me, like me." That seemed to be the unspoken shout of her presentation. And the more the audience withdrew, the more the primal cheerleader ran amok.

And yes—Marcia had no idea that she had fallen into this split.

On Wednesday, I had a private session with Ann. Ann's a senior VP of marketing for a major pharmaceutical company, newly promoted into her job, and she was gearing up for her first major presentation to a group of senior stakeholders. Like many of her colleagues in this line of business, Ann displayed a keen intellect and sharp mind that I find immensely appealing. She came dressed in the traditional two-piece navy power suit and meticulously coiffed hair, as if she had just stepped out of a Madison Avenue salon. I was struck, however, by Ann's warmth as she greeted me, her easy and generous smile, and a deep and lucid sparkle in the eye. Ann was clearly the sort of person "where the light is on"—my phrase for the individual where mental prowess is matched by an open heart and spiritual attunement.

When Ann got up to present her stakeholder speech to me, replete with a series of well-crafted PowerPoint slides, her inner light went out. Almost at once. I found myself getting angry at Ann the moment I noticed. "How dare you withhold yourself from me?" I thought. I still saw the same poise with which she had greeted me, but it was a hollow poise now, a robotic poise. Gone was the twinkle in Ann's eye and the subterranean warmth. The poise had turned into polish. Well-mannered. Empty.

Two minutes into her presentation I stopped Ann.

"What happened?" I said to her. "Where did you go?"

"What do you mean?" Ann replied, a little startled and testy.

"The person who walked into the room and shook my hand is not the person that got up and talked to me about pharmaceuticals!"

Ann, of course, had not realized that she had submitted herself to the role of the professional and her deeply ingrained sense of what it means to perform like one. For many of my women clients, it means not being "too much"—too much of whatever you believe you have "too much of"—warmth, expressiveness, spirituality, humor, soul. These, of course, are often the very qualities that have moved you into a highly visible position, and yet, the moment you inhabit this position and have to be visible, you rob your audience of these gifts. Instead of fully showing up, you hide. You strap on the neutral and lifeless mask of the professional. And Ann, that was clear from my brief chat with her, had not made a single conscious decision about how she wore the mask. The mask wore her.

Melinda one-upped Ann with her interpretation of the professional role. She came to see me in the afternoon, right after Ann had dashed off. Melinda didn't walk into the room with Ann's easy affability. While Melinda came dressed in what's commonly termed "business casual," she fully breathed the role of the professional woman, and my strong hunch was that this is not how Melinda had first arrived on this planet. It was a learned and wholly assimilated role. Melinda charged toward me before I could approach her, engaged me in a bit of quick and requisite small talk while her mind was clearly on something else. Every movement, every word had the sharp, clear focus of the endorphin-driven alpha-female.

I appreciate a client like Melinda because she's here to work and doesn't waste time. I don't always appreciate what happens to someone like Melinda when she gets up to talk.

Melinda, the director of HR at a prestigious blue-chip financial firm, came to practice an upcoming speech in which she had to deliver policy changes in front of every employee at her firm's downtown headquarters. The second Melinda began her formal presentation, I noticed the shift. Words were uttered with an even sharper, more determined pitch than before. Sentences shot and fired like well-aimed gunshots. Every phrase ended with a thudding finality, as if to indicate that opposition to the message was not allowed. Throughout I sensed an undercurrent of rage—a rage, I assumed, at the possibility of an objection that had yet to be raised. The speed and sharpness of Melinda's delivery served as the definitive preemptive strike. While Ann had removed parts of herself to hide in the professional role, Melinda seized the same role and pushed it to its darkest, boldest edge. She transformed alpha-woman into the vulture warrior control-freak.

Was Melinda aware that she had slipped into the vulture jungle? Did she notice the impact that her vulture energy had on me, the listener? I asked her, and you likely know the answer . . .

· · ·

These are just a few of my recent women clients. Rita, Marcia, Ann, Melinda. I have coached hundreds of other women, and I have coached hundreds of men, as well. Now here's the tricky part.

Not a single man I have coached has ever taken on the role of the teacher.

Not a single man has ever turned into the cheerleader. The joker, maybe, but not the cheerleader.

Not a single man has ever flipped into the vulture. Mind you, I have coached many a male vulture, but my male vulture was invariably the vulture before, during, and after the public event. The vulture didn't appear out of the dark. The vulture wasn't a hidden primal role. The vulture was fully lived.

There are other roles that I see women, and only women, channel in the heat of the public moment: The nurse. The seducer. The flirt. The rebel outcast. The brainiac.

The split into the role of the professional is the only split that is shared by men and women alike. It is in some way the saddest split of them all, because it betrays a profound sense of inner shame. At its core sits the unspoken belief that if you see me as I truly am, you will not like what you see. Who I really am is not meant for public consumption. So I will don the most neutral mask I can find. I will pretend to be like every other professional who is equally busy pretending to be like every other professional. I will fully and unequivocally submerge into this role. I will show you nothing.

Since I am a man, I sometimes wonder if you, my woman client, behave differently in front of me because I am a man. What other archetypal roles might pop up, or not pop up, if you were talking to a woman coach? I don't know, and I share these insights from my experience as a man and my way of seeing women. But since you have gone through the trouble of coming to visit me in my office, why don't you take this moment now, get up and start to speak? Simply speak and stay conscious. Speak and stay conscious. And let's see what happens in the empty space.

Remember what we said about the split? If you have it, it will show up. The act of speaking in front of others is a magnifying glass for all we try so hard to hide. But here is the beautiful truth about getting up to speak: Every time you utter a word, you will know more about yourself than you did in the moment before. The more you speak, the more you will know. The speaking game is a game with no end in sight. And that, I believe, makes it the only game worth playing.

4

Gender Roles

Roadblocks to Equality?

Risa L. Lieberwitz

The women in these three stories navigate the separate and disparate worlds of family and work. In "Dream Man," Susanna fills the traditional gender role of wife and mother, never having had a job outside the home. Susanna's daily life is vastly different from the one Wallace, her husband, inhabits in the workplace. She cares for her family. She provides for their physical and emotional well-being. In short, Susanna's work in the home frees Wallace from these concerns. Yet Wallace still wields the power at home and devalues Susanna's contribution to the family.

Society has long placed more value on the breadwinner than the home-maker. The women's movement, too, has sent mixed messages. Women are heralded for entering the workforce, but the status of full-time homemak-ers has remained low. Susanna has soaked up some of these values. Her poor self-image mirrors her husband's and son's disrespect. But Susanna begins to see her life more clearly as she finds common ground with other women filling the role of wife and mother—even those, like Marcie's mother, who had once had a well-paying professional job and is still treated with disrespect by her husband.

In "Games Women Play," women clients work with a male "perfor-mance coach" to learn how to fit successfully into the "quintessentially male" business "world of money and power." Yet these women's efforts to mimic men fail. The performance coach sees the double bind for women moving into a man's game. Can women fit into the man's world of business without losing the personal qualities that could help them succeed?

Esther Jackson, in "LaKeesha's Job Interview," is a successful manager in a bank. She interviews LaKeesha Jones for a bank teller position. Esther and LaKeesha are both African American women, but their socioeconomic status is worlds apart. Each faces gender and racial stereotypes. Esther is a successful businesswoman. Her appearance and manner exude authority and competence. Yet she is always conscious of the need to fit in. Esther must decide whether to play the game and hire "an acceptable white boy, with acceptable grammar and short fingernails." Or should she give LaKeesha a chance at the job?

All the women in these stories face obstacles in moving beyond traditional gender roles for women. Their problems replicate the experiences faced by many women—even today. Most people now agree that sex discrimination is wrong. Yet, men and women are still not equal at home or at work. What explains this? Societal values and norms influence the dynamic at home. No laws reach there to require equal respect between men and women—or an equal division of labor in the family.

The workplace dynamic is another matter. Still, almost fifty years after the passage of the Equal Pay Act and Title VII, women face employment discrimination.[1]

Are these antidiscrimination laws too weak? Or are other social forces to blame? The answer is, surely, both. Focusing on the latter, this chapter explores how one powerful social factor—traditional gender roles—helps make women unequal in the family and the workplace. Subsequent chapters address the impact of Title VII on women's workplace status.

The Same Problems of Different Treatment

Gender inequality persists. Women earn only seventy-seven cents on the dollar paid to men.[2] The pay gap between men and women who are professionals, moreover, is actually widening.[3] And women with children are treated unequally, making less money than those without children.[4] Sex-based occupational segregation also continues. At the start of the twenty-first century, two-thirds of U.S. working women still hold low-wage and low-status jobs.[5] Women compose 98 percent of all secretaries, registered nurses, and preschool and kindergarten teachers, accounting for 80 percent of school teachers overall.[6] By contrast, women hold anywhere from 2 to 20 percent of traditional "men's jobs," such as engineer, police officer, or mechanic.[7] Less than 4 percent of firefighters and airline pilots, and less than 3 percent of electricians are women.[8] A job segregation index estimates that "more than half of women would have to change jobs to achieve equal representation among occupations."[9]

Opening up the door of each occupation also shows that women are employed at lower levels than men. In 1999, women composed only 5 percent of top-level executives and 12 percent of corporate officers in Fortune 500 companies. In the 1998–1999 academic year, women held more than 58 percent of instructor positions in universities but only 19 percent of full professorships.[10]

Separate Spheres: Work and Family

Women's primary family caretaker role has traditionally shaped their workplace identity.[11] When women began entering the workplace, either because of financial necessity or by choice or both, their gender role went with them. Typically women's jobs involve supporting men, child care, domestic labor, or service—relegating them to work as secretaries, teachers, nurses, maids, or retail salespeople. Women fill the ranks of temporary or part-time workers to make their time more available for carrying out family responsibilities.[12]

Conversely, men bring their traditional gender roles home from work. Their breadwinner role has made men the head of the family. The Supreme Court observed as recently as 2003: "The fault line between work and family [is] precisely where sex based generalization has been and remains the strongest."[13]

In "Dream Man," Susanna's traditional gender role of wife and mother places her far from her husband's professional life in the business world. Feminist theorists call this the division of "separate spheres." Women's role in the private sphere of home frees up their husbands for their role in the public sphere of the workplace.[14] The *Ozzie and Harriet* and *Leave It to Beaver* television shows exemplified the 1950s idealized vision of the white, heterosexual, suburban, middle-class family. The television characters fit happily into their gender roles, resulting in well-run lives and well-adjusted children.

In the 1960s, the feminist movement exposed the cracks in this "ideal" image. Betty Friedan, often credited with launching the "second wave" of feminism, published *The Feminine Mystique* in 1963. Calling women's unhappy domestic lives "the problem that has no name," she captured the isolation that women felt in the separate sphere of the home given the expectation that their identities revolve around their husbands and children.[15]

Friedan and other leaders of the 1960s and 1970s women's movement set as their highest priority women's entry into the economic and social public sphere of work. This agenda has been successful, as women have moved into the workplace. In 1940, 28 percent of women were in the labor force. This percentage increased to 60 percent in 1999. Women made up 25 percent of the labor force in 1940 and 47 percent of the workforce in 1999.[16] Yet, the separate spheres ideal retains a persistent hold on the public imagination. Recent polls and surveys show "a curious nostalgia for returning to the sex roles characteristic of the 1950s where many women stayed home after marriage and certainly after having children."[17]

The separate spheres regulated not only gender roles but also power and control. The home may be a woman's domain. But if women are economically dependent on their husbands, they have little power in the marriage and family.

As the breadwinner and home owner, Wallace, the husband in "Dream Man," wields almost total authority in the family. He repeatedly refers to the house as his own, not "ours." Susanna, in her traditional gender role, is denied the independence and power that come with a professional identity.[18] She feels isolated in her role as full-time housewife and mother in her male-dominated home. Wallace ridicules her for her naïveté, and her son Dylan criticizes her "nosiness." She sees herself as weak and ineffectual, even agreeing with Wallace and Dylan's attacks.

In telling her story, though, Susanna starts expressing her own anger about Wallace's and Dylan's poor judgment and irresponsible conduct. Ultimately, she sees her husband as "an old gray toddler with a mustache, all belly and bravado." As she conveys her anger and alienation, Susanna moves from a state of unconsciousness—almost somnambulist—to confront the reality of her home life. She is furious that her domineering husband denies responsibility for his inappropriate conduct toward their son's girlfriend, Marcie.

Recounting her story to Marcie's mother, Eleanor, Susanna begins seeing her similarities with other women. Eleanor, we learn, left her professional life as an attorney to become a full-time wife and mother just like Susanna. What is more, Susanna discovers that Eleanor's husband is also disrespectful, dismissing her volunteer work in the local theater community.

Like the middle-class women who read *The Feminine Mystique* in the 1960s, Susanna becomes aware of her anger and alienation as she shares (if only in her imagination) her story with another woman. It was this process of "consciousness-raising" that made the early second wave of feminism come alive. Having discovered their common needs, women began making collective demands for social and economic independence.

Gender Roles in the Labor Market

The women's movement of the 1960s and 1970s was successful in bringing middle- and upper-class women from the home sphere to the workplace. Women's choices of jobs, however, were restricted by sex-segregated occupations. Although many of these women had college and even graduate degrees, they were shut out of most professional positions. Women's traditional jobs replicated their family role of support and care. Hired into temporary, part-time, or low-skilled jobs—the societal expectation was that women would be committed to their family first, not their career. As a new law school graduate in 1952, Supreme Court Justice Sandra Day O'Connor, herself, could not find a position as a lawyer in a private firm. Instead, she was offered a job as a legal secretary. O'Connor, however, persisted. She started in an unpaid position as an attorney and built a career in public service, becoming the first female Supreme Court Justice in 1981.[19]

The "performance coach" in "Games Women Play" encourages all his clients to "play and experiment with who we are." They practice their professional roles—preparing for speeches and business presentations. Men and women alike experience what he calls "the split" when they stand up to perform. This is "that millisecond when you slip into another skin . . . into the role of the public person." The similarity between his male and female clients ends there. One after the other, the women transform—for the worse—in front of the group: from a "fluid, spontaneous" personality to a low-energy "archetypal teacher"; from a person with "palpable, defiant energy" to "a suddenly desperate cheerleader"; from a bright, warm personal style to "a robotic poise"; and from "alpha-woman into the vulture warrior control-freak." Although the men also take on public personas, the coach has never seen any of them turn into "the teacher . . . the cheerleader . . . the vulture."

What explains the difference? The performance coach is witnessing the force of gender roles for women and men in the separate spheres of home and work. The women's presentations in the public sphere of the "quintessentially male" business world reveal the continued influence of traditional gender roles for women, such as the teacher, nurse, or cheerleader. While these roles did not fit well in the business environment, neither did Melinda's attempts to be more macho than the men, turning her into the "vulture warrior control-freak." The performance coach recognizes that male gender roles enable men to more easily integrate their public and private personas. Even the "male vulture" was more authentic as a "fully lived" role.

Gender roles put women in a double bind. Like the women in "Games Women Play," if they try to be the "tough" business professional, women may appear stiff or uncomfortable in an unfamiliar role. If women try to be "themselves," though, they may be penalized for displaying traditional female qualities, such as warmth and friendliness. Ann Hopkins faced this double bind when her employer, Price Waterhouse, denied her promotion bid to partnership. Several of the male partners criticized her for being "too macho" and for "overcompensating for being a woman." They told her that she should be more feminine.[20]

Hopkins's case ended up in the Supreme Court, where she made history. The Court found that the Price Waterhouse partners' reliance on gender role stereotypes provided powerful evidence of sex discrimination. The partners had placed Hopkins in an untenable position that few men, if any, face. They denied her partnership because she was "too macho." But if she had been "too feminine," the partners might well have found that she was not tough enough for the job.[21]

The Importance of "Intersectionality": Gender, Race, and Class Intertwined

Susanna's role, in "Dream Man," as full-time housewife and mother is in-extricably linked to her race and economic status as a white middle-class woman. Many women, however, never fit tidily into the idealized vision of the separate spheres of family and work. Poor and working-class women have always held jobs in the public sphere of the economy, with their second-class status in society relegating them to low-wage service jobs that replicate traditional gender roles at home.[22]

Scholars have long recognized that a major weakness of the women's movement has been its primary concern with white middle-class women.[23] From the 1960s through the 1980s, U.S. women's organizations focused on women's entry into the workplace. This agenda, while important, ignored social and economic circumstances of working-class and poor women. These women also experienced the effects of the separate spheres, shoulder-ing the primary responsibilities for family needs. But their class position al-ways required them to enter the workforce. It was (and still is) poor and working-class women of color who have done the hardest and dirtiest jobs, such as low-wage work in industrial laundries. It is these women who do the custodial work or the domestic work for middle- or upper-class families.[24] They are the targets of gender, race, and class discrimination, all of which are "inextricably intertwined."[25] The race and class privilege of white women and men enables them to benefit from the low-wage domestic and service work of women of color.

In "LaKeesha's Job Interview," Esther knows how hard it is to overcome gender and racial stereotypes. She aspires to a career in upper management at the bank, "making those fast deals. Lending millions just on her say-so." But she'll need to "play[ ] her cards right," and then "maybe she could be the one who'd transcend the glass ceiling. Every once in a while, they let somebody black slip through."

What does it mean for Esther to "play her cards right"? She knows that the "smart move" is to hire David Weaver, the white male candidate. But Esther also knows that LaKeesha is struggling, against the odds, to get ahead. She advises LaKeesha about how to get not just a good job, but a career. And part of that is conforming to racial and gender norms of a white male workplace. Esther tells LaKeesha to change her fingernails, clothes, makeup, hair, and grammar. "[W]hen you're working for white folks you want to fit in, not stand out." In the end, will Esther follow her own advice or will she take the riskier path and hire LaKeesha?

Nature or Nurture: Or Are These the Same Thing for Women?

Why do gender roles exist and persist? Are gender differences a matter of biology or "nature," or of socialization or "nurture"? Is Susanna, in "Dream Man," "naturally" suited for her role as wife and mother? Did Eleanor leave her job as an attorney because she wanted to put her family first? Did the women clients in "Games Women Play" have trouble fitting into the business world because of a conflict between innate feminine and masculine characteristics? Did Esther, in "LaKeesha's Job Interview," succeed in business by finding a way to act more like a man?

The debate over nature versus nurture reflects different perspectives about whether gender roles can or should be changed.[26] Biological explanations tend to explain gender roles as a consequence of innate sex-based differences in reproduction. They view woman's traditional primary caretaker role in the family as being a natural result of childbearing. Nonphysical qualities are also attributed to women's reproductive capacities. Women are seen as nurturing, emotional, caring, and supportive. If women have these innate qualities, this view holds, they are suited for the private sphere of the home, rather than the harsher, competitive public sphere of work. By contrast, men are described as inherently more competitive, rational, risk-taking, and tough. These qualities suit them for the role of worker and breadwinner in the public economic sphere. This economic role in the workplace translates into men's traditional role as head of the family.

Social construction theories, in contrast, challenge biological explanations by arguing that gender roles are part of social, economic, and political divisions of wealth and power.[27] These social theories reject the view that the biology of pregnancy and childbearing determine women's personal and professional abilities and interests. Such biological determinism overstates the scope of the relevance of physical differences of reproduction. Although gender roles are so deeply ingrained that they may seem natural, men and women actually share most qualities that a biological explanation attributes to one or the other sex.[28] Both men and women, at different times, are nurturing, fragile, tough, risk-taking, competitive, analytical, and emotional.[29] If women do reveal more nurturing or empathetic qualities than men, this view holds, this is due to their socialization to fit particular gender roles rather than to any innate sex-related characteristics.

Gender roles also define sexuality. A biological perspective on men's and women's traditional family roles assumes that heterosexuality is natural. But this perspective breaks down if sexual orientation, like gender roles, is largely determined by social factors. If gender and sexuality are socially constructed, they can either constrain or expand choices about the way that individuals create and care for their families.[30] Questioning gender roles creates questions about sexuality that in turn undermine the validity of a heterosexual norm—and vice versa. If women are not inherently more suited than men for caretaking, then either men or women can competently fill child care duties. This opens the possibility for families made up of two male or two female parents—all of whom are able to raise children.

What do these different perspectives mean for women in the workplace? From a biological perspective, if women are innately more nurturing and caring, they will place family needs first, preferring jobs that allow easy workforce entry and exit. Eleanor, in "Dream Man," left her job as an attorney when she became a mother. Similarly, women's disproportionate representation in part-time or temporary work, low-skilled jobs, or public school teaching reflects their priorities, not sex discrimination. Women's natural qualities of nurturing and care also lead them to jobs such as teaching, day care, or nursing.[31] From this perspective, the women in "Games Women Play" would naturally find it difficult to adopt the aggressive and competitive qualities needed for business careers.

If women's primary caretaking role is more socially than biologically determined, though, occupational segregation is not a natural result of women's interests and abilities. Instead, women have been socialized to carry the primary responsibility for the family, which leads them to choose low-wage, part-time, and support positions. This socialization reserves the better-paying and higher-status occupations for men, who are free of primary caretaking responsibilities. Eleanor may have welcomed the opportunity to share family care with her husband and to pursue her legal career. The women in "Games Women Play" aspire to responsible positions in the business world. The performance coach sees his job as helping them to succeed with the same qualities that they would draw on in the family sphere—energy, creativity, warmth, and intelligence. Esther, in "LaKeesha's Job Interview," is proud of her career and dreams of advancement. LaKeesha seeks to enter this world, as she explains to Esther, to be a role model for her sisters.

This is not to say that adherents of biological explanations oppose the elimination of intentional sex discrimination. It may mean, though, that they expect that innate differences will continue to influence men's and women's choices and roles at home and at work. In one case, the Equal Employment Opportunity Commission (EEOC) charged that Sears, Roebuck & Co. had systematically excluded women from commission sales positions.[32] At trial, Sears's expert witness, historian Rosalind Rosenberg, testified that women's nurturing and noncompetitive qualities would lead them to avoid these jobs that required risk-taking and time away from family priorities.[33] The trial judge agreed, as did the appellate court. Judge Richard D. Cudahy, dissenting, criticized the appeals court's acceptance of the employer's arguments as being "of a piece with the proposition that women are by nature happier cooking, doing the laundry and chauffeuring the children to softball games than arguing appeals or selling stocks."[34]

What Is the Role of Law?

Whether gender roles are determined more by nature or nurture, they are deeply engrained. But as more women enter the workplace, the gender role of primary caretaker no longer fits the reality of most women's circumstances. Women work because of financial pressures and career aspirations. Just like men, women should have the opportunity to work full-time and to seek high-wage and high-status jobs. For most women, though, this still means filling two shifts—at work and at home.[35]

Feminist legal theorist Martha Fineman explains that women continue to subsidize the rest of society through their free labor in the family. Both the government and employers maintain that providing for the family's basic needs falls on women's shoulders. After all, it is a woman's "natural role" to care for her family.

How entrenched gender roles are raises questions about the law's potential to achieve equality between men and women. Can antidiscrimination law help women gain all aspects of equality at work, including equal pay and representation in all occupations? Will women be free from sexual harassment on the job? Will gender equality include gay and lesbian rights? Can the law "crack the foundational myth," as Fineman has put it, that workers' family care is a private concern?[36] Can the legal requirements of equal treatment of men and women in employment be fulfilled if women and men are not equal in the family?

UNFAIR TREATMENT

5

Getting Even

Harriet Kriegel

The metal lamp barely illuminated the large black table with heavy claw-footed legs. A spark of light caught the brass ring of the table's lone drawer. In the middle lay a pad of yellow lined paper, its center ringed by a curious glow spreading into shadow. The neat handwriting was familiar, but she couldn't decipher the words. She stared into asterisks and carefully placed strips of Scotch tape fastening additional paper to the bottom of the page. The words in the circle loomed larger and clearer, as if looked at through a spyglass. Yet she couldn't make them out. She peered closer and closer and closer . . .

Julia awoke with a start and sat up, sweating, breathing heavily. Why had this dream evoked such anxiety? It hardly seemed significant as daylight patterned the bedroom wall through slits in the blinds. Visualizing the singular cursive loops on the legal pad, Julia recognized Ira's handwriting.

Reaching for a non-existent cigarette, she laughed, having given up smoking years ago. I can't believe after all these years all the money I spent on therapy, I'm still upset by Ira.

Ira had been president and CEO of Waverly Family Medical Center, a midsized hospital on the East Coast and Julia's boss. He was a brilliant schmoozer with a talent for grooming his own popularity even if it meant rationalizing some department head's obduracy or some board member's disdain. His staff was devoted to him but they were inevitably frustrated when his decision in some dispute was sought. No matter the issue, Ira managed to agree with all sides.

Damn Ira, Julia thought, always playing the nice guy, leaving everyone to fight it out and leaving me to pick up the pieces. Damn. I have more important things to think about than Ira.

She planned out her day in the shower: First, she'd give her secretary an agenda to type up for the hospital department head meeting. She thought of how best to approach the psychiatrist who apparently had lied about his credentials on his CV. She reminded herself to have her secretary ask the Dietary Department to set up a luncheon for a donor. Better wear the conservative black Donna Karan suit for the presentation at the board meeting tonight.

But despite her busy schedule, the dream and Ira resonated throughout the day. Julia had worked for almost six years during the 1980s as Ira's director of administration. He had relied on her efficiency with details, her facility with state and federal regulations, grateful for how she handled thorny patient and staff complaints and had soothed angry activists. Julia relieved him of standing up to inspectors, arguing with lawyers, negotiating with insurance agents.

Julia was aware that not everyone shared Ira's enthusiasm for her accomplishments. Why would they? She had done his dirty work—and been more demanding. How could she not have been more demanding than Ira, who demanded nothing of anybody?

Rehabilitation resented her relentless pressure to create videos to increase the hospital's visibility. They were convinced it was her own visibility she cared about, and they bristled at the extra work.

She had infuriated Public Relations by ignoring hospital protocol, taking press calls instead of transferring them to PR. Despite the PR director's angry warnings that mishandled media inquiries could damage the hospital's reputation, Julia continued talking to the press.

But it was Clyde Morgan, the development director, who was most offended. Without his knowledge and against hospital policy, Julia spent months cultivating Don Walden, a wealthy developer, until she succeeded in getting a $1.5 million naming gift for their new wing.

Clyde fumed to Ira, "What makes Julia so special that she doesn't have to follow your rules and then hammers others who do? I could have gotten a larger gift if I had the chance. Julia's meddling makes my job infinitely harder."

After Clyde left, Ira reproved her. "Oh come on," Julia replied. "You know Clyde can't close a deal. He bores donors to death. If I hadn't gotten to Walden, we would never have gotten the gift." Julia mollified Ira, conceding perhaps that she should have been more sensitive. Ira applauded her success—and he lost no time informing the board of it.

While she prevailed in most matters, she was unable to convince him that Matt Childers, his chief financial officer, was a threat to him and to the hospital.

Ironically, she and Matt had begun as allies. She flinches, remembering how Matt had congratulated her for "putting those females in their place." "Those females" had complained that they weren't paid as well as their male counterparts were. Knowing her influence on Ira, they had sought her help.

Julia responded, "You must be kidding."

The women had looked at each other, stunned.

"We're not kidding," said Nettie Sanders, chief of nurse recruitment. "Why would you think we are?"

"Equal pay for equal work," giggled Beverly Gazapoli, head of pediatric social work. Julia wondered why some women giggled when they wished to be taken seriously.

The women continued to express frustration. Julia continued to tune them out, focusing on Beverly's excessive weight, denim jumper, Peter Pan collar, Mary Jane shoes. No excuse for wearing clothes you wore in college. Thank God she's not wearing those red and violet horizontally striped stockings. I ought to talk with personnel about a dress code.

The physical therapist, Sarah Goodman, roused her attention. "Frankly, Julia, I think it's a class action suit."

"Oh please. You don't have a leg to stand on. Do you really know what men in your positions earn, or do you just have a feeling that they make more than you do?"

"I know that Frank Steinberg makes a lot more than I do," said Janet Rothman. "We're both internists, and we finished our residencies at the same time."

"There are too many variables." Julia replied. "His academic training is different from yours. Your subspecialties are different, not to mention differences in experience."

When Nettie raised her objections, Julia advised her to take it up with her union, since the nurses had a much-fought-over contract with the hospital.

"Well I don't have a contract," Beverly pointed out.

"As head of your department, what male social worker is getting paid more than you?" Beverly admitted there were none.

The group began to disperse. Julia felt pleased with herself at having averted a crisis. But Sarah moved like a ferret from the door. "You've got some nerve being so smug. Not all of us have husbands who can keep us in Saks Fifth Avenue suits. In case you don't know it, you're the house shill." The door slammed.

Julia wanted Sarah fired. She wrote to Sarah's boss and to personnel, demanding a review for insubordination. Ira told her, "Drop it. Forget the whole thing. They'll only get angrier if you don't."

Still livid, she described the incident to Matt, who was gleeful that the insurrection had been quelled. His budget would remain intact. "Ira's wrong. You should have filed the complaint. You were great, and Ira should have told you so."

Her friendship with Matt grew.

One of her most challenging assignments at Waverly had been getting the staff to work collaboratively on the state accreditation review. Vanessa Nelson, the nursing director, fiercely opposed anyone who threatened her autonomy. Vanessa had created a first-rate, disciplined staff, but she was actively disliked. She had denigrated Housekeeping for laziness, castigated Pharmacy for sloppy record keeping, and attacked some of the physicians for their failure to communicate with her nurses. And she had so irritated the head of engineering that he threatened to quit.

Ira expected Julia to impose order on the warring departments. With rewards and flattery, Julia set up competitive teams within departments and honored weekly winners. Matt encouraged her to meet with department heads individually to bolster morale and convince them to cooperate. He agreed to purchase equipment and to hire temporary help. Julia's persuasiveness, combined with Matt's assistance and Vanessa's ruthless pursuit of excellence resulted in Waverly's receiving the highest state rating. Ira was euphoric, and the board was delighted.

For Matt it was an opportunity to liberate himself from Vanessa's imperiousness. Armed with Julia's descriptions of Vanessa's behavior he persuaded Ira that Vanessa was capricious, her decisions dangerous to Waverly's welfare. Her high-handedness could lead to problems with the union. For the good of the hospital, it would be best to dismiss her, Matt insisted. It was Julia, Matt stressed, who had been primarily responsible for the hospital's ratings. And the more Julia modestly said, "It was just everyone pulling together," the more Ira respected her.

Julia was grateful for Matt's help, and no matter how often she told herself she never intended to have Vanessa fired, she was also aware that she was delighted that she no longer had to deal with her. But Julia soon found herself wary of Matt's growing power.

Without Vanessa to keep him in check, Matt became so overbearing that the staff and department heads began to refer to him as the "CBO," chief bullying officer. Department heads he favored had no trouble with budgets; those he disliked battled arbitrary cuts. No one could counter his insistence on budgetary constraints. Anyone threatening to complain faced Matt's warning, "You won't even know it when I get you. There'll be no way to trace how you ended up in shit." When Julia reported this to Ira, he laughed. "People exaggerate. I know he can get carried away, but he's under terrible pressure managing the deficit. He's brilliant with the numbers."

His brilliance with the numbers caused Julia increasing concern. She noticed irregularities in his financial reports. But when she brought them to Ira, he dismissed them—until the irregularities grew so obvious that he couldn't overlook them. One morning Julia heard them shouting at each other from behind the closed door. But Matt had already presented the financial reports to the chairman of the board as evidence of Ira's deceptive accounting. The board dismissed Ira and named Matt president.

To ensure a smooth transition, the board recommended that Julia be appointed vice president of hospital administration. But in his first memo to the board, Matt announced:

> With the increased administrative responsibilities our hospital now must handle, I have created a new Administrative Vice President, Jack Wilson. For many years, Mr. Wilson, a Harvard MBA, has handled the significant responsibility of procurement for the entire hospital with great diligence as Materials Management Director. This has prepared him to meet the requirements of the medical center in a very special and unique way.
>
> Jack will be assisted by Julia Roschak, one of the most devoted and competent members of our staff. Julia will be of enormous help in teaching Jack the ropes and in helping him over any rough spots. Together, they will make a great team.
>
> Please join me in wishing Jack success.

Dubious as some members were, the board felt obliged to support the president it had just chosen.

Julia felt stunned, humiliated, her expectations dashed. How could Jack, whose hospital experience was limited to buying supplies, manage the administration of a hospital? Clearly, he couldn't—not unless she helped him "over any rough spots." How dare Matt ask her to "teach him the ropes." Remembering all the hours of managerial crises she had endured working for Ira, she seethed. Was she to continue to handle daily crises while Jack got the credit? Did Matt expect her to teach Jack state and federal regulations? Was she to do what she always had done, work to benefit another?

At home, she stormed at her husband.

"That asshole! That moron. How can anyone in his right mind assign someone like Jack Wilson to run a hospital?"

Bob urged her to calm down.

"What do you mean, calm down?"

"Ranting isn't going to help."

"I'm expected to train someone to do my job. He gets a promotion and a fat salary, and I get nothing. Worse than nothing. And you want me to calm down?"

"So you're not the Boss Lady you thought you were." "Boss Lady" was guaranteed to make her angrier. "Matt may be an asshole and a moron. But he holds the cards. You better get used to that. As far as he's concerned, you're nothing more than a reliable fixture."

Her husband was right. But knowing that enraged her more. "I swear I'm going to get even with that fucking bastard."

"You're better off looking for a new job. Forget Waverly."

"Forget it! I'm not going to forget it."

"Don't forget it then. Julia, you're right to be pissed. But don't take it out on me."

Their tension was exacerbated by Bob's having just given up his job with an established firm to start his own law practice.

"Matt knows better than anyone how much I've done for Waverly. He knows how good I am."

"You're overlooking the one talent that Jack has that you don't."

"What's that?"

"Procurement."

"What's that got to do with it?"

"There's profit in procurement. Sometimes, Julia, I think that for all your skill, you're shockingly naïve."

"Thanks. Not exactly the message I need now."

In the end, whatever motivated Matt didn't matter. She had been humiliated, humbled. Struggling with her rage, she decided to confront Matt directly. She had no illusions about changing his mind. But she could negotiate an increase in salary and a better title.

The next morning found her armored in a buttoned down blue suit.

"He won't be able to resist," Bob said.

She grimaced.

"Lighten up, Julia. Smile."

He kissed her, wished her luck. Her teenaged daughter, Alicia, grunted something that sounded like "good luck" as she downed her black coffee breakfast.

. . .

There were two ways to get to Matt—flattery or seduction. Even if she were attracted to him, flirtation was too dangerous. She recalled how Matt had put his arm around her at last year's medical convention in Dallas, as if he were claiming her. She had gently removed his arm and smiled. But remembering the incident made her feel as if his hands had been all over her.

Julia played the game. Rich silk blouses softened crisply tailored suits which hugged her waist, lying flat on hips that she knew emphasized her curves. Her just-above-the-knee skirts flattered legs whose appeal lay in the long curve of calf. Matt had repeatedly told her he liked the way she dressed, as much offer as compliment. But she avoided what he could perceive as an invitation. And he was careful enough not to chance rejection.

She relied on flattery—at times inviting him to lunch by claiming the need for his expertise. His arrival invariably exuded a strong whiff of Aqua Velva. His tie was always a meticulously knotted silk marker against a starched shirt, his matted hair carefully blow-dried into submission. Although he struggled to keep fit, his middle hinted a paunch. The women in his office admired his grooming and took pleasure in working for a man with power. They even took satisfaction in how uncomfortable department heads were when they were summoned to his office like high school students reporting to the principal.

Matt reveled in the admiration of subordinates. Yet despite his bravado, he was uncomfortable beyond the office, and Julia found herself straining to get him to talk at their lunches. Fiscal management was her ploy and at some time in the conversation Matt would tell her she was "different" from most women—sensible, rational. A man could talk to her. If a lunch had gone particularly well, he would offer the ultimate male compliment, "You think like a man."

Impassioned about his craft, incensed that people dismissed accountants as bean counters, he bitterly confided, "Accounting can be very creative." At one of their lunches he arrived visibly perspiring, tie askew, fresh from battling a team of state officials over money owed the hospital for more than five years. Despite two court judgments, the state had not paid. She had never seen him so disturbed.

On another occasion, he arrived furious at Jane Feingold, the neurologist who insisted she be paid what her male colleagues were paid. "No one held a gun to her head when she agreed to work here. Women simply get paid less. It's not my fault. That's the way things are."

"You can't say that anymore, Matt. You'll get us into trouble."

"That's ridiculous. It's reality."

Their lunches always ended with the same ritual. She would take out her American Express card. "*I* invited *you*," she would say, knowing he would put his hospital credit card on top of hers, "We *were* talking hospital business."

. . .

Julia confronted Matt in Ira's old office. She congratulated him, told him she was certain he would do well. But when she came to the substance of the visit, he expressed surprise.

"We laid off a lot of people, Julia. And you still have a terrific job."

"Matt, my job now is to train a man with no experience to do what I've done for years. That's difficult."

"It shouldn't be. He has an MBA."

"I have a master's in hospital administration."

"So what do you want? The Nobel Prize?"

"That's not funny."

"All right, so you don't like my humor. Look, Jack's a really bright guy. An MBA prepares you for any job."

"I hope he doesn't show up in the operating room to do brain surgery."

"Don't be a smartass. You know what I'm saying."

"My degree got us through government regulations. My training kept us in compliance and helped me write Ira's position papers."

Those papers had landed Ira on talk shows and policy boards, and Matt was tempted by the prospect of TV himself, but he shrugged. "Those TV shows and policy people took too much of his time."

"They gave the hospital prestige."

"Prestige doesn't help the bottom line."

She spoke of the customer satisfaction project she had initiated.

"It was expensive. A waste of time."

"I helped Ira develop major donor strategies."

"Which made Clyde so grateful that he left."

"He didn't leave. He was replaced."

"Not exactly a positive outcome."

He stood up from his desk. The meeting was over. Desperately, Julia continued, Her salary was lower than Jack's. She was training him, and *her* salary was lower.

Matt shrugged, "So women get paid less. We've had this conversation."

"In fairness, at least change my title to associate vice president."

"I can't have two vice presidents of administration."

"That's bullshit."

"Listen, you worked for Ira for about five years. Right?"

"Almost six."

"You're making my point. If you were so terrific then he should have made you vice president."

Trembling, she rushed to her office, knocking into her secretary's desk. Ignoring Rose's "Are you all right?" she slammed the door behind her. She wasn't sure who had enraged her more: Matt or Ira. Or was she herself to blame? Matt was right. Ira should have changed her title. He always put her off. She should have insisted, but she had allowed herself to get caught up in the daily demands, to bask in his praise. She had behaved like a file clerk, not an executive.

Julia raided the files for her annual reviews—the laudatory notes from board members, congratulatory letters from colleagues about the awards she had won. She copied everything, from the CV she had submitted to the last report she had written for Ira. She even copied her cover notes. It took her a week to copy everything.

Unsure of what to do next, she shielded herself, flitting from a dramatic resignation to the cautionary idea that she would be better off if she got another job first. She weighed the idea of a lawsuit. She didn't know whether she had a case. She didn't know whom to ask. Would it be a federal, state, or city claim? Christ, if she didn't know, how were other women expected to know? She called Bob for someone who specialized in employment law.

· · ·

"You filed a complaint with the state?" Matt exploded.

"I didn't file. I inquired whether I *could* file. And Waverly, it turns out, is in violation of Title VII."

"Don't give me that crap."

As Julia tried to explain the statute, he bellowed, "I didn't ask you, did I? Why ask you when I can get advice from a professional? We have lawyers, you know." He paused. "I don't understand you. I didn't fire you. I didn't cut your salary. And this is how you repay me?" The state! Damn it." Glaring at her, "I can't have someone on my staff I can't trust."

By the time she returned to her office, Matt had already told Jack to fire her. She had three hours to leave while Jack stood alongside her, nervously watching her pack.

· · ·

Part of her wanted to be fired, so that she could sue. Matt had strengthened her case by retaliating for her visit to the Human Rights office, as she had hoped. Being fired meant she could also collect unemployment insurance. It wasn't the money she was after as much as the irritation it would cause Matt. Still, her dismissal was another humiliation.

Liberated from the straitjacket of tight scheduling, she found leisure disorienting. She had taken pride in how much could be achieved by intelligent time management. Now simple household tasks stretched over days. She spent hours reading—newspapers, magazines, medical journals, convincing herself that she was widening her horizons. She dutifully went to the unemployment office every two weeks, polishing and repolishing her CV.

At first, Bob had been understanding. "Don't worry, you'll get another job."

"Every hospital has a job freeze."

"It'll open up. We're not starving."

"I'll never get as good a job."

"You're joking. Matt's a bastard, but he was right about Ira. You worked your ass off, and he never gave you what you deserved. You should have pushed for a promotion."

"Yeah. Maybe."

"You know I'm right. I'm also right that you'll find something better."

Months passed before she found the energy to turn to her case. The Human Rights lawyer's advice consisted of pages of statutes and volumes of background material. Overwhelmed by the mass of documents, a need to clean her closets overtook her.

She cleaned—closets, medicine cabinets. She cleaned the basement. She sent out CVs, went on job interviews, and listened as personnel manager after personnel manager told her she was overqualified.

Maybe this was her chance to break out of hospital management, to do something more creative. When she heard that a filmmaker specializing in pharmaceutical and medical products was looking for a manager with a health care background, Julia rushed to the interview and was elated when she got the job. But the Antonioni of medical films tormented his staff and frustrated clients who couldn't understand why they should pay for his celluloid perfection with rarely met deadlines. His tantrums matched their anger. Within the month Julia resigned.

She painted the kitchen.

Reorganizing the linen closet one weekend, Julia remembered Memorial Day weekend, 1985. Ira, apologizing profusely for imposing on her just before the holiday, had stressed the urgency of the application for a state nurses' housing grant. It was due in a week. With his customary ambivalence, Ira had decided to apply at the last minute. "I'm really sorry, Julia," he said as he left the office that Thursday. She sought consultants, but they had all left for the long weekend. The only one she could reach had been hired by St. Bart's three months earlier.

Bob and her daughter were banished for the weekend to the house they were renting on Fire Island as she attacked the proposal with two secretaries on double overtime and a junior administrator from Nursing. The two hundred–page proposal was handed in forty minutes before the deadline. Three months later, Waverly received funding for a new building.

"That son of a bitch!" she murmured into the carefully folded sheets.

"You OK?" called Bob from the bedroom.

"I'm fine." She could do for Ira what everyone said was impossible, but now she was too daunted to make a case for herself. She was a fool to settle for depression and self-doubt. That afternoon she removed the dusty cover of her rarely used Olympia and began typing.

She was a poor typist, used to a secretary transcribing dictation on a large Selectric. She constantly re-edited what she had written. Her drafts—both handwritten and typed–were blotched with notes and crossed out text. Corrections in tiny letters were glued like hieroglyphics above blocks of inked-in handwriting that even she found difficult to read. Curved arrows went every which way, repositioning paragraphs to preceding or succeeding pages. Wite-Out and ribbons of correction tape decorated every page.She called NOW and was given Shelley, a legal counselor. "I don't have time," Shelley apologized. "I'm working on my own thing." Then, voice tinged with guilt, Shelley added, "Put everything, everything, into your document. Even stuff that seems minor. Put it in."

So much for Sisterhood, Julia thought. But she put everything in.

. . .

"You're doing *what*?" Aunt Sophie yelled, nasality shattering the air. "Bob, for God's sake tell her to stop."

"How do I stop her?"

"Believe me. I've seen what happens when employees complain."

"Sophie, the world's changed since you were working."

"Some things never change."

"My lawyer says I have a strong case."

"Julia, you're so naïve. You'll end up blacklisted."

. . .

The brief grew.

"Julia, I don't want to interfere," Bob said, voice a mixture of apology and irritation. "But you've got to get a job."

"I know."

"I don't think you do. We're running short of money."

His new practice had hit a rough patch. He had recently lost his most important client.

"I can't help it if I'm overqualified."

"I know what this case means to you. But you're not going to get any money."

"We'll get money."

"Julia, you're giving yourself a song and dance."

• • •

She typed. As obsessive as she had been about closets, she now became about her case. She relived the past even as she wrote, watched herself thwarting the activists who came to trust her, developed new strategies to convince Don Walden to donate money to Waverly. She again cajoled staff into creating the best customer service program in the Northeast. Recalling each success stoked her anger, spurred her on.

Why hadn't Ira acted swiftly when she showed him the evidence against Matt? Inertia or faith in Matt? Had Matt threatened him? Or had Ira, too, profited from procurement?

After all these years, she still found the memory of Matt's behavior in Dallas revolting—his attempts to paw her, his clumsy effort to lure her to his room. Not that she was adverse to adventure. She had, in fact, flirted with the handsome orthopedic surgeon whom she sometimes met for lunch to talk about the Yankees and the movies. His cynical sense of humor made her laugh.

"Will I see you in Dallas?"

"You will."

Bob had had his flings. Why shouldn't she?

But Matt eagle-eyed her every moment. She couldn't open her door without sensing his presence. She laughed at the irony that it was Matt who had kept her virtuous.

• • •

Alicia burst into her room.

"Mom, can you fix my cheerleading skirt? It's an emergency."

"When do you need it?"

"Tonight."

"Put it on the dining room table. I'll take care of it when I get back from the interview."

"Why can't you fix it now?"

"I need to finish what I'm writing, take a shower, and prepare for a job interview."

"I'm so sick of your damn case. Daddy's right. You don't think of us. And we're not getting anything out of it anyway." Alicia half-slammed, half-pushed the chair next to her mother, which ricocheted against Julia's leg. "Shit, I didn't mean to hurt you!"

"Son of a—"

"Bitch?" finished Alicia as she raced out the door.

Julia pressed gauze to her bleeding shin. Was Alicia's behavior her fault too?"

• • •

"You need to show a pattern of gender discrimination," the lawyer said. "Get salary lists. You have to show women are paid less than men." Julia felt guilty, remembering the women who met in her office. But Rose, her former secretary, now in personnel, had no compunction about giving her the information.

Eight months after she began her brief, she submitted two large loose-leaf binders to the lawyer. A week later he called. "Your brief looks good. But there are so many variables."

"What do you mean?"

"Jack Wilson could have had managerial training you didn't know about. Or they could massage something into his background, making it more meaningful than it was. Who knows? In this business you prepare for surprises. We'll see."

• • •

At a cocktail party an artist Bob knew approached them, his heavy silver peace amulet gleaming on his bony chest. "It's been a long time," he smiled. They nodded. "What have you two been up to?"

Bob mentioned his law practice.

"Terrific," the artist said.

Julia mentioned her case. The artist just stared. "Jesus, Julia, you're an angry woman," he said. Julia felt as if she had been slapped.

• • •

The economy dipped, hospitals cut staff, Julia called Don Walden.

"It must be really tight out there if you're having trouble. Let me make a few calls."

A call to Carter General led to a fund-raising job. There, Julia quickly discovered it was one thing to cultivate a single donor like Walden, quite another to solicit large gifts from scores of donors. She found herself plagued by lunches, dinners, plaques, mailing lists, mailing houses, and most horrible of all—the annual dinner journal.

As irritation and fatigue deepened, she reluctantly applied for an administrative internship at a nursing home. But a director of administration position opened at Morley, a small private hospital near Philadelphia, for which she had been interviewed almost a year before. When the board chairman made an offer, she accepted immediately.

Seven months later, Julia was contacted by the state's Human Rights division. A settlement had been proposed. Waverly (now called Bolton Medical) would give her two years' salary, tax free since she had sued for damages. "Of course, the state has to agree," the lawyer said. "I don't foresee any problems. The good thing is that they fired you. But there're always possible variables."

"Such as?"

"It's highly unlikely, but you never know when someone finds a loophole in the law. On the other hand, you've got a good case. And I think you could get more if we went to court."

Too much time had passed. Her desire for vindication, like the names, facts, and figures she had assiduously collected, had ebbed. She had even forgotten parts of her brief. The time needed to prepare for court would jeopardize her position at Morley. That was her priority now, not what had happened at Waverly.

She took satisfaction that her case had been threatening enough for the hospital to hire a white-shoes law firm to handle the suit. The state's approval would confirm the justice of her case. And two years tax-free earnings would help with Alicia's law school tuition. It would be helpful especially now that she and Bob were in a trial separation.

The satisfaction she sought in "getting even" with Ira and Matt was illusory anyway. There wasn't anyone to get even with. Matt had been dismissed a year and a half earlier for manipulating hospital funds and accepting kickbacks. Jack Wilson had simply disappeared. The chairman of the board had taken over—within the year all the other members of the board had resigned, and Waverly Medical Center was merged into the Bolton Medical System.

· · ·

Julia got home late from the board meeting. Her presentation had gone well. She flipped through the mail on the foyer table, including the stack she had not yet opened from the day before. Julia spotted the envelope with the state's stark black letters. She stared, sighed, picked it up, and slit it open.

6

Trading Patients

C. G. K. Atkins

The new, female patient lay in the far bed near the window. Late afternoon sun lasered through the broad glass panes of her room, making it difficult to see. Elisa leaned forward a little trying to get a better view of her through the partially opened door. But the patient's face remained hidden by a vase of flowers and a stack of books on the bedside table. Wanting to advance, but not daring to—another patient lay reading in the bed by the door—Elisa retreated to the hall.

She walked slowly back down the corridor, smiling and nodding vaguely at other patients leaning on canes or clustered in wheelchairs. She needed to start her rounds on the east side of the ward.

The first thirty minutes of every shift began with a quick survey of all her beds. As she scanned her own duty roster, she noted that no new patients had been admitted to her section. Mrs. Q's bed remained empty—she had died two nights ago when Elisa had last been on shift.

Elisa silently hoped that no one new arrived tonight . . . she hated the paperwork—if only she could write in Tagalog—writing in English always brought back the flushed shame of the nuns calling on her to recite from the English primer back in the Philippines. Her hand seemed to convulse under the pressure of writing foreign words. Her fingers cramped, turning her script into a topsy-turvy scrawl.

The unit director, Joanne, had documented two complaints about Elisa's illegible penmanship. Recently, Joanne had suggested, "Why don't you look for a pen that makes it easier for you? Look, I use a fountain pen—I find it helps me—my husband gave it to me when I graduated from business school." The older, blonde-streaked woman rotated a blue lacquered, gold-nibbed stylus back and forth in her hand. She leaned forward sympathetically, "Maybe it's something more fundamental. Maybe you should do some English night classes?"

Elisa's heartbeat had thudded in her ears, but she didn't respond. Unsure of what the manager wanted, she returned Joanne's wistful smile.

"Either way, I've recorded Dr. Jensen's and Dr. Peterson's complaints in your file—I had no choice." The manager paused, waiting for a response. When she got none, she continued, "You understand what that means don't you? It constitutes a warning about your performance." Joanne's eyes darted across Elisa's face, trying to penetrate the younger woman's seemingly implacable gaze. "I encourage you to try to find some way to improve your writing. Maybe you should talk to one of the other girls? I know that Mercedes did a course last fall; maybe you should talk to her?"

The remarks had infuriated Elisa. She didn't have any problems with English—she understood and read it perfectly—better, in fact, than most of the Filipinos on the floor. After all, the others often asked *her* what this or that word meant in a manual or patient chart. Even the black women asked Elisa for help from time to time. What would a night class accomplish except empty her pocket of money? Money that she needed to save or send back home! Joanne was nice—well-meaning, even—but stupid. Where the hell did the doctors get off complaining? Their writing was always bad. Jensen was the worst; her writing looked like an EKG—full of sharp up-and-down peaks with no breaks between words. On top of that, she stuttered terribly, which made her heavily accented Norwegian English even more difficult to understand—the staff made fun of her for it behind her back.

For Elisa, carving out English words always brought her back to the austere rule of Sister Jerome and the stark powerlessness of grammar school. Sister Jerome had had long hair and dressed in the robes of the other nuns, but to the little girls, she walked and talked like a man. She had a dark-shadowed upper lip—it looked like she shaved it—and four, long black hairs protruded from a large mole on her cheek. The girls tittered whenever they saw her—they nudged each other, and tried to imitate her gait—and then, they would then bend over and stagger with laughter.

One day, Elisa overheard two of her classmates comment, "Did you notice? Elisa looks just like Sister!" These words shot a current of fear through her. Elisa didn't know quite what they meant. But she knew that Sister Jerome *was* strange—the older girls talked about her "unnatural desires" and Elisa grasped that their inferences were sexual. These memories caused a heat of shame to rise across her face, breaking her reveries—Maybe a different pen would help. She sighed.

"What was that for?" Jesus, the head nurse for the evening, looked up from the desk in the corner.

"What?"

"The moan."

"I moaned?"

He clarified, "Well, more sort of sighed." He brushed off the page in front of him. "It doesn't matter. It just seemed you had a lot on your mind."

"I don't know. I didn't even know I sighed.' Elisa smiled, "It was probably just gas or something."

Although they were both Filipino, Elisa remained wary of Jesus. He had been here much longer than any of the others. He had come to the United States over twenty years ago and it seemed that he held little patience for new arrivals from back home.

Ten years ago, Elisa had been the head nurse of a cardiac unit of the general hospital in Naga City in the Philippines. Her parents owned a small stall in the main open-air market. They made enough to put her through college, but then it fell to her to finance her two younger siblings' education.

But one day her job at the hospital quietly disappeared when one of the vice presidents cut the cardiac department's budget. Eventually, she found a job taking care of an elderly, Spanish widow who lived in a grand, stuccoed house near the waterfront. The woman lay in bed most of the day, and so nursing duties centered on shifting the patient's emaciated body from one pillow to another. A cook brought food up on a tray, and a maid kept the room and bedlinen clean.

When the ailing widow slept, Elisa and the cook, Corazon, would sit on the veranda just outside her room and talk. Cori had been all over the world, living in Singapore, Dubai, and New York, working as a cook but sometimes also as a nanny or housekeeper. She told elaborate stories and gave Elisa sly glances; vaguely intimating about the strange sexual practices of foreigners. She would then would giggle slightly and quickly dismiss what she had just recounted with the sweep of her hand, saying, "You don't want to know! . . . You don't want to know."

Elisa never knew what to say. One day, as she listened to Corazon describe the late-night party of an American artist she had worked for in New York, the older woman eyed her carefully and asked her again, "You don't want to know about this—do you?" She paused to watch Elisa's reaction and without breaking her gaze, she leaned into the younger woman's face and kissed her on the mouth. Elisa pulled back sharply in response and bit her lower lip. The two then stared at each other almost in contestation.

A groan from the next room broke the tension, and Elisa rose to tend to their elderly mistress.

Even though a part of Elisa wanted to flee, she also felt curiously excited by the sinuous tie that now existed between Corazon and herself. They never spoke of the kiss but a fibrous current passed between them whenever they met.

Within a few weeks, the Spanish widow died. An acne-scarred, American man came to the house. He pared and cleaned his fingernails with the blade of a small penknife as he dismissed Cori, Elisa, the driver and maid.

Afterward, the servants walked out of a pair of French doors and onto the gravel drive. Each carried a small bag or bundle of clothing. They walked as a group along the grassy verge which gently arced toward the security gate. Without a word being spoken, Cori and Elisa slackened their pace, creating a gap between themselves and the others. Soon, the driver and maid reached the main road without them. As they did so, the driver turned and motioned impatiently at them—either waving goodbye or signaling them to hurry, it wasn't clear. Both women ignored him. When they looked up a few minutes later, he was gone.

Hardly aware of her own gesture, Elisa reached her hand out to Corazon. Their fingers and knuckles knotted tightly together as they ducked between the lower branches of a hedge. Underneath the shade of a large tree, their bodies fell into each other with longing. Lips penetrated clothing, braising skin as they made love in the humidity of the midday. A torrent of desire washed away any fear of being caught.

For the next several weeks she and Cori met in darkened corners of the city to kiss and fumble one another. Elisa felt curiously free—she had never considered that such a love was possible but it now flooded her. They began to speak of finding a small house to live in together—Cori had savings from all of her years abroad.

But Elisa's joblessness fretted her parents. Late one evening, as he was locking the market stall for the night, her father suggested that she emigrate to the United States. His cousin worked in the U.S. Consulate and had told him that the Americans were always looking for nurses and nursing aides. "You could get a visa. You're not married. It would be easy for you."

His daughter's chest tightened as he spoke. She did not want to leave Cori. "I don't know, you and Mama need me here—what if one of you gets sick?"

"That's right!" His hand struck the wall of his shop firmly. "What *if* one of us gets sick? We don't have the money for doctors or medicines! If you go to America, we would have those things." He pleaded with her, "and your brother has two more years of college to go."

Despite her new infatuation, Elisa acquiesced. If she had felt these things for a man, it might have been different. A wave of relief swept through the family when the visa papers arrived. Her father laughed and hugged her, "Maybe we will now get a second storey on the house!"

Elisa found a job working at a hospital just outside Manhattan. At the suburban hospital, Elisa looked after "catastrophic injuries"—often the result of car wrecks, drug overdoses, workplace injuries, hugely disfiguring cancers, and the final ravages of crippling diseases such as ALS and muscular dystrophy. Bodies arrived with a surfeit of orifices, bedsores, festering wounds, and contractured limbs. Those who were conscious and coherent when they arrived harbored hopes of someday going home—but few ever did. Most spent years hospitalized. If they improved medically, they might move to a less intensive unit—which only meant moving to a higher floor with better views but staying in the same dingy, overcrowded, urine-reeking ward-rooms.

Elisa liked her job—and she tried not to resent the fact that she could work only as an aide rather than as a full-fledged RN, as she had in the Philippines. Although she passed all the qualifying exams for nursing, the hospital administration treated her Philippine qualifications with suspicion. She remained in one of the lower ranks of the hospital. Indeed, almost everyone who labored on the floors came from overseas; with Filipina nurses workings as subordinates to their Caribbean-trained peers.

By retaking his degree at a U.S. university, only Jesus managed to dissolve the invisible tether that seemed to hold Filipinos back. He not only functioned as a full RN, but Joanne quickly promoted him to head nurse. His challenging of Elisa was typical of their interactions. She found herself off balance in his presence—never quite able to respond appropriately to his questions.

This evening, she was paired with Precious, a statuesque, black nurse from Jamaica who wore her curly, gray and black streaked hair drawn tightly back in a bun. Until recently, she had also worn a starched nurses cap; a remnant from her training in London two decades ago. But during her last performance review, Joanne had gently but firmly told her to get rid of the outdated hairpiece.

As Elisa contemplated the evening ahead, she knew that she wanted to talk to the female patient who lay by the window. Her admission had caused a lot of chatter in the lunchroom and charting area—her medical file indicated that she was a lesbian and that she had a same-sex spouse and children. The boldness of this information accompanied by the woman's striking features had caused undulations of whispering talk.

One nurse had tisked during report, "How could a woman look like that and not like men?" She pursed her lips and clicked her tongue. "She could pass as normal! How stupid to have 'lesbian' written into her chart! She should be ashamed! . . ." Murmurs of assent rumbled around the table.

Elisa remained silent, watching her colleagues. Jesus sat in the corner. His face gave away little of his thoughts, but Elisa imagined that she caught a scowl flit across his mouth as he straightened papers on the table.

"And how did she get her kids? They can't be really her kids?" The woman continued, ". . . Well, a man must have been involved at some point! No objections to a . . . well, you know a . . . P-E-N-I-S when she wants a kid!" A small spasm of laughter accompanied this final remark.

During the first few days, hushed stage-whispers and laughter continued intermittently and then seemed to ebb. The lesbian patient, it seemed, was likable.

Elisa pondered this as she returned to the stockroom beside the nursing station. She reached back and forth, gathering sheets, blankets, pillow cases, towels, and face cloths onto a small metal pushcart.

Precious interrupted her, "C'mon girl—what are you doing in there? We move this slowly, and the patients might die before we check them again!"

"I'm coming, I'm coming. Don't be so impatient." Elisa rebuffed her partner, "I had to wait till housekeeping brought up more towels."

"They're always behind, those people. If I did my job the way they do," Precious chastised, "I tell you, I wouldn't be keeping it."

The two women turned into the first ward room. A hissing of oxygen dominated the space. Their crepe-soled shoes squeaked against the linoleum tiles as they briskly moved between the beds. Three lay empty, their occupants were either in the lounge at the end of the hall or in therapy sessions. A man occupied the fourth. He lay behind a phalanx of machinery and computers, propped on pillows with an oxygen mask tipped against his throat. He breathed nosily through a tracheotomy while his left hand fingered a well-worn keyboard lying on the mattress beside him.

"How you doing today Reggie?"

The word "GOOD" appeared on a screen mounted beside him.

"You want anything? Water? Pain meds?"

"TOWEL" and "PAIN" appeared on the monitor.

"Okay, here you go." Elisa patted him on the shoulder as she lay two clean hand towels on the side of the bed. "Precious will give you your meds and change your dressings. And don't forget, tomorrow you get your shower and we change your bed."

A murmur of insurrection seemed to rise up from his inert body.

"No, no Reggie. That's the way it is. You know that." Elisa smiled at him and turned away. As she brushed by Precious, she arched her eyebrows, crinkled her nose, and mouthed emphatically, "He needs a shower."

Elisa and Precious worked well together. Despite her stern demeanor and the fact that she was in charge, Precious didn't mind helping aides pull and roll sheets from underneath infirm bodies, remake beds, or wash patients' backs and legs.

As they finished turning one of their comatose charges, Precious tucked a pillow behind the patient's back and turned to Elisa and said, "Oh yes, I forgot to tell you, we have that new woman patient—you know the one—Amanda traded her to us because . . . well you know . . . It's against her 'religion.' So she took Mrs. H instead." She peered at Elisa quizzically, "You don't mind, do you?"

Elisa shook her head.

Precious clucked her tongue, "I will look after anyone: a black man, a white man, a criminal, and even a 'batty boy.'" She corrected herself with a knowing smile, "Well—even a 'batty girl.'"

Elisa tried to suppress her quickening heart. She didn't want Precious to guess at her interest in the patient. Two nights ago, she had slowly picked her way through a union brochure. She scanned the small, glossy booklet for any mention of families and spouses. Amidst the recent rumors on the unit, she had heard that the hospital recognized same-sex spouses—people claimed that even the CEO himself was gay.

To her surprise, when talking about benefit plans and health insurance, the booklet stated that it considered a spouse to be "an adult of the same or opposite sex who has continually co-habited with said employee for one full year." Elisa read and reread the phrase "same or opposite sex." Her disbelief gradually dissolved. A small reserve of glee slowly built within her—America was such a wonderful country! Not like back home. Here she had rights. Here she and Corazon could have a life together!

Corazon was due to arrive from the Philippines in just a few days. She had found a job as a housekeeper with an old employer in Manhattan and, after ten months of waiting, had finally managed to obtain a U.S. work visa. On her weekends and evenings off, she would share Elisa's rented room in the Hudson valley.

The women's yearning for one another had not abated since Elisa had left Naga City. But, to her current housemates and coworkers, Elisa had mentioned only that a "cousin" would be coming to stay.

The United States was making her brave, and she wanted to know how she might be able to write Cori into her benefit and medical plan. Maybe she could even have a child—her parents, she was sure, would adjust—anyway, they lived half a world away if they didn't. Instinctively she believed that the lesbian patient would be able to help her.

"Do you want to do her now, or take your break?" Precious queried Elisa.

"Oh, I'll do her now—if you want to go, it's alright by me. You can do her meds afterward."

"You're sure?"

"Yeah, I had big lunch; I'm not ready to eat yet."

"Well, I didn't eat lunch, so if you don't mind, I'll go for break now."

"No, that's okay. I can manage." But even as Elisa said this, the muscles in her chest tightened.

Precious closed the binder in front of her. "I'll just go lock my cart in the cupboard." The tread of her shoes squeaked as she strode away down the curved corridor.

Elisa pushed her own cart toward the entrance of the lesbian patient's room. She drew in a breath, girded her courage, and stepped into the doorway. "Hi there!"

The closest bed now stood empty, but the lesbian lay in hers. She didn't respond.

"Hello?" She called out again, this time waving her forearm and hand in a maladroit gesture that left her elbow glued to her side and her fingers down by her thigh.

The woman looked up from a small laptop computer on her lap. "Oh, sorry." She smiled. Her thin face exuded a pale, soft translucency. The woman wore a clean white T-shirt and a pair of khaki pants. A blue sweatshirt lay across the head of her bed. Three pillows supported her upper torso and another pillow supported her knees. Half-open books and yellow legal pads lay scattered around her on the blankets.

"I'm Elisa and I'll be your nurse this evening."

"Really? I thought a different nurse was on."

"She was needed on the other side, so we had to trade—me and Precious are your nurses now."

"Oh."

"Is there anything you need?"

"My meds are due in half an hour."

"Precious will bring them," Elisa tried to assure her. And then she asked, "How long have you been lying like that?"

"Oh, you've got me. Probably too long." The woman guffawed, "But I'm trying to finish a brief for one of my partners."

"You'll get a pressure sore."

"I know, I know." She looked down at the keyboard in front of her.

"Maybe we should try changing the position of your legs and hips?" Elisa suggested. "And then later I'll help you move onto your side."

"Oh, all right." The patient tucked a pen into the crease of a book and folded it shut.

Elisa pulled the pillow from underneath the woman's legs. She then grabbed the waistband of her trousers on each side. "Ready?" I'm going to tilt you a little toward the window, okay?"

"Yeah."

Elisa tugged upward and then sideways, shifting the patient's pelvis so that she could tuck the pillow behind one hip. "There—that okay?"

"Can you put a pillow between my knees?"

Elisa reached for a towel from her cart. "If I roll this up, will it do?"

"I'd prefer a pillow but that will work if it has to . . . we never seem to have enough pillows in this room!"

"There aren't enough on the floor—and then they get left downstairs in the therapy gym or in x-ray." Elisa smiled at her, "What are you working on?"

"A case," The woman tucked some stray hairs of her lank, brown hair behind one ear, "I'm a lawyer."

"That sounds hard. You must be very smart."

Her pale green eyes reflected the evening light and seemed to light up her face as she laughed at Elisa's remark. "I don't know whether you have to be smart, hard-working, or lucky—maybe a combination of all three." Her left hand settled lightly on the back of a book, "I like it though . . . I'm really lucky that I like my work . . . and it seems to like me."

"So since you're lawyer, you don't mind if I ask you a question?" Elisa started carefully.

"No, I guess not—though I don't know whether I will be able to answer it."

Elisa glanced toward the doorway and saw that it remained empty. She then stepped backward to lean against the wall, tucking her hands behind her and pressing her palms against the cool plaster as she probed further, "You're a lesbian, right? You live with another woman?"

"Yeah . . ." The woman answered cautiously, "I do."

"How did you decide to do that?"

The patient sounded a little irritated, "Do what? Be a lesbian?"

"No, no," Elisa's cheeks reddened, "No, I mean, how did you decide to put that on your chart?" She felt her body begin to overheat with embarrassment. "You know, to be 'out.'"

"Oh. . . . Oh, I see."

But Elisa knew that she didn't. She quickly interjected, "You see, I like women." She paused. "I'm a Filipina—and well, Filipinos don't talk about it. About being gay." She added, "We're Christian. We're a Catholic country."

Any irritation seemed to disappear from the patient's voice. "Oh, I get it. So you want to know how to come out?"

Elisa nodded and checked to see if the doorway was still empty.

"Look, I can't tell you how to do that—it's different for everybody. But if it helps, my partner was Catholic—she doesn't go to church anymore—but her family accepts us." The patient became more animated, "Frankly, if you have kids, you really can't avoid being out. You can't really lie to your children." She played with a bracelet on her wrist, "We think honesty is best—even if it is uncomfortable."

"But wasn't it hard—the first time?"

"Absolutely. And it still is sometimes. I don't really like having to say I'm a lesbian—and I don't often do it—only when I have to. Like on forms and paperwork, for those who recognize that the name I write down as my spouse is a woman's name, they know—but since she has a Greek name, people often can't tell whether it's a male or a female." The patient laughed. "So you see, sometimes you can come out without really doing it overtly. It all depends on the situation. At my kids' school, we had to be up-front about it because we both want to be involved with their education—*and* we want to protect them from discrimination."

Elisa tried to nod in response but the muscles of her neck remained rigid with nerves. The skin of her face felt taut and unnatural as she grinned back at the woman.

"I forgot; what's your name again? Mine's Isabel—most people call me Izzy." The patient extended her hand.

"Elisa."

"Hi."

The nurse stumbled forward, grabbed the fingers limply, and mumbled softly, "Hi." She then looked down and quickly stepped backward to the cool shelter of the wall.

"So why do you want to know?"

"Well, my friend is coming from the Philippines and I want to put her on my health plan—but there are problems."

"Problems?"

"Well, I don't want to tell my union steward—everyone who works on the floor is from back home or from the West Indies—and they don't like gays either." Elisa winced slightly, "So I'm afraid."

"Well, you shouldn't have to tell your steward—you should just be able to go to HR—you know, human resources. Only they need to know. . . . Does this place cover same-sex spouses?"

Elisa nodded, "They do—that's why I want to do it—but I'm scared. It would be very bad for me if anybody found out."

Isabel frowned slightly, "The nurses seem to treat me okay—but I get that it might be different for you. You see at my partner's work we just asked that they change the wording of their plan and have us included—and they did. It was real easy." A wisp of hair fell back into her face and she retucked it behind her ear. "Only *you* can decide whether it is worth the risk. I can't tell you that—only you can."

A rattle of metal carts and nurses' voices suddenly echoed in the hallway. A renewed veil of worry descended across Elisa's face. She pushed herself off the wall and stood erect. "I should go now."

"Well, look if you want to talk again—it doesn't look like I am going anywhere soon." Izzy grimaced wanly, "Okay?"

She nodded, "Okay." The rush of anxiety that had seized her began to ease. "I'll remind Precious to bring your pills." As she stepped out of the room, she sensed that no one had overheard their conversation. She turned and called awkwardly, "Huh—thanks!"

"Sure. No problem."

"See you later."

"Yeah, see you later." Elisa squinted up the dark corridor. She could see Jesus and Precious standing together near the nursing station. They appeared to be arguing. The head nurse repeatedly slapped the back of one hand into the open palm of the other. His chin jutted forward as he continued to rant. Although Precious was taller than Jesus, and she loomed over him in silhouette, her posture looked defensive and unnaturally still. As Elisa moved closer, Jesus' aggressive attitude lessened and his voice, while still indistinct, became less shrill. As she came within an arm's length, Elisa could finally catch his words: "Look I'm sorry to be so firm about this—but I feel very strongly that it is unprofessional." His mouth straightened in disapproval, "When Amanda gets back from break, tell her that I want to see her *before* she goes on rounds." Jesus abruptly turned and walked away.

"What was that about?" Elisa inquired.

"That we shouldn't have let Amanda trade with us."

"Oh."

"I thought I was doing the right thing—I didn't want the gay woman to have a nurse who was prejudiced." Precious looked quizzically, "What do you think?"

Elisa shrugged impassively.

"I had no idea that it would be such a problem. I haven't seen Jesus go off like that in a long time."

Elisa remained mute.

"I mean it's only one patient—and she is a lesbian after all—he can't expect everybody's going to be fine with that." Precious nudged Elisa's arm, "I wouldn't want to be Amanda tonight! Jesus is in a real mood—oh, that man!"

Finally, Elisa spoke, "Is she back yet?"

"No not yet."

"Isabel—you know, *the* patient . . ." Elisa cocked and jerked her head to one side, "She wants her pills."

"Okay. I'm heading there now." Precious pulled a black binder from the counter behind her and stowed it in a canvas pocket hanging from the trolley. She began to push the cart slowly up the hall.

"I'm going on break now." Elisa called after her.

"Okay."

Elisa turned into the stairwell and began to skip down the stairs. Every other floor, a large window gave a view of the parking lot. A red Mercedes wagon was pulling in below. She saw the hospital CEO come out the side doors and walk toward the car. He wore an expensive-looking, beige suit. Its silken weave flashed in the sun. He swung a dark brown, leather briefcase in one hand and carried a small, blue duffle bag in the other. He looked fit and happy. A young, blonde man got out of the driver's seat. The two embraced and then kissed quickly on the lips—or was it the cheek? Elisa stopped abruptly as she came to the landing. She was unsure of herself, had they just kissed? She watched them through the glass as they stood close to one another. After a few more seconds, the younger man handed the car keys to the CEO and walked around the front of the car. The CEO tossed the keys in the air with one hand and opened his own door with the other. A moment later, Elisa watched the rear of the Mercedes turn out of the driveway and into the street.

7

FLINT

Ellen Dannin

Perhaps it is not the stars we are born under but the minerals we are born with. I was born under the sign of Leo but in the town of Flint, though we moved from that industrial Michigan city while I was an infant.

As a child, I searched out flint arrowheads between the endless hot rows on my grandparents' Ohio farm while I picked beans and tomatoes each summer. I wanted to stroke the flaked edges and feel their silky surfaces and reach through time to the hands that had made them. And, of course, I wanted to learn how to strike a flint with steel to send sparks flying and release the fire locked within.

But the flints I found were just unworked rocks, and not even glamorous rocks. They come in muddy shades not so different from the earth in which they were buried. But their homely beauty caught my eye better than would a cut diamond, for flint was in my blood.

We were the poorest family in a tiny town that my mother had left after high school. She returned, with three children under five, the only divorced woman except for the town floozie. I was the dark daughter of a father who was half Turkish-Jewish in a town where everyone else's ancestors were from Britain and Germany, and I was their target, hit and shunned in school and beaten, taunted, and thrown into the dirt walking home from school.

So I escaped. I wandered through the old beech woods on the hills above my grandparents' farm and wished I could live there forever. I read and read. And that was the best I could do. I was never able to release even one spark in the unchipped flints I found. And I never found one arrowhead. Not a single one. The dusty rose-colored arrowhead buried at the bottom of my jewelry box was given me by my grandfather. He let me choose it when I was eight from a cigar box he had filled over the years. He found them as he plowed the fields deeper and deeper each year, walking the fields, examining the soil, learning what it had to say. By the time I knew him, years of hard labor had transformed him, body and soul, into something very nearly made of rock.

So twenty-nine years passed between my parents' leaving Flint and my finding myself there again. I had left home at seventeen, put myself through college and law school, married and divorced a man who had beaten and tried to kill me, traveled abroad. I learned that inside me was a fire for justice, and that put me on the road back to Flint, a new government attorney, preparing for my first solo trial of any complexity and my first out-of-town trial.

We National Labor Relations Board agents traveled constantly. Fortunately I've never had trouble finding my way if I had even the most rudimentary map. A lucky talent in the days before computer mapping.

In this case, on my first return trip to Flint, Kiyanna Lock, the woman I was to represent, had been able to give only the most impressionistic directions. I thought that maybe she wasn't very bright. It didn't occur to me then that people who don't drive, who take buses, and who don't and can't leave Avenue A in Flint, Michigan, can't give directions from freeways they do not travel.

Once off the freeways and in the city of Flint, I drove with one eye on the map grasped in my right hand which was also resting on the gear shift and one eye open for landmarks—a nervous and uncertain way to drive through an unfamiliar city.

Avenue A could have been transplanted directly from some Agee picture of suffering sharecroppers mired in the Depression-era South. Nothing in the poverty and dilapidation of Flint's main streets had been a prelude for this rural poverty in the midst of a major city. No, it was even worse. I had grown up in rural poverty. In the countryside there was space for a large garden, and we could and did find our own food in the woods. Morels, raspberries, wood strawberries, loganberries, hickory and hazel nuts, asparagus. Foods that now are pricey luxuries were abundant and available for a walk through the woods. But in Flint, this rural poverty of unpainted ramshackle homes was unrelieved by woods or gardens.

This was where Kiyanna Lock lived, so this was where I was going to spend a lot of time over the next few weeks as we prepared the case to get her job back.

Of course, where else could she live, a licensed practical nurse in a Flint nursing home with a wage of five dollars an hour who had been fired months before.

I parked across from her house, got out, and tried to lock my car nonchalantly as though I always locked it wherever I parked it. Everything about me spelled out "government agent." As a matter of fact, I always did lock my car. But the squalor of this street was so profound that the newness of my car seemed to demand elaborate apologies. No one who lived here would have a car they would need to lock, if they even had a car. Kiyanna herself would make it to the hearing only by begging rides from a friend. She told me that when she arrived a little late the first day of trial and, thank goodness, choked off my start at telling her it was really important for her to be on time.

Kiyanna Lock's house was two flights of steps up the side of a slope. It was brown, weathered, unpainted wood amidst a street of houses tar-papered over or with peeling paint. This was not a once-good neighborhood fallen on hard times. These buildings were built to house the poor—intended from the start as basic shelter and no more, built to hold furniture from second-hand shops or from stores where everyone bought on terms. Not for these houses the touch of hands ever filled with even enough.

Over the phone, Kiyanna Lock's voice had been slow and her speech slurred. Was she a drunk? On drugs? When I asked Carol, the investigator, she told me I would have a big surprise when I met Kiyanna. Carol wouldn't tell me what the surprise was but wanted me to tell her what I thought after I met Kiyanna. All Carol would say was that Kiyanna Lock's husband had shot her in the head on Mother's Day a few years earlier, leaving her with deadened nerves on half her face. That explained the slurred speech.

I understood part of the surprise when I stepped inside Kiyanna Lock's house. The decay and desperation outside did not intrude into this place. In some way this impoverished single mother kept her home clean and neat. What space she had dominion over—and there was a lot of space because she didn't have much furniture—she kept spotless. Even more than that. The living room seemed perfect in its spareness. It had a still, almost Zen quality, as if—were she to be offered more furniture—Kiyanna would turn it down as unwanted. I wondered at the will that existed in this small woman that she could so gracefully and successfully forbid entry to the slatternliness of the street.

From the moment I walked into her house to this day, Kiyanna Lock has and will always be a puzzle to me. I have always been certain that her employer treated her unfairly and broke the law when it fired her. But how could this woman have been consigned to the life she has led? Where is the reason and justice?

Kiyanna Lock was like her house. She had a slim sensual body with full hips, skin that looked as if it would be silky but firm if stroked, and a queenly walk. But her face was a ruin. On the side where she had been shot, her lip sagged and she had no expression. Losing half her face meant she could not control her speech. It was a human tragedy and deserved sympathy, but mere sympathetic feelings were irrelevant. I had a case to try and win, and to do that I had to persuade a judge to believe her. Anyone hearing her would think she was a drunk. A judge might reasonably and easily reach that conclusion while listening to her testify and be sympathetic to the accusations her employer would lodge against her.

So I sat at the kitchen table of a woman I had just met and talked about her face and her speech. I told her I already knew about the shooting. I told her that, even though it had nothing to do with our trial, she was going to have to talk about it in public and to strangers. I explained that the judge would be looking at her and the way she testified and at every witness to help him figure out who was telling the truth. She would have to be prepared to explain why she talked the way she did.

I hesitated with each word. I was, after all, breaching normal etiquette, baldly pointing out a defect in this woman I had just met for the first time. Every word felt like a stone thrown at an innocent victim.

But Kiyanna listened calmly. And that was no pose. In fact, when I asked her to tell this part of her story on the witness stand she did it as if it were natural to explain to strangers why she only had half a face. Perhaps she badly needed someone to listen to her. Hers had been a hard life, and I think few ever stopped to hear her story. But she never asked for sympathy. She did not accuse. She did not complain. She just answered the questions.

At her kitchen table, I spread out my papers and went through my list of questions. To assure myself I would not make mistakes in the stress of my first real trial, I wrote down the exact wording of the questions I planned to ask and the exact answer I expected to get.

I asked Kiyanna if she had ever testified at a trial before. She told me that she had—twice. Once was for her divorce. The other was shortly before that when she had testified against that husband who had blown her face off on Mother's Day two and a half years ago. That testimony sent him away for a long time but not long enough.

When I asked her to tell me about herself, Kiyanna told me how she had almost finished her LPN training when she was shot in the face and ended up a patient herself, spending months in the hospital and in rehabilitation. Then she'd had her two stints as a witness that had ended her marriage and locked up her ex-husband—and, that finished, she finished her degree and started her first nursing job. Things had seemed to be improving for her and her children.

Actually, things hadn't just seemed to be improving. Things were great. At the trial, I got her personnel file, and they showed she was a good employee. When Kiyanna had started work as a nurse on the critical care floor of a nursing home, the nursing home had been solicitous of her because of her problems and had written in her file that she would need an extended period of training. But that's not what seemed to happen. Her first evaluation said she was doing excellent work and was well organized and careful with the medications. At her ninety-day evaluation in October, there were more positive evaluations, and the nursing home gave Kiyanna a raise and even gave her some assignments overseeing the work of aides and taking doctors' orders directly. The dark days were over and gone.

And then in mid-November, Kiyanna got a letter from her stepmother in Picayune, Mississippi, asking her to come help her recover from a serious illness. When Kiyanna asked for leave from her job to take care of her stepmother, the supervisors expressed real solicitude for her stepmother's situation. They agreed that the leave would be open-ended so Kiyanna could assess her stepmother's needs.

But on her last day at work, a union steward asked Kiyanna for information about what had led to the firing of an aide. Kiyanna agreed to write a letter to be used in the aide's grievance meeting the next week after Kiyanna left town. Lock's version turned out to be the key in saving that other woman's job. The other woman went back to work. Kiyanna Lock did not.

When Kiyanna got to Picayune, Mississippi, her sick stepmother accepted care from her while telling Kiyanna how worthless she was and how she had never measured up to her stepmother's real children. After two weeks, Kiyanna decided that she was no longer the child who had to take this kind of treatment. She decided it was time to go home and back to her new job.

So Kiyanna called the nursing home to tell them she was ready to return to her job. Her supervisor said that before they could schedule Lock to work, they needed to talk about a letter about an aide's discharge. She asked Kiyanna if she had written it. When Kiyanna said she had, her supervisor asked why she had done a thing like this. Kiyanna explained what had happened. The supervisor paused and then told Kiyanna that the nursing home had been left tight by her leave and the resignation of two other nurses, so they had done some hiring, and now it just wasn't so clear she could get her job back. But they would see when she got back to town.

After arriving back in Flint, Kiyanna repeatedly called the nursing home to tell them she was ready to go back to work. Each time they put her off.

Finally, when she called on January 17, Kiyanna was told that her work had been poor and that she had shown no improvement so they had to let her go.

Kiyanna said, "That's not the real reason, is it? It's because of the letter I wrote, isn't it?" Her supervisor said, "Well, you really didn't have any business being involved in that union business." She told Kiyanna that if she would just resign, the nursing home would stop fighting her unemployment benefits. Kiyanna said she was not going to quit, so they fired her.

So that's the human story. A woman does the right thing for another worker. That's solidarity in union terms. Gets fired for doing the right thing. Gets fired even though she does her job well. It happens all the time. Most of the time it is perfectly legal to treat a worker this way.

But Kiyanna got lucky when she was fired because it is illegal to fire a worker for helping a union with a grievance. It was not a huge amount of luck, but better than no luck at all. So to make Kiyanna's lucky break mean anything, to get her justice, I had to prove the nursing home fired her because she helped her coworker and not because she was a bad worker. And all I had to do was to get the judge to believe the story told by my only witness, this impoverished, beaten up woman. I could not find a single person from the nursing home who would or could lift a finger to help her. So Kiyanna had a chance, but she had to make her own luck.

Ranged against us would be at least three witnesses, all confident, all convincing in their belief in the rightness of the decision to fire Kiyanna Lock. They would all be articulate. Whatever they said, they would tell their stories with whole faces, with white faces. Their speech would be clear and easy to understand. It would not be slurred, it would be educated . . . the language of the judge. So I had to show that these very nice and very reasonable people had taken revenge on Kiyanna for supporting her coworker, had lied and broken the law when they fired Kiyanna Lock, and for all this, they owed her back pay and her job back. Not easy.

The first step was to take Kiyanna Lock back to this bad time and see how much detail she remembered. It had been months since the investigator, Carol, had taken Kiyanna's written statement. It would not be surprising if she recalled almost nothing. She was going to have to testify about date after date and incident after incident. Many conversations involved the same people in the same places and were similar enough to be confusing. And confusion means traps on cross-examination.

But prepping Kiyanna Lock was like opening a surprise package. She recalled it all, dates and conversations, people, places, what was said. With only slight probing, she seemed to have it down. She talked about the tones of the voices. She pointed out the inconsistencies in what her bosses had told her. I thought that perhaps she had memorized her NLRB statement.

So I tested her. I asked for details that were not in her statement. Kiyanna answered my questions without hesitation and later could repeat it all. It was all convincing, and it all hung together. The long process of probing and checking, of trying to trip her up and having her come through unscathed convinced me I should have no reason not to believe her. But what I thought did not matter. What would the judge think?

I know from my life and from my work that people are not eggs. Just because society stamps us grade A—or not—says nothing that matters about us. But I still make at least initial judgments based on status, and most likely the judge would too. To see who Kiyanna Lock was you had to get past the shells of the poverty of her street, her house, her life, her lack of opportunity, and the mistreatment she had suffered at every turn.

Kiyanna Lock became a major topic of conversation between the Carol and me. She had struck us both in the same way: fascinating, someone easy to sympathize with, someone life had wronged, someone we had a chance to help.

The trial, of course, was like all trials—completely predictable and always in danger of being out of control. The employer's witnesses all testified at length—and convincingly—about the terrible employee Lock had been from the moment she put on her uniform. The judge, unfortunately, sat on Kiyanna Lock's bad side and never had the opportunity to see the mobile, expressive side of her face. A witness I had found at the last minute and brought into Flint at great trouble changed her story once she was on the stand. The prisoners in lockup in the room next to the courtroom the NLRB had rented for this trial yelled and whooped all through the proceedings so that sometimes you could not hear. Through it all, Kiyanna Lock sat there, queenly, steady, and just was the person she was.

But the judge did not seem to see that. I saw him nod sympathetically when the employer's witnesses told us what a bad employee she was. As they presented their case, I felt doubts eating into my conviction. If Kiyanna Lock had done what they said, made the wrong decisions and nearly killed a patient, then I could be committing a culpable act in getting her job back. I could be responsible for putting her in a position where she could harm others. What if I had misjudged Lock? And if I felt this way after having spent so much time with her, how could the judge who saw her only briefly possibly find in her favor?

When the case closed, Kiyanna Lock thanked me and sailed out. While I packed up to leave, the other side was holding an informal victory celebration at their table. The judge thanked us all and could barely look me in the eye. But they were only looking at the surface of the evidence and not what was buried there if you only had eyes to look.

On this day, as it turned out, Kiyanna's last name was Luck. And her luck came from the employer's bad judgment.

The employer's witnesses said that Kiyanna Lock was a terrible employee from the start, but they had kept her on out of sympathy. Then just when they decided to fire Kiyanna for having nearly caused the death of a patient she asked for the leave to care for her stepmother. They figured she would never return, and the problem would be solved.

But their own documents and actions told a very different story.

You would think that a nurse who had nearly caused the death of a patient would be fired immediately or at least suspended pending investigation or at the very least given work where she could cause no harm. But Lock was not suspended. Instead, she continued on with her normal work, including being scheduled to work alone as the only nurse on the floor with the heaviest patient load. What is more, sympathy can only go so far. Lock's evaluators had always rated her very good. Put together, they seemed to be rewriting the past.

The employer should have left it at that, but the attorney decided to prove that this employer fired bad employees. To do this, the attorney asked to put into the record the files of five other nurses who had been fired. I looked at the documents and agreed to have them put in evidence. The attorney seemed surprised. The records were irrelevant because they had nothing to do with firing Kiyanna Lock. Had I objected they would never have been admitted. They were jubilant at getting the records in and must have assumed . . . I have no idea what they assumed about me and what I was thinking. But I'll tell you what I was thinking.

I was happy to have them there, and I did not want to let them know just how happy. Every one of those five employees had files that carefully documented the dates and details of incidents that eventually got them fired. They all had evaluations that rated them as poor and had been given written disciplines before they were fired. But Kiyanna's record was completely different. Good evaluations, promotions, no disciplines. And best of all was the evaluation that was supposedly written on Kiyanna's last day at work. Unlike the careful evaluations in the files of the five fired nurses, this was a rambling, impressionistic story that said she was a terrible employee, but mentioned not a single incident. It did not even mention nearly killing a patient, something that had supposedly happened just two weeks earlier.

Everything about that document told me they wrote it to cover up their real reasons for firing her. It made no sense that a nursing home would risk keeping on such an incompetent employee for so long, all the while writing inaccurate evaluations praising the employee.

But the other side so clearly felt that victory was theirs as we all packed up that it was hard not to feel that I must have made some terrible error. Their certainty convinced me that I could lose.

It was many months later that I got the news we had won. But why?

Well, we won because of Kiyanna Lock, but we also won because the other side just could not tell a consistent story. We won in part because I was able to show the inconsistencies in the employer's evidence. And we won because only Kiyanna Lock's story hung together. And all this persuaded the judge that this woman had been wronged. The judge's decision even mentioned Kiyanna's bravery in the face of tremendous adversity.

It was a wonderful, sweet moment of victory.

Kiyanna Lock got her job back with back pay. But she continued to live on Avenue A. She worried about whether her employer would try to fire her again. And they did. They claimed that this time she had caused the death of a patient who was scalded in her bath. But we got Kiyanna her job back once more.

Months after all this, I received a call from Kiyanna Lock. Her fifteen-year-old daughter was pregnant by a twenty-three-year-old man who was in jail, on his way to prison for armed robbery. She told me she couldn't bear the way her daughter looked at her. She was so disappointed, she wanted to throw her out of the house, but she couldn't. She made a long-distance call to me about this. Hours of work at five dollars gross spent on that call. And it was all wasted on me. Way beyond my powers to do anything more than just say how sorry I was she had to deal with this.

It has been years since all this happened. My memories are not so much of victory but of how much it hurt to witness this painful, wasted life.

When I think of Kiyanna Lock, I think of her as she walked in her queenly way. I see her walking away from me down the hall. I think of my files all spread out on her kitchen table. And as I think of all this, every painful detail of Kiyanna's life floods in. I have not spoken with her for years. For all I know she could have given up on life. She has every right to. Or she could have found happiness, love, and respect. But most likely she still lies, a piece of unworked flint, of potential, buried in the mud of her life on Avenue A.

If this were a fair and just world, she would have been a treasure lifted up from the mud, her edges delicately flaked and then tied to an arrow and sent flying into the heavens. Or her flint would meet steel and the sparks would make a blazing and beautiful fire.

But that is not this life and this world. There is no justice for her. The only justice I could get for Kiyanna Lock was so small for all she had suffered and will always suffer. And even that is more justice than so many get in life.

And it is bitter to me that her whole life seems to be a fight against being buried and crushed. She will never be found by any kind hand that releases the fire within. And so these days I do not try cases. I try to teach. And I try to have faith and the courage that at each moment we each do the best we can, and I approach each learner as having the possibility of becoming so much more.

8

Bad Intentions

Risa L. Lieberwitz

The women in these stories face all sorts of job problems—hiring, firing, promotions, and receiving equal pay for equal work. Yet they would encounter problems if they walked into the courtroom trying to prove that their employers intentionally held their gender against them. To be sure, their employers treated them differently from other employees. The challenge is finding the smoking gun.

Julia Roschak, in "Getting Even," must prove that hospital president Matt Childers was motivated by gender in passing her over for promotion and then firing her. To make a case under Title VII, it's not enough for Julia to show that Matt was underhanded and dishonest. If he abused both men and women "equally," no sex discrimination occurred.

In "Trading Patients," Elisa worries about the official warning regarding her performance that unit director Joanne placed in her file. She's especially anxious about it because she needs this nurse's aide job to send money back to her family in the Philippines. What if Elisa is suspended? Or worse, what if she's fired? Would she have a Title VII claim? If there is no discrimination because she's a woman, could she claim sex discrimination because of her sexual orientation? Because of her national origin? Does her union contract provide more protection than Title VII?

Kiyanna Lock, in "Flint," also works in health care, as a licensed practical nurse. Like Elisa, Kiyanna is poor and must hang on to her job to provide the basics. Yet, Kiyanna does the "right thing," helps out a nurse's aide in her grievance against the employer, and is subsequently fired for this good deed. Kiyanna files her discrimination charge, not under Title VII, but under another federal statute, the National Labor Relations Act (NLRA).[1] The NLRA prohibits employers from intentionally discriminating against employees because of their union activities. Kiyanna wins her case under the NLRA. But would she also have a discrimination claim under Title VII on the basis of race or sex or both?

The Meaning of "Discrimination"

American antidiscrimination law is concerned more with what an employer must *not* do, rather than what an employer *must* do. Title VII of the Civil Rights Act prohibits Julia's, Elisa's, and Kiyanna's employers from making employment decisions on the basis of their race, sex, national origin, and/ or religion. Similarly, other federal antidiscrimination statutes forbid employers from taking into account an employee's or a potential employee's age or disability.[2] State antidiscrimination laws provide analogous prohibitions, with some state laws adding other grounds for claims, such as sexual orientation or marital status.[3] But Title VII and other antidiscrimination laws do not require more than this—that is, employers are not required to treat employees like Julia, Elisa, and Kiyanna fairly.

What does this mean? The U.S. framework of workplace regulation gives employers an enormous amount of power and authority over employees. Under the legal rule of "employment at will," an employer can hire, fire, or discipline an employee for "a good reason, a bad reason, or no reason at all."[4] Laws such as Title VII limit employer power, but only to the extent of specific categories, including prohibitions on sex discrimination. Antidiscrimination laws do not, though, require employers to act fairly or even rationally. In the words of the employment-at-will doctrine, statutes such as Title VII eliminate only some of the "bad reasons" that employers can use when they make employment decisions. Under Title VII it is unlawful for an employer to take action because of someone's race, sex, national origin, or religion. But this does not mean that employers must have "good reasons" for their actions.

The employment-at-will approach differs from virtually all other industrialized countries, where employers are obligated to make employment decisions based on "just cause."[5] Certainly, there is some overlap between antidiscrimination laws and just cause; neither would permit decisions based on sex or race. But just cause requirements go further, mandating that employers prove a valid reason for an employment decision. For example, an employer could show that financial exigencies necessitated layoffs or that an employee was fired for substandard work. Just cause requirements limit employers' unilateral power, placing discretion in the hands of neutral judges or arbitrators who then decide if employers acted in fair, evenhanded, and reasonable ways.

In the United States, unionized employees' collective bargaining agreements usually contain just cause protections. Under her union contract, Elisa, in "Trading Patients," could file a grievance claiming that her supervisor disciplined her without just cause. Her employer must then justify its decision to issue written performance warnings. Elisa's unit director Joanne, Dr. Jensen, and Dr. Peterson could testify before an arbitrator that Elisa's handwriting was illegible. It is then up to the arbitrator to decide if this constitutes just cause for discipline. Elisa would also have a separate right to sue her employer under Title VII.

Less than 8 percent of private sector employees in the United States are unionized.[6] State civil service laws covering government employees also require just cause. There are even a small number of employees who have individual contracts with just cause protection.[7] This leaves most employees, like Julia and Kiyanna, with no right to claim that they were discharged without just cause. They must prove that the employer discriminated against them under antidiscrimination statutes such as Title VII.

The Challenge: Who Proves What?

Title VII regulates employers, labor organizations, and employment agencies.[8] As in Julia's, Elisa's, and Kiyanna's situations, most Title VII complaints concern employers.[9] Such complaints deal with a broad range of conduct, including hiring, firing, promotions and demotions, transfers, compensation, benefits, and job assignments.

Employment discrimination "because of [an] individual's race, color, religion, sex, or national origin" is unlawful. Although Title VII does not contain the word "intent," the courts have developed a long history of cases defining "intentional discrimination."[10] In the Civil Rights Act of 1991, Congress amended Title VII to clarify that employer actions are unlawful if they are motivated at all by race, sex, religion, or national origin, even if the employer also has other nondiscriminatory reasons.[11]

While it seems uncontroversial that intentional discrimination should be unlawful, proving intent or why someone did something is not easy. A subjective concept, intent is an abstraction. From the perspective of a judge or jury, it is difficult to know a person's state of mind.

Julia, in "Getting Even," believes she has a strong case that Matt denied her a promotion to vice president because she was a woman and that he ultimately discharged her because she complained about it to the state human rights division. It's easy to imagine Julia telling her story to an attorney. She would describe her qualifications and accomplishments at Waverly Family Medical Center, and conclude with statements such as: "My job [was] to train a man with no experience to do what I've done for years . . . Jack Wilson . . . gets a promotion and a fat salary, and I get nothing." But, will her evidence hold up?

Most employers do not admit that they fired employees because of their race, sex, national origin, or religion. They rarely share these sentiments, keeping them at least out of the employee's earshot. Julia will try to prove her employer's motivation by showing that her employer treated her differently—or "disparately"—from male employees. She would argue that she was more experienced and a better employee than the man who was promoted. She would also testify to Matt's many derogatory statements about women employees. He congratulated Julia for " 'putting those female [employees] in their place.' " He even complimented her for being " 'different' from most women—sensible, rational"—that she " 'think[s] like a man.' " Matt told her that women are just paid less than men, and that this was the reason her salary was lower than Jack Wilson's. This seems like solid evidence, showing that gender motivated Matt not to promote Julia to become the hospital's vice president.

Proving Illegal Intent: Sex Stereotypes and Mixed Motives

Julia's case looks strong, especially when compared with Supreme Court decisions where women successfully proved sex discrimination. In one case, the Court concluded that gender stereotypes can be powerful evidence of an employer's motivation. When Price Waterhouse refused to promote Ann Hopkins to partnership, she sued, alleging that her gender predisposed her employer against her. Hopkins had an impressive work record, having brought several large new accounts into this nationwide accounting firm. The partners, however, turned down her bid for promotion based on her poor "interpersonal skills." Several of the male partners also commented about her appearance. They criticized her for being "too macho," for "overcompensating for being a woman," and for being "a lady using foul language." They told her that she should "walk more femininely, dress more femininely, wear makeup, have her hair styled, and wear jewelry."[12]

The Supreme Court held that Hopkins had successfully proven Price Waterhouse's unlawful motivation by showing that the partners relied on gender role stereotypes in denying her a promotion. Justice William

J. Brennan explained that an "employer who objects to aggressiveness in women but whose positions require this trait places women in an intolerable and impermissible Catch 22: Out of a job if they behave aggressively and out of a job if they do not. Title VII lifts women out of this bind."[13]

Price Waterhouse argued that it had legitimate reasons for turning Hopkins down for partnership given her poor interpersonal skills with colleagues and staff members. The Court agreed that Price Waterhouse could rely on this evidence in its defense. But the Court concluded that Price Waterhouse must prove that it would have made the same decision to deny Hopkins a partnership in the absence of the evidence that they considered her gender.[14]

This is called a *"mixed-motive" case*—where legitimate and illegitimate reasons both explain an employer's action. First, Hopkins had to prove that Price Waterhouse had used an illegitimate reason—her gender. Price Waterhouse could then defend itself by showing that in the absence of sex stereotyping, it still would have denied Hopkins a partnership for legitimate reasons—here, because of her poor interpersonal skills. The Supreme Court sent the case back to the lower courts to apply this mixed-motive approach. And one year later, Hopkins won.[15]

Like Ann Hopkins, Julia can maintain that gender stereotypes influenced her employer when he denied her a promotion. Matt's sexist statements show that he views women employees differently. He even admitted that women are paid less—"that's the way things are." Julia tried to be a tough, yet feminine, woman in the male-dominated world of hospital management. She "dressed for success," seeking a professional image, even as she remains sexy by choosing "silk blouses [that] softened crisply tailored suits which hugged her waist, lying flat on hips she knew emphasized her curves." She partially succeeded. Matt told her he considers her "more like a man." Still, Julia is caught in the *Price Waterhouse* catch-22. No matter what she does, she still doesn't "fit" in. Matt's physical touching and flirtation at a convention reveals that he considers her first as a woman—not equal to a man.

Julia also gets some help from a more recent Supreme Court decision in 2003, where a female employee proved that she was treated differently from men.[16] Catharina Costa, the only woman forklift operator in a warehouse at Caesars Palace Casino in Las Vegas, was fired after a "physical altercation." A coworker had trapped her in an elevator and then shoved her against the wall. While the Casino suspended him for five days, she lost her job. At the trial, Costa revealed that one of her supervisors stalked her and that the Casino treated her differently from her male coworkers. She received much harsher discipline for her misconduct than the men. Costa did not get as much overtime as the men either. Finally, she testified that her supervisors repeatedly made sexist comments, calling her "a bitch," "a lady Teamster," and saying that "she had more balls than the guys."[17]

Costa's case helps individuals like Julia prove a mixed-motive case of intentional discrimination. The Supreme Court made it clear that Costa could make her case with circumstantial and/or direct evidence of her employer's intentional discrimination. An example of direct evidence is a statement by a supervisor admitting that he fired Costa because she is a woman. Costa, like most employees, did not have a "smoking gun" directly proving her employer's illegal intent. But she did have powerful circumstantial evidence, meaning that there were facts which, considered together, indirectly proved her employer's discriminatory intent. These facts consisted of evidence that Costa's supervisors treated her differently than the male employees and aimed sexist comments at her. The Casino must now prove that it would have discharged Costa in the absence of this evidence of sex discrimination. The jury decided in Costa's favor, awarding her more than 350,000 dollars in damages.[18]

The Civil Rights Act of 1991: Congress Gives Employees Relief

Julia receives more help from the Civil Rights Act of 1991, which made a crucial change to Title VII mixed-motive cases. Under the 1991 amendments to Title VII, the employer's defense relates only to the level of remedies awarded to the employee. This means that if Julia proves that gender influenced Matt's decision not to promote her, she'll win her case. Waverly Medical Center can still attempt to reduce the remedies it must pay by showing that they would have treated Julia the same way if they had not considered her gender. If Waverly succeeds, a court will order them only to cease their unlawful action and to pay the employee's attorney's fees.[19] But, if Waverly fails to show this, Julia will receive additional remedies for Waverly's decision not to promote her and then to discharge her. She could win job reinstatement, a promotion, back pay, front pay, and compensatory damages to alleviate "pain and suffering" as well as damages for collateral consequences, like a mortgage foreclosure due to the loss of wages.[20]

If Julia proves her case, does Waverly have enough evidence to diminish the amount of remedies? Matt might testify that he would have promoted Jack Wilson anyway because he was better qualified than Julia. Ironically, Waverly might even rely on Matt's obnoxious conduct toward both men and women to argue that there was no disparate treatment on the basis of sex. Matt is a rude boss to everyone—the staff called him the " 'CBO,' Chief Bullying Officer." Or Matt could contend that he eliminated Julia so that he would not have to face a powerful workplace rival. This type of competitive conduct, after all, had nothing to do with Julia's gender. He would have engaged in it with a man.

If Waverly fails to prove its defense, Julia might also increase her remedies by proving that Waverly acted "with malice or reckless indifference" to her federally protected rights. In this case, the court will award punitive damages.[21] The 1991 legislation caps compensatory plus punitive damages. The employer's size sets the maximum amount of the award that ranges from 50,000 dollars for employers with under 101 employees to 300,000 dollars for those with more than 500 employees.[22]

Julia also benefits from the 1991 Act's provision that gives any party the right to a jury trial in cases that involve compensatory or punitive damages. This means all cases alleging intentional discrimination may be heard by a jury.[23] Julia would likely want a jury trial. Many jurors would empathize with her workplace experiences, either because the juror has experienced unequal treatment or because he or she recognizes the difficulty of working for a living.

Wages and Retaliation

Julia has two additional claims against Waverly. She could argue that Waverly paid her less than Jack Wilson because she was a woman. Matt even admitted this. A watershed Supreme Court case in 2007, though, creates an obstacle for Julia. Lilly Ledbetter sued Goodyear Tire Company for wage discrimination on the basis of sex. She had proof that over many years she was paid less than men in similar jobs. The Supreme Court dismissed her case, finding that she filed her claim too late. Under Title VII, an employee must file a charge with the EEOC within 180 days of the employer's alleged discriminatory action. The Court concluded that Ledbetter was required to file her claim within 180 days from her employer's initial decision to pay her less than the men.[24]

The Supreme Court's *Ledbetter* decision makes it impossible for many employees ever to sue for wage discrimination. Now, a woman or person of color must file an EEOC charge within 180 days of her employer's specific compensation decision. The fact that each paycheck perpetuated an earlier discriminatory decision is not enough.

Justice Ruth Bader Ginsburg wrote an angry dissenting opinion. As she explained, it may take years before an employee realizes that her wages are lower than a similarly situated male employee. Employers often keep wage information secret. Even when employees do have information about wages and raises, the cumulative effect of compensation differences may not be apparent immediately. Justice Ginsburg called for Congress to "correct [the] Court's parsimonious reading of Title VII."[25]

Julia has a stronger claim for discrimination under the "anti-retaliation provision" of Title VII. This provision protects employees' right to oppose an employer's unlawful conduct under Title VII, including employee complaints at work or formal employee legal charges or testimony.[26] Recently, the Supreme Court held that employers must not engage in retaliatory employment actions or even retaliatory conduct away from the workplace.[27] Such unlawful retaliation, for instance, might consist of an employer filing false criminal charges against a former employee who had complained about discrimination.[28] Julia must prove that Waverly retaliated in a "materially adverse" manner, meaning that she would reasonably be discouraged from bringing a discrimination charge or acting in support of another person's claim.[29] Since Julia was discharged after she filed a complaint with the state human rights agency, she has a strong Title VII claim. Matt even admitted his retaliatory motive, saying, "I can't have someone on my staff I can't trust."

The Intersection of Race, Sex, and Other Categories: Complex Motives

Elisa, in "Trading Patients," is also the victim of stereotyping by her employer. Like Julia in "Getting Even," she works in a hospital, but at a much lower level as a nurse's aide. Although Elisa had been head nurse of a hospital cardiac unit in the Philippines, U.S. hospitals do not accept her registered nurse (RN) credentials. Unit director Joanne shows no appreciation of the fact that Elisa understands and reads English perfectly. All Joanne sees is that Elisa's handwriting is hard to read. Instead of being impressed with Elisa's multilingual skills, she suggests that Elisa buy a new pen. Adding insult to injury, Joanne gives Elisa written warnings about her handwriting.

Do Joanne's disciplinary warnings to Elisa constitute intentional discrimination on the basis of sex or national origin? Or could Elisa prove that Joanne's attitudes reflect a combination of national origin and gender discrimination? Women have filed these kinds of lawsuits, called *intersectional claims*, under Title VII. They allege that a woman's experience depends on her gender in relation to—or intersecting with—other factors, such as her race, national origin, sexual orientation, and religion. For example, sexual stereotypes about African American women increase their vulnerability to sexual harassment.[30]

The courts have a divided response. Some courts recognize that an intersectional claim alleges a unique form of discrimination. For example, one federal appeals court held that a woman could claim that she was denied a promotion and discharged because of the intersection of her race and sex. "Discrimination against black females [could] exist even in the absence of discrimination," the court said, "against black men or white women."[31] Another appellate court agreed.[32] A federal trial court in Pennsylvania even permitted a woman to claim discrimination against older women, an intersection of two federal statutes.[33]

Other courts have rejected intersecting claims of race and sex discrimination. In one case, a trial judge held that the women claimants could attempt to prove that an employer laid them off because they were women or because they were African American, or both, but not because they were African American women. Claims that combine different types of discrimination, the court feared, "clearly raises the prospect of opening the hackneyed Pandora's box."[34]

Elisa, a Filipina woman, would face an uphill battle in the courts to prove intersectional sex and national origin discrimination. Joanne does favor Jesus, a male Filipino RN, whom she "quickly promoted . . . to head nurse." Even if a court were open to such an argument, the case will be hard to make—probably impossible. To win her Title VII case, Elisa must show that Joanne treated similarly situated individuals differently. But Elisa and Jesus are not in a similar situation. Jesus has more experience and education after requalifying as an RN in a U.S. university. Joanne could legitimately promote him because of his better qualifications. That Joanne gave preferential treatment to Jesus does not prove that she was motivated by gender and national origin in issuing written warnings to Elisa.

Elisa will fare no better with a Title VII claim that Joanne is motivated by Elisa's sexual orientation—alone or in combination with national origin. There is no sign that Joanne believes that Elisa is a lesbian, which she has attempted to hide from other employees. Even worse, no federal court has concluded that "sex" in Title VII includes "sexual orientation." For example, Donald Strailey lost his claim that he was fired from his position as a teacher at the Happy Times Nursery School because the employer found him too effeminate for wearing a small earring.[35] Strailey argued that the employer's reliance on gender stereotypes constituted sex discrimination. After all, the employer fired him for displaying the same "feminine" traits that were essential qualities for child care employees. Strailey lost his case. This was a case of sexual orientation discrimination, the court concluded, not sex discrimination. Title VII only protects the latter.[36]

Elisa may have a weak case under Title VII. But she has added protection under her union contract, which prohibits her employer from discharging or disciplining her without just cause. If the union takes her "unjust discipline" grievance to arbitration, the employer must prove that it had just cause for its actions. The just cause standard does more than prohibit race or sex discrimination. It requires the employer to have a "good reason" for its actions. Elisa's collective bargaining agreement also provides benefits coverage for same-sex couples. Combined with just cause, this gives Elisa strong protection against sexual orientation discrimination. Her contract provides more rights than she can find in legislation.

Kiyanna, in "Flint," was a licensed practical nurse in a nursing home where the nurses were not unionized. The nurses' aides, though, did have a union and a collective bargaining agreement. Kiyanna wrote a letter that helped the union win a just cause grievance for a nurse's aide. Without a union contract for the nurses, Kiyanna could not file such a grievance after she was fired. But she could file a charge under the National Labor Relations Act (NLRA), which is the federal law that protects employees from discrimination based on their union activities. Kiyanna claimed that the nursing home discharged her in retaliation for helping the union with the nurse's aide's grievance.

The National Labor Relations Board (NLRB) attorney recognizes that Kiyanna is the target of race, sex, and class-based stereotypes. The attorney is embarrassed by her own assumptions about Kiyanna, realizing that she "still make[s] initial judgments based on status" and fearing that "likely the judge would too." Yet Kiyanna wins her case under the NLRA when these stereotypes are proved wrong. Her excellent memory and calm and open demeanor contrast with the employer's arrogance and lack of credibility.

Kiyanna could also file a claim under Title VII if she has evidence that her employer treated her differently from other employees based on race, sex, or some combination of the two. Clearly, the employer did not fire her legitimately since she proved that the employer's reason—that she was a bad employee—was untrue. Her employer retaliated against her for her union activities. But she'd need more evidence of racial or gender motivation to bring a Title VII suit.

A Fly in the Ointment: The Supreme Court's Ambiguity about Proving Intentional Discrimination

Employers sued under Title VII try to keep their cases from ever reaching a jury. They often file motions for *summary judgment*, which means that the employer asks the judge to dismiss the case prior to a trial. Employers argue that their employees do not have enough proof that gender motivated them. And indeed, federal trial judges have granted employers' motions for summary judgments at a high rate in Title VII cases.[37] Judges have dismissed cases especially where employees rely on circumstantial evidence.[38] This kind of evidence can be viewed as fitting together pieces of a puzzle. For example, Julia, in "Getting Even," will show that she was more qualified than Jack Wilson, the man who was promoted to vice president. She can also testify about Matt's sexist comments. Julia's evidence does not directly prove that Matt was motivated by gender in denying her the promotion. All of these pieces of circumstantial evidence, though, come together to create a picture of sex discrimination. Julia will argue that her evidence is strong enough to infer that the real reason Matt denied Julia a promotion was because she was a woman, not because of her qualifications.

As discussed earlier, most employees do not have direct evidence of discrimination—that is, a "smoking gun" that directly proves illegal intent. If Matt had told Julia that he would not promote a woman to be vice president, this would be direct evidence of sex discrimination. What about Matt's comments that women are paid less than men? Some judges would find that these statements are strong enough to be direct proof that Matt denied Julia a promotion because she is a woman. But other judges would decide that these sexist comments are only indirect or circumstantial evidence that he considered Julia's gender in refusing to promote her to vice president.

Why do judges dismiss circumstantial evidence cases so often? Much of the problem is attributable to an older Supreme Court decision from 1973, where an employee had only circumstantial evidence of discrimination.[39] Employees had a heavy burden to prove the employer's illegal intent—that an employer was motivated by sex, race, national origin, or religion in decisions such as hiring or firing. In contrast, employers had only a light burden. To defend himself, an employer had only to "articulate" a nondiscriminatory reason for his or her actions.[40] The employee would then have to show that the employer's articulated reason was a *pretext*—that it was false or was a cover up for unlawful discrimination.[41] Since it was so hard for employees to prove discrimination, many federal judges dismissed their cases before getting to trial. The judges "transformed the circumstantial evidence case into a 'toothless tiger.'"[42]

Sixteen years later, in 1989, another Supreme Court decision evened the playing field between the employee and employer. This was the case where Price Waterhouse denied a promotion to Ann Hopkins for both legitimate and illegitimate reasons; that is, for "mixed motives." She proved that the employer's decision was motivated in part by gender. It was then up to the employer to prove that it would have made the same decision for legitimate reasons. Most federal judges, though, reserved this mixed-motive approach for cases where employees had direct evidence of discrimination.[43] Since these "smoking gun" cases are so rare, most employers did not have to prove the more difficult defense. Federal judges continued to dismiss many cases before getting to trial.

The Civil Rights Act of 1991, together with a later Supreme Court decision in 2003, gives employees stronger ammunition.[44] The Court made it clear that employees can use direct and/or circumstantial evidence to prove a mixed-motive case; that is, to prove that the employer was motivated, at least in part, by sex, race, national origin, or religion.[45] After this Supreme Court interpretation of the 1991 Act, some lower federal courts have decided cases using only the mixed-motive approach.[46] This means that more individuals protesting discrimination can get their cases to trial—and in front of juries.

Many other lower federal courts, though, still use both the newer mixed-motive approach and the older Supreme Court "pretext" approach that makes it harder for employees to win in circumstantial evidence cases.[47] This leaves Julia and other women and people of color vulnerable to having their cases dismissed on summary judgment motion. Given the discrepancy among the lower federal courts, the Supreme Court should step in and finally clear up the confusion.

Discrimination Against Women as a Group

Julia, Elisa, and Kiyanna can each complain that their employers discriminated against them because they were women. Each woman would attempt to prove that her employer treated her differently from male employees on issues of promotion, disciplinary warnings, and discharge.

Sex discrimination can also affect women as a group. These types of claims fall into two main categories: explicit exclusionary policies and an employer's pattern or practice of discrimination. As an example of the first category, Kiyanna's nursing home employer might have an explicit policy that only male nurses can perform certain procedures, such as catheterization, on male patients. This policy affects all women nurses.

In the latter category of group-based claims, Julia could join with other women to sue Waverly hospital for its pattern or practice of paying women employees less than men—which Matt said is "the way things are." She and other women might also bring a claim under Title VII based on Waverly's "glass ceiling." They could argue that Waverly intentionally discriminated against women for years by refusing to hire or promote them into high-level management positions.

Exclusionary Policies and the Bona Fide Occupational Qualification

Title VII prohibits most explicit group-based exclusions. Kiyanna could argue that her employer violated Title VII if it excludes women from performing certain types of nursing procedures. To preclude women from doing certain jobs, employers must prove that the exclusion is based on a "bona fide occupational qualification" (BFOQ) "reasonably necessary to the normal operation of the business."[48] This is difficult for an employer to do. Employers cannot rely on gender stereotypes for such exclusions. For example, an employer could not refuse to hire women with school-age children based on assumptions that women's caretaking obligations would lead to excessive absenteeism. In just such a case against Martin Marietta, an aerospace company, the Supreme Court ruled that Title VII does not permit one hiring policy for women with young children and a different one for men with the same-aged children.[49]

In another case, the Supreme Court rejected an employer's paternalistic assumptions about pregnant women. In *UAW v. Johnson Controls,* the Court held that a battery manufacturer violated Title VII by excluding women of childbearing capacity from jobs with lead exposure or that could result through transfer or promotion in jobs with lead exposure. The Court rejected Johnson Controls' argument that it was excluding women to protect the safety of fetuses. "Concern for a woman's existing or potential offspring," Justice Blackmun wrote, "has historically been the excuse for denying women equal employment opportunities."[50] Such a broad exclusion of women "is limited to instances in which sex or pregnancy actually interferes with an employee's ability to perform the job."[51] But Johnson Controls failed to prove "that all or substantially all women would be unable to perform safely and efficiently the duties of the job involved" in manufacturing batteries.[52]

The Court also applied the Pregnancy Discrimination Act (PDA), which amended Title VII to prohibit discrimination on the basis of pregnancy or related conditions.[53] Added in 1978, the PDA made it clear that pregnancy discrimination was a form of sex discrimination. Women capable of doing the job, the Court said, "may not be forced to choose between having a child and having a job."[54]

Kiyanna would have a strong argument that exclusion of women nurses from such work as catheterization comes from an old-fashioned and outdated image of women. Even so, she might lose. To protect the privacy of patients by assigning only male (or female) nurses to perform certain medical procedures on a male (or female) patient, the courts have allowed employers to exclude women employees.[55] Hiring an actor (e.g., a male actor for a male role) constitutes another example of an exclusion that is permitted—for authenticity.[56]

The Supreme Court has even used gender stereotypes in allowing the state of Alabama to exclude women from positions as guards in state maximum security prisons. A woman's "very womanhood," the Court ruled, endangered her and others in those prisons.[57] Justice Marshall, in dissent, castigated the Court for using "ancient canards about the proper role of women" as a basis for treating them unequally.[58]

Pattern or Practice of Discrimination: Intentional Discrimination Against Women as a Whole

Even without explicit exclusionary policies, sex-based occupational segregation continues. At the start of the twenty-first century, two-thirds of U.S. women work in traditional "female jobs," including secretary, sales employee, waitress, nurse, day care worker, domestic worker, and elementary school teacher.[59] While women have entered higher paid and higher status professions such as law and medicine, men still dominate these professions. Like Julia in "Getting Even," women also hit a glass ceiling that keeps them out of the higher ranks of management.[60]

Group-based discrimination claims can be brought by the government or as a private class action suit. In a *"pattern or practice" claim*, a group of women or persons of color must demonstrate that their employer disproportionately excluded them as standard operating procedure.[61] They can find proof in statistics. Long-term discriminatory patterns in hiring, job assignments, wages, or other working conditions must be shown. Julia and other women at Waverly would try to prove that over a period of years, Waverly's hiring and promotions practices excluded women from upper management. The women would have an even better case that Waverly systematically paid women lower wages than men.[62] To "humanize" the case, lawyers often bolster the statistics with "anecdotal" evidence about some of the women. Julia and others could testify to their own experiences at Waverly, including Matt's comments about paying women less than men.

Claims alleging patterns of systemwide discrimination are hard to prove. Even so, since the mid-1990s, there has been a "sharp rise" in such class action suits.[63] Legal scholar Michael Selmi has studied these cases in the securities industry and the grocery industry. While these employment settings are very different from each other, the evidence has much in common. In both industries, women hold a low percentage of management jobs.

These suits led to large settlements for the women bringing them.[64] What remains discouraging, however, is that women's representation has not significantly increased in management.[65]

In the securities industry, Selmi describes the situation: "As of 1996 when many of the cases were filed, approximately 15 percent of the more than 100,000 brokers nationwide were women, and women held fewer than 10 percent of the senior management positions. By 2003, the figures were nearly the same . . ."[66] The class action suit against Smith Barney was the most notorious. At this brokerage house, women protested systematically being excluded from highly paid broker jobs and being relegated to low-paying sales assistant positions. The few women who did make it into broker jobs alleged they encountered discriminatory treatment, including severe sexual harassment.[67] Merrill Lynch and Morgan Stanley, other well-known firms, faced class actions alleging systemic sexual discrimination.[68] All of the firms described above settled their cases for millions of dollars, although the amount individual women received in the class varied widely.[69]

Even as recently as the 1990s and 2000s, women filed as a class and sued their employers for relying on oppressive gender stereotypes. In the securities industry, sexual harassment at Smith Barney grew out of crude sexual stereotypes of women and men. In the other securities firms, "women also contended that they had been excluded from golf and strip club outings with clients."[70] Similar to Matt's sexist remarks to Julia, women in these lawsuits were targets of gender role stereotypes, including questions about the salary of one woman applicant and negative remarks about another woman's status as a working mother.[71]

Stereotypes about working mothers remain strong, resulting in unequal treatment at the workplace. Feminist legal scholar Joan Williams created an innovative legal claim called "family responsibility discrimination." Williams suggests that women hit a "maternal wall."[72] Once women employees have children, employers treat them differently than their male counterparts.[73] Employers believe women with children are less committed to their work and less competent than they were before they had children.[74]

Similar gender role stereotypes arise in employer defenses to group-based lawsuits. If Julia and other women bring a claim that Waverly Medical Center systemically excludes women from management positions, Waverly might assert a "lack of interest" defense. This defense uses stereotypes that "naturalize" women as wife, mother, and caregiver who choose family priorities over work advancement in nontraditional jobs. Employers argue that most women are just not interested in taking managerial jobs that require work schedules, relocation, or other working conditions that could interfere with their family priorities.[75]

The 2001 class action filed against Wal-Mart alleges systemwide sex discrimination in wages and promotions to management positions.[76] This well-publicized lawsuit of "the largest Title VII sex discrimination class action ever and the largest civil rights class action in U.S. history" holds the promise of making a loud statement about continued workplace sex segregation.[77] In 2007, a federal appellate court affirmed a federal district judge's decision that the lawsuit can proceed as a class action.[78] The class consists of 1.6 million women suing the largest employer in the world for sex discrimination since 1998.[79] Delivering on the lawsuit's potential requires casting out gender stereotypes about "women's work." Wal-Mart asserts that women's family responsibilities account for their lack of interest in management jobs.[80]

Will judges or juries accept Wal-Mart's contention that women choose nonmanagerial positions? Judges may, but perhaps juries will not. Legal scholar Vicki Schultz conducted a study of the fifty-four sex discrimination cases between 1972 and 1989 in which the employer argued that women were not interested in certain types of jobs due to their family priorities.[81] Most of these cases alleged classwide discrimination. Schultz found that judges were persuaded in almost half the cases that women were underrepresented in certain jobs because they were not interested in them.[82]

Before the Civil Rights Act of 1991, judges, not juries heard these class action cases. Now that women and people of color have the right to jury trials, the case outcomes may change. Juries tend to award higher damages than judges.[83] Jurors, coming from more diverse backgrounds than judges, can empathize with Wal-Mart employees' workplace realities. The statistical evidence, enlivened by women's testimony, may lead to verdicts and damage awards that get employers' attention. The negative publicity surrounding the class action suit already has made an impact on Wal-Mart, lowering its rank from first to fourth place in the Fortune 500 survey of America's Most Admired Companies.[84] The fear of continued bad publicity, of course, increases the chance that Wal-Mart will try to reach a settlement agreement long before a trial.

Improving the Law to Achieve Gender Equality

Title VII's prohibition of intentional sex discrimination promotes "formal equality." Women with the same skills and qualifications as men should have equal standing with men. This legal approach and the women's movement's hard-fought battles have opened doors for women to enter a "man's world" in education, training, and occupations.[85] Women have moved out of the private domestic sphere and assimilated into the public sphere of the workplace.

Women have also entered the political sphere as elected officials, political ap-
pointees, and judges. These are important gains, but there are also limits.
Under a theory of formal equality, women have the right to equal treatment if
they can prove they are "just like men."[86] In reality, though, men's and wom-
en's lives are not the same. This may be due to biology or socialization. Whatever the source, women's daily experiences differ from men's experiences.[87]

Defining equality by making men's lives the norm does not create full
equality for women.[88] For women to be just like men, they must fulfill the
role of the "ideal worker," who does not have constraints of family
caretaking.[89] Since gender roles still create a norm of woman as primary
caretaker in a heterosexual family, women cannot be similarly situated to
men. Even if women conform to the male norm by eliminating their responsibilities for family care, they still are not equal to men. Women who
do not have children or who hire other women to do child care remain
constricted by gender role stereotypes. Ann Hopkins, in the *Price Waterhouse* case, was punished for being "too macho." Julia, in "Getting Even,"
tried to be a tough business woman dressed in suits that still emphasized
her feminine curves. Neither of them could avoid the catch-22 that kept
them from fitting into the work world defined by gendered, heterosexual
norms. Gender stereotypes limit men too. They can be subject to discrimination for failing to act masculine enough.[90]

What is required to move beyond formal equality to greater substantive
gender equality? The courts and Congress should more actively promote
women's equality.

Price Waterhouse improved the law through the Court's insight into the
effect of stereotypes about women. The courts should now take these insights to their logical conclusion. Both men and women should be protected from discrimination because of stereotypes about masculinity and
femininity.

Additional legislation is still needed—including enactment of the Employment Non-Discrimination Act (ENDA), which would amend Title VII,
prohibiting sexual orientation discrimination.[91] The most inclusive legislative change would mandate that employees, like Elisa in "Trading Patients,"
be protected from bias on the basis of sexual orientation or sexual identity.
This would prohibit discrimination against transgender individuals as well
as gays, lesbians and bisexuals.[92]

Increasing gender equality also requires more attention to group-based
claims. How much progress overall have women made in the workplace? A
shift in focus from "equality treatment" of individuals to "equality of outcome" for women as a whole should occur. What is more, judges should be
skeptical of employers who argue that women do not want the higher-paying
jobs traditionally held by men.

Affirmative action programs promote equality of outcomes by increasing the number of women in all kinds of occupations. Male or white plaintiffs, in so-called reverse discrimination suits, have challenged employers' affirmative action plans as violating Title VII. The Supreme Court, though, has upheld voluntary affirmative action plans that employers use as temporary measures to correct large gender or racial disparities, where few women and people of color hold certain types of occupations.[93] Such programs make race or gender a positive element in hiring or promotions.

Employers do not need a formal affirmative action plan to take positive steps to expand workplace opportunities. Nor do employers need to act only when there is pronounced occupational segregation. If employers help women and people of color advance, the workplace becomes richer and more diverse.

Acting Collectively to Gain Equality

Women can improve their working conditions by joining together. The publicity about the Wal-Mart litigation places a spotlight on gender inequality. As a Title VII class action composed of more than one million women, the lawsuit calls attention to the power of collective action. One commentator has labeled the class action as women's way of having a collective voice that they've been unable to achieve through unionizing.[94] Unions have not yet made headway in their organizing campaigns at Wal-Mart, a company well known for its antiunion policies and actions.[95] After the meat-cutters at a Texas Wal-Mart voted to unionize, Wal-Mart closed all its meat-cutting departments.[96] The NLRB has issued multiple complaints against Wal-Mart, alleging that it has coerced employees to discourage them from unionizing and has fired employees who were active in the union organizing campaigns.[97]

Women and other workers face an uphill battle in unionizing. The current private sector unionization rate in the United States is less than 8 percent.[98] Yet a union collective bargaining agreement provides benefits that women will not achieve through litigation. Perhaps most important is the difference in employees' participation. No matter how involved employees are in a class action, attorneys run litigation. By contrast, employees help create union contract proposals and can help negotiate better working conditions. Elisa in "Trading Patients" has the right to "just cause" under her collective bargaining contract. This protects her from sex discrimination, including discrimination based on sexual orientation. As discussed earlier, just cause goes beyond protection against discrimination. The employer must have a good reason for its employment decisions.

Elisa and other unionized employees also negotiate for better wages and benefits. In 2000, union wages were 27 percent higher than nonunion wages. Unionized workers receive significantly better insurance and pension benefits. What makes this more significant is that women's representation in the labor movement has grown from 17 percent in 1954 to over 40 percent in 2000.[99] Unions have negotiated for child care subsidies, flextime, and paid vacations and family leave.[100]

Substantive equality requires the elimination of intentional sex discrimination. But it also requires structural and institutional changes that will "accommodate" the reality of women's lives. Rather than measuring women's qualifications against the traditional male norm, substantive equality would restructure social and workplace policies and practices to make the workplace open to women on a truly equal basis.

SEXUAL HARASSMENT

9

Plato, Again

Stephen Kuusisto

It was spring in the college town where Caroline Moore was wasting her day. Caroline had been wasting dozens of days. She watched young girls and boys on the college lawns and saw how they danced without knowledge like Plato's figures—people in the dark since their childhoods. That's what she thought. Young people . . . And not one of them was ill . . .

Everything is easy, she thought. The doctors had been easy; the cancer had been quick to come; chemo, radiation, surgery—all of it had been a dark season but strangely beyond her control and now, eight months "in" it was mostly behind her. Easy enough.

She set a cup of Starbuck's coffee on her knee and cradled it as she pulled her rolling briefcase closer to the bench. A girl with a blonde ponytail that swayed from the back of her red baseball hat stopped abruptly and caught a Frisbee, turned, thrust out her left hip and sailed it back to a stand of boys who were rapt with attention.

"Things are easy in the Platonic shade," Caroline thought. "Easy in the shadows; in health or illness; until you want to keep your job . . ." She thought that Plato in fact didn't mention jobs in his allegory of the cave. Just votive objects, the easy things . . .

Now here she was: fifty-two years old; a black woman with a master's in computer programming; post-irradiation, post-chemo, post-surgery— votive, upright, half in darkness, and most likely a victim of sexual harassment and disability discrimination: and good work she thought, all she'd had to do was "show up." All she'd had to do was stand behind a closed door with Bill Densk, the chief information technology officer of Grandville College. He'd asked her into his office. She'd gone in. Easy . . .

Now she sipped her coffee. Watched two college boys: one black and wearing a T-shirt that said "Corporation T-shirt" who was playing keep away with a football, dodging around his friend, a cheerful-looking boy who might be Korean, athletic, fast, but laughing too hard to succeed. She watched as they fell to the ground, each gripping the ball, laughing in breathless spasms. A home video . . .

She'd gone into Densk's office her first morning back. She'd had the first mastectomy. She'd had the full course of chemo. She was back at work. She remembered being euphoric: They'd given her steroids; she was happily wound up. She'd been ready to work on course management software. A thing she hadn't much cared for before her illness. But she was back and ready. And she thought Densk was going to outline the project; tell her how important it was; put her in charge after her hard months on medical leave.

She'd never really looked at him before that moment. She remembered now how surprised she'd been to see that Densk was so round-faced and hairless. He looked like that band leader on the *David Letterman* show, a smiling, smirking, little white guy who thought he knew a good joke. He'd looked her up and down there behind his office door, appraising her body in that exaggerated, grinning examination that certain men employ to make you feel small. She remembered how fast things went just then.

"Does it hurt?" he asked. He was looking askance, his head tilted, still with the smile. He was staring from her face to her chest.

She knew this wasn't the right question. It was that jaunty grin. And her mind had been moving fast: "Compassionate people," she'd thought, "don't ask this question first thing. It was the pronoun *it* that was the giveaway." She remembered that she'd sensed this. She'd been alert but things were running too fast for evasion.

"No, it doesn't hurt." She said. She remembered pulling at the bottom of her blouse.

She recalled how he repeated her answer. How he smiled.

"So it doesn't hurt?"

And she remembered how he touched her just there, where her breast had been. With his index finger tapped at the loose fabric. A tentative touch as if he was touching a bird's nest. She recalled how he kept smiling.

And then she'd had presence of mind. She'd said he shouldn't do that. She had stared into his vulgar face.

In turn he'd shown no sign that her reproof had bothered him: He made a courtly sweeping gesture with his arm—suggested that she sit down on his office couch. She'd sat then.

He took a chair to her right: one of those black alumni association chairs with the gold seal of the college displayed for status. Harvard had them. Grandville had them. She remembered thinking that the chair had no status of its own. She remembered her heartbeat and the odd way that Densk was still appraising her blouse. He looked both smug and coiled, as if he might touch her again where her breast used to be.

Then he plunged into his speech. He was smiling as he talked. He kept his eyes on her blouse.

"We are pleased to have you back after your medical leave," he said, "and we recognize that you will soon be having another procedure."

She couldn't believe that he was staring at her remaining breast. He was staring unguardedly. She noticed that his eyes were small and gray. They seemed ill matched to the pinkness of his skin. She had been taking steroids and her thoughts were quick. She decided that Densk was really Pinkerton, the womanizing naval officer in *Madame Butterfly*. All he needed was a little white naval uniform.

"You will be back with us for about two months, is that right?"

She saw he was asking her a question. She thought that the question was unnecessary. She was coming back to work. There would be another mastectomy soon. It might come in about two months. She didn't know. She leaned forward just slightly, the engaged and professional shift of position and said that she was back full time. Said she would likely need another medical leave soon. Repeated that she was back full time . . . Ready to work . . . Prepared for something new . . .

Densk had waved his hand then. A sideways gesture.

"We are bringing you back, but with a new assignment," he said. "You will be working for Lori on the payroll system."

"You will of course continue in a full-time position. Continue with benefits . . ."

His smile was like molasses. She remembered how her grandmother had used that expression. And now she understood it. The man had the slow, sweet smile of power.

"You will of course see this as a step down," he said. "But Lori Gustafson needs emergency help with the new payroll software and we're of course hopeful that once this situation is straightened out we can reexamine your old position."

He was telling her they'd taken her job away while she was undergoing surgery. She was being demoted. The words were rolling across the floor like beads from a broken necklace. She wanted to reach down and gather them up.

In Plato's allegory of the cave all the men are chained in place. They see only a small glimpse of the world. As a college student she'd thought this had been about aesthetics. Caroline had left Densk's office speechless but clearer about *The Republic*. And things got clearer after that. Time on the job began to speed up. Where formerly she had enjoyed her coworkers, there was now an unmistakable look in their eyes. People were in a hurry to get past her. Sandra at the front desk actually looked at her wrist as if she'd been wearing a watch. Then she'd smiled sheepishly and grabbed a stack of mail and run away.

Lori Gustafson with whom Caroline had always had a good rapport was also either diffident or critical. A soft-spoken woman from Minnesota, Lori was a friendly but reserved number cruncher. But now she was clearly troubled by Caroline's every piece of work.

Caroline was the one with the master's in computer science and the undergraduate degree in literature. Lori was a high school graduate and a junior college accountant. On their first day together she'd actually said: "We are pleased to have you back after your medical procedure." Densk's words.

After that almost all of Caroline's work was wrong.

It wasn't that she got the numbers wrong. But according to Lori her reports weren't centered on the page in the right way; she used staples where she should have affixed a paper clip; had used the wrong colors for highlighting figures for review.

She'd been back in the office for about two weeks when her oncologist called. She'd be going back in for more surgery in ten days if her blood counts stayed good.

She knew she shouldn't tell anybody. She figured it would be best to wait and make the announcement a few days before the hospitalization. She thought of the word *tenor*—the tenor of the office was wrong. Where formerly she had been employed at a managerial level she was now an administrative assistant. Her work was being devalued as well. Densk had returned her federal withholding report because she'd used a blue paper clip when he'd specifically said that red was the color for federal reports. He had conveyed this through Lori who hadn't even looked apologetic. There was a new, stern look about Lori Gustafson. She'd actually said, "You better get it right."

Then time had collapsed like a star. The second round of surgery and chemo and radiation had been harder. She would always remember the lights of examination rooms: fluorescent strobes had been everywhere. Nausea. And brutal headaches. One afternoon she'd thought her entire body could hear. She'd been unable to stand. She remembered the unanticipated compassion of a nurse who brought a damp cloth for her head. Her legs had felt like there were insects walking just beneath her skin. Then she'd had the strange sensation that her internal organs had been rearranged so that her heart was down by her kidneys and beating there like a caught bird.

Then came her first steps out into the late winter light. She had felt a kinship with the trees. Nothing was budding yet.

Then it happened: Back at work she saw that Densk had filled her old job as codirector of information technology. No one spoke to her about it. Lori Gustafson brought a clipboard to Caroline's desk. First day back.

"We'll have to work out your hours," Lori said. She said it without inflection. There wasn't a hint of embarrassment or the whispered half tone of apology that happens when shy honesty is called for. Nothing. Just the de facto part-time hours marked on a chart.

She thought of her paper trail then. Her work had been exemplary. It couldn't be that cancer was the problem. It couldn't be Densk's desire to touch her blouse. Caroline had imagined the Republic was a more evolved arrangement.

She'd walked out the door then. She saw Lori Gustafson standing with the clipboard and she could see two or three other women holding in place like shaded figures standing back from the mouth of a cave.

10

BE WHO YOU ARE

Aurelie Sheehan

Wendy doesn't think it's right that the glove compartment should be out of bounds. Certainly, if we're going to clean a car, we really need to *clean* a car. Clean it, and, if possible, know it from the inside out as it were.

"Out of bounds" anyway—what's his problem, saying that? Of all the people in the world, Chuck knows that these things are, shall we say, *flexible*.

The first car of the morning is bubble-gum pink, and that's awesome, a real eye-opener. "Check it out," says Dwayne. The pink Mustang rumbles slow as it gets close to the entrance, turns, and then teeters forward.

"Pretty in pink," Dwayne says then, flicking Wendy on the butt with a rag.

"That's for sure." At least it's different. At least it *is* different. But who's driving—an old lady? Well, appearances can be deceiving; Wendy knows this if she knows anything.

The pink car halts smack in the middle of the carwash esplanade and you can see the woman inside—can't quite tell how old she is yet—peering around.

"Check out the sign, Mad Maxeena," mutters Wendy.

"C'mon, Wendy, the sign's not *that* obvious."

Mad Maxeena doesn't seem to notice the ten-foot sign, ENTER HERE. Chuck's up by the welcome stand ushering her in, leaning forward and sweeping the seven a.m. air. Finally she catches sight of him. Does she notice the *fuck you, stupid bitch* look? It's a look he specializes in when he's not sucking up to the customers.

"The lady finds the very large door," says Dwayne. Then he turns to Wendy and starts kind of standing really close to her.

Dwayne is pretty tall, and his chest is curved in like a spoon. He bothers Wendy, because he has these magnet blue eyes, blue as chrome, fierce and a little beautiful. But then he has pockmarked skin galore, and a chin that isn't quite there. It's like all his anger is in the eyes and the rest of him was just done half-assed and haphazard. He's stepping toward Wendy and she's stepping back in some kind of a dance, the car wash tango.

"Get out of my face," says Wendy. Fucking Dwayne, with his morning Gatorade. All she can see is the green rim around his mouth, and she can smell the sweet tiptoeing breath of her coworker.

His anger has no follow-through. He's not her type at all.

· · ·

Besides Detail, the best place to find anything is on Vacuum, and Wendy and Dwayne are on Polish. But still, after the pink Mustang goes through the automatic wash, two-and-a-half minutes of sloshing joy, the old lady loiters in the store looking at the Christian greeting cards and the leather-scented air freshener, and Wendy has her moment. Dwayne's doing windows and she's got the inside of the car.

At first it looks like Old Mad Maxeena doesn't have much, just some science fiction book and a hospital bracelet hanging from her rearview mirror. She's some kind of old fucking organ donor. What you do is you lean over like you're wiping down the other door. What you do is look past the dash, past the instrument panel and the steering wheel, into the crystal ball.

Wendy releases the glove compartment latch, let's the door fall—but nothing. Just maps, receipts, a half-melted roll of duct tape, pencils with no erasers.

And then here. A photograph. Give it a look. It's a little girl.

It's me, Wendy thinks, holding the blue rag to her chest, reaching for the picture. The girl is wearing a straw hat and heart-shaped sunglasses. She's leaning on a tree. There are flowers.

It's me, when I was a movie star. When I was a little tiny innocent girl.
Dwayne raps on the window. *What the fuck?*

Wendy slams the glove compartment shut and pulls herself back up, giving the wheel a last swipe, then readjusts the mirror.

"Whaddya find, sexy?" asks Dwayne, a concavity in his bright blue WASH PLUS polo shirt. He's got two pairs of pants he wears to work, alternating days.

"Nothing."

"You're stealing from the old farts now, aren't you? You've got no morals at all."

"Shut the fuck up, Dwayne."

. . .

Wendy and Dwayne make $7.10 an hour. This is because they've worked at WASH PLUS for over six months. You get a raise then, moving up from minimum.

"Oh shit," Dwayne says, at the wheel well. Here comes fucking trouble in the form of C-H-U-C-K—Chucky boy.

"Wendy, I need to talk to you," says Chuck. "Now. In my office."

He turns toward his truck, parked behind the car wash proper.

Wendy's interior: *I was a movie star and a little girl, and I lived in a tree house. It was the kind of tree they only have in California, wispy and tall with purple flowers. Purple flowers everywhere and when they fall it's a snow of lavender.*

There's a funny feeling you get from the cleansers, a smooth slick feeling, like your hands are made of silk and it doesn't matter where you put them anymore. And there's a kind of grit that cars have, too, like sugar.

"But we're about to get hammered here," says Wendy. Her voice is smaller than she intended, ineffectual. "Dwayne—"

"Now," Chuck is saying, and in the background, like some kind of saloon in a movie set, is his vehicle, a yellow flash with flames off the front wheels all the way to the back and his rims, man, those rims are something else, even in Tucson. They'll murder you for your rims here. Leave you in the desert with a distinct lack of life in your body and four unadorned tires.

So Wendy throws the blue rag in the barrel and she's going to miss saying "Have a nice day!" to the old lady who owns the Mustang, now hobbling out to her shorn car.

Movie-star Wendy is invisible. She slouches toward Chuck's office, the cab of his Ford.

. . .

"Wendy, Wendy," Chuck says, after he's turned on the truck and gotten the AC on medium and the radio on low. Chuck is a thirty-year-old man. What do people do with so many years, where is it stored? Is it in their shoulders, their stomachs? Wendy can hardly imagine being that old.

Chuck's fingers don't have bones, they have metal bars inside, same with his arms. He's part robot, she knows that. Or like he's from one of the old bag's *One Hundred Best Science Fiction Tales*, some kind of half-man, half-machine. When she's with Chuck she has two instincts at the same time, like she, too, has been transformed into a kind of mythical creature—a mermaid, or a dodo bird.

He's taken her silk-cleanser hand and put it on his trousers.

"I've been meaning to talk to you," he says, laying his head back on the seat. "You take too fucking long with the polish, little girl. You've got to shape up or—"

"Or what, you're going to fire me?" Wendy says to the man's profile.

• • •

The next car Wendy violates is some kind of boring minivan. Her hand reaches all the way under the seat, instinctively dismissing the McDonald's toy plastic bags and instruction sheets, in eighteen languages including legalese. She's searching for something better, for treasure. She should toss the bags, right? In fact, Vacuum should have already gotten them. But there's often a kind of *who-gives-a-fuck* going on with the guys in their blue shirts, and so sometimes, even here on Polish, there can be pockets that have been left undiscovered.

There's like twenty zillion tan minivans, and each one smells like vomit even after they squirt the juice under the seat—this time, Vanilla. This particular tan minivan's got the Christian influence, a bamboo cross suctioned onto the windshield, and some kind of Prayer of the Day book with a fake white leather cover wedged sideways in the drink compartment, and it's not long at all before she finds what she's looking for, one token to Chuck E. Cheese's—a fake coin with a fake Mickey Mouse on it with fake value but real value to someone, somewhere. Real value if you're three and it's the last coin you need to maybe win some stupid-ass made-in-China teddy bear. She slips it in her pocket, next to the photograph. I will use it someday, the last coin necessary. Or I'll just take the coin and throw it into the arroyo, throw it as far as I can, and it will go nowhere.

There's always a lot of business between 7:30 and 9:30; Wendy would say that's about the busiest time of the day—not counting Saturdays. The cops come through sometimes, and if she's got Vacuum, Wendy would say that these are probably some of her favorite moments, besides Detail. Detail provides the ultimate privacy, though you've still got a quota to fulfill. You've still got Chuck or Jamie—he's okay, for a dork—keeping tabs on things. Eight cribs, ten hours a day. Do the multiplication, blue shirt boys.

At WASH PLUS, Wendy works from 7:00 to 3:00, most days. She used to work second shift just as often, but Chuck changed her schedule. He likes her to be around when he's there, in the sunny morning. She takes home $208.10 a week.

Today—today if she gets a sign, maybe she'll quit this place.

She's had this thought before.

• • •

My Wendy, says Dwayne. My Wendy.

Chuck has separated them now, and she's on Vacuum and he's still Polishing away. Oh, but you're sexy in the blue shirt, even in the blue shirt, Wendy Wendy. Wasn't there some kind of fairy tale girl called Wendy?

But I, I am just a pitiful nerd, thinks Dwayne. For I bespeak not of love to those such as dear Wendy. Dwayne catches a glimpse of himself in the rearview mirror, takes a glancing assessment of his black-blue eyes, his horrid horrid skin and chin. *Skin & Chin job, please*, he'd say, just like the cheap bastards who rumble up and say, *I've got a coupon for the Shine n' Go? $4.99?* What the hell do you think you're going to get for $4.99, dude? Meanwhile, her youth is slipping away. My stunning and royal Wendy. *The coupon actually expired two weeks ago, but can I still use it, please?*

Dwayne takes the spray cleanser and draws a big W on the car's interior window. A big W, and then he fills it in with scribbles of sunlight. He's been doing this for almost ten months now and he has systems, man, systems and plans and all manner of education to impart on the baby-washers, like Wendy, who came in a couple months after him, and like that kid John who lasted, what, two hours? Couldn't handle Chucky-boy's attitude. You have to take it with a grain of salt or like a whole fucking cup of salt, that's what he would have told him!

Ah well. Dwayne is done, throws the towel, drops the spray bottle back into the trench. Back in the old days, when No was working here—those were good times. No with his weird fucking name, right? But he knew how to make the hours pass. *Game a' chance*, that's what he always said. *Game a' chance.* It was his mantra. Then No passed on to another land.

The horizon from here is all zigzag with buildings. You've got your Western Wear Outlet, your Zenith Plumbing, your Mickey D's. And then there's the layer of wires and lights. And then, if you look closer, you've got the puzzle pieces of pavement: road, and sections of sidewalk leading no real place really. So it's like these layers, and then way back, way way back, which you can only see if you're on Vacuum, are the mountains, the color of baby mice. That's what No said, the color of baby mice, and now every time Dwayne sees them that's what he thinks.

Wendy, Wendy, Wendy. What if Wendy ever met his mother? He smiles when he thinks about that, a kind of skull-smile. Dwayne's mother doesn't meet people well. It's not a skill she's learned in her forty years on this planet. Maybe next week. Maybe next week she'll learn about Meeting People. And then after that maybe she can learn how to Have Conversations with Acquaintances, or maybe even Hold Down a Job, or even, Dress Normally for Outdoors.

"Bitch!" calls Chuck from the other side of the yard. "Rag wash. Now, yo." Yo Yo yourself, Chuck. Fucking Yo Yo. Yo Yo Ma.

Dwayne wheels the garbage pail of rat-tail towels around the periphery of the property and opens the industrial steel washing machine. Once they found a pair of panties in there, some kind of Victoria's Secret jobs. It was depressing, kind of, mainly because Dwayne would never see such things himself—in use, that is. Never has.

Calling the mountains the color of baby mice: that's depressing, too. It makes them seem smaller than they really are.

．　．　．

So then comes one of those asshole types, one of those guys who likes to keep his car madhouse clean, right?

Dwayne knows them all. Besides the car-holes, as he calls them, you've got the company men. Someone else is paying to keep the car clean—these are the cops, the insurance agents, the sorry-ass travelers with shirts hanging in the backseat. These guys come in and the car's not even dirty half the time, and the guy's got it all expensed out so it's a major yawner, in Dwayne's estimation. Of course most of them don't tip worth shit. It's like, if it's free to us, why should we spend one frigging dollar on you, little blue shirt man? Then you've got the fucking Kirby vacuum cleaner dudes and their crazy purple van. Then you've got your housewives, and they're okay sometimes, but the vehicle's usually trashed, smells like puke or urine and it's like someone's ground sandwiches into the upholstery. If you're on Vacuum they'll come up and be all rolling the receipt around in their red hands and saying, *How much just to get that little spot taken care of? Really? That much, huh? Wow. Well, maybe next time.* And then there's all manner of other boring folks. Blah, blah, blah. And then there's the goddamned old ones. Not like the crazy old lady and her Mustang this morning, she was different, a sweetheart—you'd want your grandmother to be like that—but these people, and the men and the women look the same, they're all about what would you say 180, 200 pounds and about four-feet tall and wearing old washed-out green sweatshirts and greased-up eyeglasses and after you've polished the sweet hell out of their ugly as shit van or Dodge or some other junk heap, they shuffle on over and stoop down to give your job the half-blind once-over. *Hey, you missed a spot, sonny boy. You missed a spot, and, wait a minute now, the antenna didn't used to be this loose, what did you do to my antenna?*

Fucking oldsters.

Not that there aren't exceptions. The other day this dude, he had a bum arm, he searched out Dwayne and slipped him a five, slapped him on the shoulder with his good hand. "Way to go on my Infiniti last week," he said. "I couldn't find you last time." Keeps you guessing, anyway. Anything is possible, that's what Dwayne ends up thinking. Sometimes.

But the absolute worst, truthfully, are the guys like this one right here. These muscle guys. Yo, I'm a nerd, man. I'm way too nerdy for this job. I'm not like in a gang, I'm not like a gang wannabe, I've got a life, I've got plans (or I could have plans). This guy and his 4x4, and it's got one of the custom paint jobs, sparkle blue, and a flat top and major tires and spinners too, blinding chrome—and there he is squatting right next to Julio who has the shine lotion and he's squeegeeing that on the black rubber and the guy's on his cell phone and watching Julio like a hawk, doesn't want him scratching the rims, doesn't want him to miss a spot of rubber, not one little sliver or the guy's manhood is at stake and he's liable to go break some bones to get it back.

"Hey, Julio, where the hell did the sponges go?" Dwayne says, mainly because he thinks the guy's about to eat his coworker alive, little Julio who says even less than him on the line, who comes in bruised but never brags like the others about what he did over the weekend, whose ass he kicked, what park he skated or girl he plowed through.

Julio throws him one, doesn't look his way because the sun's behind Dwayne, throws the bright yellow sponge up like a softball against the brilliant blue Tucson sky. Only another six and a half hours to go.

• • •

Why is Welcome so hard for these morons, Chuck asks himself, looking on. Fucking greet the customer and sell the product. This place could be a machine, a gorgeous machine, but the concept of *greet-and-sell* kicks their ass every time. You've got your Honest Johns, fucking dimwits, and you've got your BS artists, and they're probably worse in their own way, because they give this yellow smile and you can see the people in the cars getting all terrified and closing up to the possibility of the deal. But the fact is Chuck, who prides himself on his job, learns a little something from the dimwits and the assholes; he studies them. At the bar he tries out Honest John, he tries out BS Artist, and then he tries something new, one of the techniques he's made up or perfected on his own. He likes the I'm Your Best Friend approach, and then there's also We're All in It Together (that's like, *Hey listen, I'll take an extra five off, just don't tell the manager*). And he likes the Practical Asshole approach. *Two days left of this sale and then not again until summer.* Summer's always around the corner, too soon, too long. It's always fucking summer here.

They look at you in horror, like you're Jacko in Thriller, that old-time video Chuck's mother used to dance to those bad afternoons. And even he has to admit that it gets old, tiring, putting on the smile when all the time you're thinking two things exactly. One, you dumb motherfucker. I'm giving you ten dollars off, is that what you're going to think now? Two, you dumb motherfucker. You're not just dumb but you're scared, too? Don't want to engage me in conversation?

You can do a lot with those two emotions, dumbness and fear.

Fact of the matter is he's preoccupied lately with other developments. He's got it all balanced out like on the nose of an elephant here.

It was going to be the best time yet, like in the theaters. Just Chuck and a useless criminal in the desert. Payback, girls. All he was supposed to do was a simple stalk and lure, a simple crash and burn. All he had to do was off some unnecessary scrap of nothingness, and it would be fun, new, and he would be Vin Diesel, Willis, and there would be ketchup everywhere.

And he'd get it on his phone camera, of course. Some of the choicer moments. Maybe not all the action, but some stills to share.

But now, certainly, his patience has grown thinner. With the eight employees here at WASH PLUS, with the ignorance of the owner, who rolls down from the Foothills once a week like he knows something, to empty the cash register. The employees, they're children. They need discipline; they need order. Chuck astonishes himself thinking of how little these people learned growing up. What, you never learned how to do a job well? You never learned the value of personal responsibility? Someone has to lead the blind from darkness, to get them to fucking clean a car.

So yes, lately, there is this tension. He'd call it a lack of focus on his part. Everything's balanced out and if he moves the wrong way something's likely to—he's got more on his mind than before.

The owner has a caramel-colored Jaguar. He smokes a pipe, and so he's always got his window open a crack, and when you see him coming and you're looking through the tinted window it looks like he's got a helmet of gold hair and that he's on fire. The fucking inside of the car is on fire.

What the hell's this, another pink Mustang? Didn't we see one of those before?

. . .

"GET THE FUCK OVER HERE, DWAYNE, before not after the wax dries on this Vee. What, you want us to lose business? Every goddamned customer?"

He starts loud and small and ends big and in Dwayne's face and whispery hoarse, and it feels, to Dwayne, like a visual/aural seesaw. But the fact is there she went again, diving down into another personal adventure, his Wendy. Only what the hell, that's a cop's car, Wendy, my maid, my lass, my princess, do be careful when you're expressing your inner desires in the vicinity of a brigade of Tucson police officers. I know not from personal experience, but the men in their thick polyester britches, they're rumored to be unreasonable about things like that, you know? Rifling through their pads of tickets, fondling their spare 45, the keys to their 'catch em 'copter.

One last look at the lass and he's back to the Humvee. Don't think I don't know what you're doing with Wendy, woodchuck Chuck, Dwayne says to the hubcap of a Hummer. A nerd like me, I'm not social like this, I'm not about this, I can't compete, I'm not funny, I'm not going any place, particularly, I just want to make my paycheck—so just pass me by, angel of assholeness, with your damaging eyes.

"Julio, my main man," Dwayne finally says out loud, to the Guatemalan. Everyone thinks he's Mexican, but he's not, he's from Guate-fucking-mala. Once he told Dwayne his family is gone. What? *I loss family*, he said. Dwayne kept that in his head for a while, through a pair of Accords, a Cherokee, an Outlander. *I loss family*. It sounds, even the words of it, like an error.

It's a bitch cleaning the windows on the Humvees and the Escalades; you've got to lean out as you lean over, try like hell not to scratch the finish with your belt or your zipper. And the owners on their cell phones watch from the Guest Yard, just the other side of the sad little tip box, and most of them don't put anything in at all. Once Dwayne saw someone pretend to drop money in, a quick flip of the hand because she saw them watching her. A shitload of them are probably doing the same, gesture of kindness, but what you've really got is a shadow passing over the $9.50 that, at the end of the shift, all eight workers will share. Just don't give anything, my friends. Just walk past, proudly. Hell, I'm already making $7.10 an hour.

Still, there was that one guy last week. Armless Joe, the generous wonder.

Oh Wendy, sweet Wendy, but we could drive up to the top of Mount Lemmon and knock our feet against the boulders, view the city from a distance, dream together.

. . .

"Chuck?"

"What?" He's going through the order book frantically, blame in his hands. "Why the hell is this detail job in this pile? Who the hell's handwriting is this? I don't see no fucking initials on this receipt."

Wendy stands next to her boss, her paramour, and all around her trim little pretty little frame she's got things hanging, things she's stolen from the cars of the day. She's got the 52nd card in a deck from one car, a spare key, a photograph. And from the cop's sedan she found some kind of nut or bolt, the important last part to something cops need. At the end of every shift she's a Christmas tree.

Despite everything, she could give notice, or suggest that they date like civilized people, after hours, or even that they break off this torrid, reckless, heartbreaking affair. She hesitates, weighed down by trinkets and fear.

Here's a new car rolling off the ride. One of those squashed up girlie SUVs—a Jimmy or a CR-V. The bumper sticker says *Be Who You Are.*

"Never mind," Wendy says, and turns back toward Polish. She's got another three hours. She'll catch him later.

. . .

These men love cars. But of course: It's a car wash. As an ideal employee, you've got to have an essential passion for The Vehicle. Just like the folks at Burger King are truly gourmands at heart, and the people selling vacuum cleaners want to remake the world.

But it's different for Wendy. So she's not a man, obviously, but the fact is she likes to be outside, and it did beat out the one other job she was offered: wearing a tent sign for a perpetually going-out-of-business store, standing around like a moron for eight hours a day on the corner of Broadway and Kolb. No, she didn't want that, sandwiched between plasterboards and breathing the neon lie. It would be like the worst kind of unnatural jail in the world.

Wendy polishes a tire. The sun has gone high and hot like a stranger tapping her shoulder. She believes people can change, that goodness will find a reward. The talent finders are out there, picking up their Starbucks and then crossing the street to WASH PLUS to find her, to notice and rescue and discover.

She has to be vigilant and put all the pieces together. She has to be ready. She has to be ready, careful, patient, prepared.

Wendy is the flint of a match. Wendy is a diving board.

Nonetheless she finds it odd that here's another bright pink car, this one a convertible, pulling up to Welcome. No one's around, so she throws the rag and picks up a clipboard.

. . .

Methinks if you captured the dreams of me coworkers, you would have one of everything, muses Dwayne, hopping into a sedan and bringing it to the end of the line. Julio, for instance, wants to be a preacher. He told Dwayne that, and Dwayne remembers. A preacher in a car wash, now that's a laugh. The kid is from Guatemala, all right? Dwayne doesn't even know where Guatemala is, but he imagines it's a hell of a spit from here, a hell of a drive in a pink car.

When Julio's not swabbing the cars, he's got his arms wrapped around himself, like it's cold here, cold at a hundred degrees.

Dwayne worries that he will never become a preacher.

Dwayne thinks of his own mother, lying on the couch at home, watching her "favorite shows," which are all the shows on TV it turns out, all lined up in a row. At first she liked to complain about the reality shows, but now she's on board. Now she discriminates between the good ones and the bad ones. Discrimination: always the first sign of the fall.

The apartment complex on Fifth advertised one-month free rent, but when Dwayne checked into it, they meant you had to live there first, for a year.

Wendy's not the only girl here. There's also Maribel. She's got a baby at home that her mother takes care of while she's at WASH PLUS, scrubbing hubcaps. Maribel with a homemade tattoo above her wrist, some kind of love-me love-me-not daisy, the petals an even number.

And the floaters, all the blue-shirted floaters. Some days they terrify Dwayne, swarming as they do, and all he wants is to scrub and clean and polish. There are the power plays, the towels tossed, the cars half finished like Maribel's tattoo. Like me own thoughts most days, he thinks, this season of woe.

Not that there aren't perks. They get half-off a basic car wash, coupons that come in with their paycheck, and if Dwayne had a car he might use them, too. And there are days like this, two pink car days. That's worth something.

And then there's Wendy, too.

. . .

"I've got to get in the car," she says.

"Yeah, we all want to get in the car, sweet thing."

"Dwayne, Dwayne. C'mon. Hey, I'd even kiss you if your lips weren't green."

"Methinks the girl is in love."

"You're making me laugh. Look, here it comes, after the SUV. It's the next one in line."

"But Chuck will have me head, Wendy."

Now she's moving in, close to his body.

"He's at lunch, Dwayne."

Dwayne gives up and she watches his concave body motor over to the Welcome station. He has wraparound mirror sunglasses that were in style about two hundred years ago, but he still has a baby-cuteness to him, like some kind of sad sack loser boyfriend.

Anyway she's where she wants to be, blue washcloth in hand.

. . .

The pink car has entered the landscape. The owner is some kind of freak, a zombie. But the car! The car is not aware of itself. The car maintains the pleasure principle, the splash, the rub, the polish, the slide of cloth around the interior. It enlists zombies to drive it here.

Wendy lets herself in. She wipes and scans. Sometimes the glove compartment is too obvious. Plus you don't have much time, often. Quickness is important.

She remembers the zombie's dark eyes, the plea for a wax job, $29.99.

She's got expert hands, that's what Chuck says. She wears rings on five fingers. Ambassador Diamonds, a store Wendy passes in the bus every morning and every afternoon—she, like Dwayne, can't afford a car herself, has no use for the discount cards—advertises the cost of gold and silver on the marquee. Gold: $424.70 an ounce. Silver: $7.09. The rings Wendy wears on her ecstatically, other-worldly soft and smooth hands, worn smooth by the dirt of cars, worn smooth as pearls in the ocean, drift their way along the top of the upturned visor in the pink car, then between the seats, a blushing girl's legs.

She's about to find something when she discovers the eyes of the car owner, staring down at her from outside. The coma victim has left the greeting card selection and has come to see what Wendy is doing. The coma victim is screaming.

. . .

He's trying to hear his friend give instructions over the cell phone, but his friend is driving—driving away, fast—and the instructions come in patches, and Chuck, despite his mastery of the universe, feels the sting of sweat under his arms. Feels like fire ants are biting him. "What? Sorry, you cut out there. What did you say, then?" At times like this, when he's under siege, he starts talking country, starts getting polite and confused and saying *you betcha* and *what, then?* The fact is that even now, twenty years after his dad was transferred to Davis-Monthan, he still gets that balloon-about-to-pop feeling in his head from the sun. You wouldn't want to be a mole here, in the desert. You wouldn't want to be a natural human being. It's a bad luck place, with all the sand and the way the lizards and scorpions come crawling out of nothing like they've been transformed from sun and sand into live things. All his luck in the world depends on if he can hear his friend's instructions. Originally he'd said to leave the car there, with the trunk locked. Now he seems to be telling him he has to go back, back to the location on the edge of his dreams, back to the car, go back to the car and do something. But what?

Fuck, there is no body, man, he wants to whine. *Hey, man, it was a fake, an illusion. A scam. I freaked out. I'm a coward, man.*

"I'm sorry, I can't hear you, what?" he says again.

Did his friend say this is only the beginning? No, his friend didn't say anything. Chuck takes the phone away from his ear and looks at it. He's disconnected. *Welcome to AT&T Wireless,* the phone tells him.

Riddle: What's worse than being a ruthless killer?

Punch line: Not being a ruthless killer, being a no one.

He hears a fucking vicious scream. Someone is screaming at the polish station. *Hello? Guest Services, may I help you?* Chuck stands up from where he was leaning.

. . .

All the employees look up, a flock of blue birds noticing something. Chuck never moves fast; it's not appropriate for him. Still he seems to be barreling forward, and then here comes Dwayne, back from the bathroom where he'd been using wet paper towels to clean up the green around his mouth. Wendy is in the car. She's practically lying down, relaxing.

The woman holds her hands over her ears, and it's like her hands are mittens, and she keeps screaming.

Wendy understands, and she would like the woman to know she understands. She gets it now. She is in the arms of the jacaranda tree, she's in the Hollywood hills, and it is springtime.

She wants to tell the woman in pajamas that no, she won't take the piece of string she's already located, already touched with her smooth hands. It's a six-inch piece of string, but it holds everything together. So lady, like, you can stop screaming. Take six steps back, don't step on the Windex.

I have the car keys, Wendy is thinking. The car keys are in the ignition.

. . .

Chuck and Dwayne stare down at her.

"Wendy, why are you crying?" asks Dwayne.

Chuck's eyes are glazed, not understanding. In a minute he'll give the coma victim, who has now moved on to some kind of low moan, two discount coupons, redeemable within two months maximum. He'll scrawl his signature on the bottom line.

Dwayne wipes his chin, moist and cold. He's in love. He's in love with Wendy for sure now. For her, he'd do anything.

But Wendy is going to drive away, and she'll scatter all the things she's stolen. Out the window they'll go: a map of Texas, a girl's photograph, a token. She'll drive away, under the blue prison sky, past all the car washes in Tucson.

11

HWANG'S MISSING HAND

Eileen Pollack

I had lived fifteen years in Paradise, New York, without ever climbing to the offices and apartments above the shops on Main Street. The town was so tiny that it seems inconceivable I wouldn't have explored every square inch. But in small country towns, where no grid of streets maps out the status of anyone who lives at a given address, each family must chart its own forbidden neighborhoods.

When my father was young and still delivered mail on the hills above Main Street, he classified people according to whether their houses were silent or trembling with noise—not just the frenzied yapping of dogs, but the curses of a husband berating his wife for a weak cup of coffee or an imagined affair; the wails of a child being slapped for no reason; even a radio turned up too loud. If my father had to knock and ask for a signature, he hoped that nothing more threatening than a woman in a housedress would open the door. If her robe wasn't tied, if she flirted or scowled, he warned us against the family that night. When he grew older and was given the route the other men wanted—he'd have to climb stairs, but he wouldn't have to lug his bag up those hills—he cautioned my mother: "If you *have* to shop on Main Street, please, for God's sake, keep your feet on the ground!"

I came to imagine that second-floor world as an island that floated over my head like Gulliver's Laputa, its inhabitants rich in some dangerous knowledge I needed to learn. I would look up and see the stockbroker's office where Lorna Berg had worked before she stole money and was sent off to jail (her son was the handsomest boy in our grade, kind, though aloof), or a man in an undershirt, the expression on his face not quite desire and not quite disdain. Each window seemed to illustrate an emotion whose name I couldn't yet pronounce. It was maddening to stand there like a backwards first-grader, not knowing the words to describe what I felt.

And now, at fifteen, I finally had a reason to ascend to that world: I had been granted an interview for my very first job, for a firm that insured camps and resorts throughout the Northeast.

"Over my dead body," my father said at dinner. "You don't know what's up there."

By "up there," he meant the floor above Sears.

"Don't you trust me?" I asked.

"Of course we do!" My mother wiped her hands on her apron and sat down to eat, though my father and I already were done. "It's not *you* we don't trust. You're too young to know what can go on in an office like that."

For a moment I thought she might actually tell me—if she knew it herself. But I saw her reconsider.

"All I can say is, no matter what time I walk by that building, two or three men are leaning out the windows"—she lowered her voice—"*watching women go by.*"

I reminded my parents that I had to start saving money for college.

"Not like *that*," my father said.

But the only other choice for girls in our town was waiting on tables at the local hotels, where they lost their virginity and learned to use drugs. In the end, the very name of the business calmed my parents. ("*Insurance,*" they whispered in their bedroom debates.) And how could they fear for my safety in a place where my history teacher, whom they knew and respected, earned extra money by working part-time?

My teacher, Mr. Noble, had informed me of the interview a few days before.

"Rothman," he said, "I lied to these people, I said you were competent."

I love his brusque speech, the way he called me "Rothman" instead of "Dianne." He had to disguise how much he favored me over my classmates; in the back of the room, two other students were planning the trip we would soon make to Gettysburg.

"It's a shame they won't let you be an adjustor, but the boss will never change. He'll never let a girl go out in the field. Still, in that office . . . Keep your eyes and ears open and you'll pick up a lot."

Like everyone else, I knew about the office where Mr. Noble worked. He often told cryptic stories in class about being an adjustor; their point seemed to be that the world wasn't the safe, rational place the rest of our teachers had led us to think. Like the R.O.T.C. captain who came to recruit seniors for the Army, Mr. Noble seemed to advertise a life that was more exciting and serious than the one that my parents had planned out for me. I wasn't supposed to be drawn to such stories. I was meant to pass through high school, and after that college, without being touched. This would earn me a job that would let me pass through life in much the same way. I didn't have to do anything. A's flew to me, clung. They formed a spiky armor that kept away trouble and boys my own age. I had never gotten a B. So what if I did? B's were just ink on paper.

"You'll have to take a test," Mr. Noble said. "But even a girl with your limited intelligence ought to squeak by."

He put his hand on my shoulder and walked me to the door. This display of affection, naked as it was, meant less than the insults. Dale and Andy looked up, then went back to their road maps, the gesture no more troubling than the sight of Mr. Noble, who also coached football, with his arm around a player.

We stood in the hall. Other kids passed by, but he didn't drop his hand.

"Don't blow it, okay?" He said this as if the test were a gauntlet that I might not get through; but, if I did, he would be standing at the finish line, arms stretched out wide.

My interview was set for a quarter to four, but I got to the building a half-hour early. I killed some time inspecting the window of Ruthie's Fine Dresses. None of my friends went into Ruthie's except to make fun of the double-knit pantsuits and long-line brassieres; we never wore anything but tight straight-legged Lee's, T-shirts, and work boots. For the interview I'd had to squirm my way into the only dress I owned, a stretchy blue mini I had bought in seventh grade. Earlier that day, when I had stopped by to see Mr. Noble for last-minute hints as to how to get the job, he had slammed his desk shut and looked at me hard. I thought he would tell me to go home and change. Instead, he whistled softly through the gap in his teeth.

"Well look at that," he said. "Rothman's got legs. And nice ones at that. Can't figure out why you girls go around like a bunch of storm troopers. Especially girls who look so nice in a dress."

No one had ever bothered to comment on my body before this. Beauty and dress were not categories on which I was judged. Until then, I had existed in just two dimensions, and suddenly Mr. Noble had added a third. I examined my reflection in the window of Ruthie's, shyly, as though I were peeking at somebody else in the nude. I studied the way the elastic of my dress—the top part was gathered in puckery rows—stretched across my breasts, bunched at my waist, stretched again at my hips. I had pulled back my hair and I hadn't worn makeup so my face was a pale, featureless oval like the faces of the mannequins. My reflection was standing next to a dummy in a clingy red nightgown, hips thrust toward the glass. Only when a friend of my mother caught me staring ("You're a little too young to be shopping for a trousseau!") did I force myself to leave.

At last, at three-forty, I entered the door between Sears and the deli. The stairs rose before me like a rickety ladder. I had assumed that the office would be right at the top; instead, I found a maze of gloomy halls with warped floors. I passed DR. HAND, PODIATRIST, a photographer's studio, a taxidermist, a door with a sign in gold script that said NOVELTIES AND JOKES, but the frosted-glass panes showed no lights inside.

I reached a dead end. A round, beveled window coated with filth looked out on Main Street. I had come several blocks, right through the walls of three or four buildings! I shivered with the thrill of finding connections where none were before.

Finally, a light behind one of the doors. COLONIAL CONNECTICUT IN-SURANCE, PLEASE ENTER.

The clock on the wall said three-fifty-two. I was seven minutes late! I almost walked out. I thought that a single mistake, like the faintest of taps on the end of a lever, would swing my whole life through a radical arc; I would never have another chance to succeed.

But the front desk was empty. Maybe they would think I had been waiting all along. . . . I sat on the bench that ran down one wall. From a room I couldn't see came high, nasal voices like strings being tuned, the rhythmic percussion of fingers on keys, syncopated by bells. I sat on that bench and listened with the same tautness in my chest and tingle in my thighs that I had felt when my music class had traveled to New York and entered a theater as immense as a universe, a galaxy of crystal over our heads, and listened to an orchestra pluck, hum, and whistle, preparing for Carmen to appear on the stage.

"Can I help you? Oh, never mind. I *know* who you are. Don't tell me you've just been sitting there waiting!" The women who said this seemed less like a diva than a Kabuki performer. Her lacquered black hair was piled on her head, with a bright yellow pencil stuck in the top. A big crimson circle spotted each cheek and a heavy black eyebrow rose like a roof over each eye. She inspected me closely.

"Quite an outfit," she said. "Too bad we need a girl who has more in her favor than tits and an ass."

This woman seemed to hate me simply because I was younger than she was and had long, pretty legs! How could she think that she knew who I was? And what better sign that I had entered the life for which I had been waiting than being mistaken for somebody else?

"Jane!" she shouted. "Jane! That new girl is out here!" She turned back to me, a smirk on her red kiss-shaped lips. "You're Jack's girl," she said.

Jack? I thought. Jack? Mr. Noble's first name! This woman had the power to call Mr. Noble "Jack"!

"He sends us a different girl every few summers. They seem to come in cycles . . . a blonde, then a redhead. . . . You must be the brunette."

She made him sound like a pimp.

"He raves about them all." She glanced at me to see how I would take the news that I wasn't as special as I once might have thought. "But most of Jack's girls don't have what it takes."

What could this all-important quality be? Did I have it or not? And who in our school, the principal included, would have presumed to speak of Mr. Noble in this finger-wagging tone?

A high-pitched man's voice called from an office: "Cybil! Where'd you go? I *said* that I needed you."

"Oh, phooey," she said, flapping her hand. But the gesture didn't fool me. Her power was false; it only extended to young girls like me.

She huffed from the room. A few moments later an older woman appeared, tall and thin-boned, with sparse grayish hair. Her lipstick was white, as was the powder on her eyelids and cheeks; she seemed to be trying to cover her features as she might have used Wite-Out to erase a mistake.

"I'm Jane Givens," she said. "And *you* are Dianne. I've heard wonderful things about you, Dianne!"

Unlike the other woman, she seemed eager to believe them. She was handing me a gift: her innocence, her faith. I had been so looking forward to a dangerous adventure, and now I'd be burdened with this delicate gift.

"All right," she said cheerily. She held out a loop of brilliant blue plastic about six inches wide. "There's an easy little test. I'm sure that a girl who comes so highly recommended . . ."

I stood from the bench. The tops of my pantyhose showed beneath my hem. As I tugged down my dress I saw on her face that she had *wanted* to like me, now wondered if she should.

"You *can* use a Dictaphone? I hope Jack wouldn't waste my time with a girl who has weak Dictaphone skills."

For Mr. Noble's honor I would have to say yes. But this didn't seem a lie. If other girls knew how to use this machine, I could figure it out.

"I know," I said. "I can."

That's all it took to restore her good faith. "Of course you do!" she said. "I'm sure you'll do fine."

She led me through the room where the secretaries worked. All six wore earphones. The wires seemed to link them to a force that let their fingers vibrate so fast. And they talked as they typed, like an acrobatic troupe weaving scarves as they danced. I paused to watch, spellbound, but my guide hurried on; I was still an outsider, not privileged to witness this private display.

The rooms that we passed through grew smaller and darker. We picked our way between stalagmites of furniture and office machines and rusted gray file cabinets whose labels read EXPIRED, CASE CLOSED, or DECEASED. I was starting to worry that I should have unraveled a thread from my purse when we reached the last room, the smallest and grimiest, with a dented metal desk and a chair with no back. On the desk was a gray, boxy machine I assumed was a Dictaphone, a massive old typewriter, and a Styrofoam cup with brown gum at the bottom.

"All right then." She gave me the blue plastic belt. "All you have to do is type what you hear, just the way you hear it." She patted my head. "I'll be back in half an hour. Take it easy. Don't rush."

So. There I was. The shiny blue plastic, rippling with waves, called to me like a Caribbean sea. It wasn't hard to guess how the Dictaphone worked—slip the belt on the drum, slide the drum in the box. And surely the earphones belonged in my ears. My foot found the pedal. Prideful, I flicked the typewriter switch. The machine must have been the first electric model ever designed; when I opened the lid, I saw the flaked skin and fingernails, eyelashes, hair, and pink eraser nubbins of the many secretaries who had used it before me.

The drawer was full of paper, yellow and creased as an old woman's skin. I rolled a sheet in the typewriter, stepped on the pedal of the Dictaphone and listened.

"Day of a curse . . . They stripped the clay man. . . ."

Instead of some sort of legal dictation, they had given me a sermon! That couldn't be right. But hadn't she told me to type what I heard? It must be a trick to test my obedience.

"Manna overcame the curse. . . . Destroyed in our sight . . . In Jews and asses . . . Ne'er goes she I shun . . ."

The man seemed to be preaching with a mouth full of sand. And the *r* on my typewriter kept getting stuck, so by the time I had finished, he was preaching in brogue: "Day of a currrrrse . . . Manna overrrcame the currrrrse. . . ."

I tore up the paper, rolled in another, made the Dictaphone back up. But when it went forward, like a recent acquaintance who regrets that he has been too confiding too soon, it skipped everything I had heard. Nothing I did helped me recover the start of the tape. I pushed on to the end, and when I looked back I saw that I had typed more gibberish in brogue.

Just as a girl with no knowledge of sex can often be seduced by the first boy who tries, so too a girl who never has failed gives in to despair at the smallest mistake. As I stared at that page of nonsense I panicked. The room had no windows, but I guessed it was dark out—I had been here forever. I couldn't face Jane Givens. I looked for a door that wouldn't take me back the way I had come and was finally expelled to the hallway outside. A small spill of light washed over the tiles at the top of a staircase. These weren't the same stairs I had come up, but once on the sidewalk I took my bearings from the Methodist church. The sky behind the steeple was blue, pink, and white, as cheerful as icing.

I hated that sky, as I hated the smell of the young grass, the breezes that tickled my legs as a grown-up might tickle a grumpy little child. I climbed the hill to our house, where my mother was anxiously awaiting my arrival, staring out the window and tenderly molding salmon croquettes in the palms of her hands.

I slept little that night. In just a few hours I would have to tell Mr. Noble that he had gone to all that trouble to set up an interview for a girl who didn't have it. I almost stayed home, but what if he learned how badly I had done from somebody else?

It's easy to say that I gave Mr. Noble powers of judgment no one deserves. But at that age I needed so much to learn what it means to be human that I was grateful to any adult with the courage, or maybe the vanity, to stand up before me and reveal who he was.

Mr. Noble had lived a more dramatic life than anyone I knew. His father and uncle had died in a coal mine not far from Scranton. He lied about his age and ran off to join the Navy, reaching Korea just in time to be wounded—a gun had exploded, burning his chest. Back home at eighteen, he talked his way into some little college, then took a teaching job in Paradise, where the industry—tourism—was as spotless and safe as a freshly made bed. By the time he woke up and missed the excitement of his earlier life, he was married to a woman as Catholic as he was and the father of six.

He wasn't the most popular teacher in school. He scared kids too much. But he was the most powerful. He was manly and rough, with a strong, well-lined face. Unlike Mr. Busey, whose fly was always open, or Mr. Walsh, who wore the same shapeless suit every day, Mr. Noble wore trousers that fit him the way a man's trousers should and white cotton shirts with the sleeves pushed way up. He would cock his fingers like a gun and order some kid: "Tell us everything you know about Eugene V. Debs."

He taught American History, 1850 to the Present, and something called Government. He didn't try to be objective. His vision of history was the only one he saw, so he thought it was fact. Week after week he repeated his "facts" until each of his students had absorbed by hypnosis: "Sacco and Vanzetti were martyrs to bigotry"; "The unions saved America"; "If Truman hadn't dropped the bomb on Japan, a million GIs would have died on its shores." No matter what politics his students later adopted, they would find themselves teaching their own kids these maxims at dinner some night, as they would find themselves singing Mr. Noble's favorite song, "Lips That Touch Liquor Will Never Touch Mine," when their husbands or wives asked for a drink.

His views about sex were more complicated. "All this freedom to lay anybody you want isn't going to last," he cautioned the boys. "Better get it while you can." "Ask them all," he advised. "A lot will say no, but you'll be surprised how many will say yes." "The quiet girls," he said, "they're the ones who are hot."

Then he cautioned the girls: "Don't let them fool you. Men don't want women as equal partners—in bed or anywhere else. That's just a line. Be your own person. Don't give it away."

One time he asked: "I see what the guys get from all this free sex. But what do you girls get?"

"Fun," I said softly. Then, taking heart: "We get fun, Mr. Noble. Don't you think a woman enjoys having sex as much as a man?"

I spoke rarely in class—I was one of the quiet girls whom Mr. Noble teased. But nobody snickered or made a lewd joke; I had brought information that few of them had. Of course I was bluffing. I never had slept with a man. But how could I let Mr. Noble assume that girls were inferior? And I knew I was right. Just a hand on my shoulder could flood me with warmth. The *thought* of unbuttoning a man's shirt and kissing the hair on his chest could make me cry out.

"You think so?" He studied me. "I sure hope you're right." But in Mr. Noble's mind a woman was either a virgin, a wife, or a good-hearted whore, and he couldn't understand where I fit in this scheme.

. . .

That morning in class, after I had failed my test for the job, I tried not to be noticed. I didn't hang around to talk about the latest Watergate news, school gossip, my future as a union organizer. As I slipped out the door I sensed his eyes on my neck, but when I glanced back he was wiping his scribbles from the board with a sponge, and with them, it seemed, any concern he had once felt for me.

I couldn't leave it that way. After dismissal I dawdled through the parking lot.

"Hey, Rothman, get over here!" He was standing by his Ford. He took off his jacket and tossed it on the seat. "Don't you owe me the courtesy of letting me know how yesterday went?"

"I fucked up," I said. (Like him, I was rude so no one would guess how deeply I cared.)

"What's that supposed to mean?"

"I fucked up the test. It was my fault. I couldn't do it."

To the side of the parking lot a boy in white flannel was batting pop balls into the outfield, where his teammates stood waiting with hands and gloves cupped, eyes lifted in prayer. Below us, on the track, girls in red gym suits scissored their legs and leapt over hurdles, threw their arched bodies over high poles. And those moments when they floated, suspended in air, made me understand why most other people preferred to be weightless, to live in the light. Maybe I would learn to prefer it as well, now that I had to.

"Ahh, you sound just like them." He motioned at the athletes. " 'Boo-hoo, Mr. Noble, I couldn't do this test. It was my fault. I'm stupid.' What a load of horseshit. You didn't try hard enough. Or maybe you got spooked. Or maybe it was *their* fault, ever think of that? Those machines you were using, ten to one they were junk. That Eicher is the tightest—"

"Watch out! Heads up!"

The ball bounced near our feet. He bent, scooped it up, then kneaded the leather as my mother would knead a salmon croquette.

"I suppose you'll give up. Just like the rest. I say to them: 'Okay, you can take the test again,' and they look scared as hell. They'd rather lay down and play dead."

He snaked back his arm and sent that ball soaring over the fence, over the heads of the guys who were waiting to catch it in the outfield, all the way to the pitcher; the ball smacked his glove. Nothing, I thought, would ever be more beautiful than the muscles in that forearm, tense against the skin, the ripple of his shoulder under his shirt, the flex of his wrist as he unfurled the ball, its arc through the air.

"It's your life," he said. He got in his car. "I'm just disappointed. I would've enjoyed having you around this summer."

He drove from the lot. For a long time I watched as the girls my own age kept running around that cindery track, kicking off, floating, legs long and taut, like thoroughbred horses being trained for a steeplechase, around and around.

· · ·

Instead of going home I went back down to Main Street. It wasn't the pep talk, the obvious psychology of "I suppose you'll give up." It was just the information that I wasn't to blame. Why couldn't I have *seen* that?

I didn't get as lost finding the office as I had the day before. A dumpy, dour woman was sitting behind the receptionist's desk. "What do you want?"

"I'd like to see Miss Givens."

She regarded me as though I were up to some mischief, then turned and called: "Jane!" Jane Givens hurried in, hugging a stack of files to her chest.

"I was nervous," I said. "I shouldn't have left without telling you. Could I please take the test again?"

"You were nervous." She nodded. "I understand," she said. She had spent her life avoiding anything that scared her. "But I have to get these finished. You know where it is. Go ahead and try it. And then, well, we'll see."

On my way to the room I forced myself to open one of the file drawers—it smelled of rotting paper—and I peeked in some folders. In each was a sheet labeled ACCIDENT REPORT. So this was the "sermon" I had heard on the tape! Not "Strip the clay man" but "Description of Claimant," not "Manna overcame the curse" but "Manner of Occurrence," and so with the rest: "Description of Site," "Injuries and Losses," and "Negotiations." The longest part was always "Manner of Occurrence," the story of whatever calamity had struck some worker or guest at a place we insured.

The blue plastic belt was just where I had left it, inside the machine. With my eyes shut I focused every brain cell on drawing that disembodied voice through staticky space. I still couldn't decipher most of the words, but I didn't let that stop me. I filled in the gaps with whatever seemed right, as you try to make sense of a dream the next morning or fill in your memories of a childhood event.

A second-cook named Lee had saved many years to bring his fiancée over from China. He got her a job washing dishes. Several months later, he found her in the pantry with the first-cook, named Hwang, who was holding her wrists and kissing her neck—or trying to kiss it, as the woman maintained. Lee seemed to accept that his wife was too frail to fight Hwang's advances. He didn't even seem to bear ill will toward Hwang; they had been very close friends, the only Chinese who had worked at this place before the wife arrived. But the next week, while the men were hacking apart an order of beef, Lee brought down his cleaver just below Hwang's wrist. According to Lee, the cleaver had slipped. Witnesses claimed that he had taken revenge. Either way, our company had to pay for Hwang's hand.

I typed very slowly and made few mistakes, though the *r*'s still repeated. "The typewriter's broken," I complained to Miss Givens when I gave her the sheets.

"Isn't it *dreadful?*" She smiled at me knowingly, as some women smile when deriding men's flaws. "All of them have something! We've been asking for new ones for the past twenty years."

I looked around the room at the other secretaries, who were still typing busily and tossing conversation at each other's heads. But I saw something else now. Every so often one of the women would smack her IBM, throw open its lid and poke at its guts. The women grimaced and swore, but this seemed an act in which they found pleasure. They had martyred themselves to these faulty machines and the men who gave dictation.

Over in the corner a small black-haired woman shook a fist at her Dicta-phone, a tiny Ralph Cramden. "Oooh, I'm gonna kill you. Straight to the moon." She switched on the intercom, which shrieked like a cat. "Alphie, come out here. I can't understand a damn thing you're saying."

A few moments later, a rumpled, sad-eyed man slouched toward her desk.

"Alphie," she said, "I've warned you and warned you, if you're going to dictate you gotta put that thing down."

"Aw, Agnes, get your ears cleaned."

From just this one sentence, which he mumbled around his enormous cigar, I recognized the garbled voice on my belt. He leaned down toward Agnes, transferred her earphones to his own ears and listened.

"*I* don't know," he groused. "It's something about the claimant getting kicked in the *tuches* by a horse."

"I'll kick *you* in the *tuches!*"

It upset me to learn that the world of adults—outside our house—was broken, disordered, anything went, a big unwatched playground: "I'm going to kill you! I'll chop off your hand!" But this also allowed the mystery and passion that my parents' planned universe seemed to preclude. In the spaces between the words you heard clearly, possibility dwelled; you were free to invent whatever meaning you chose.

Miss Givens asked some questions about how I did at school, my father's occupation, was I able to operate an adding machine, and from just these few hints she constructed a story about who I was. Because of this story, she decided to hire me. She decided to *like* me.

"Wait here, Dianne. I have to find the forms you're supposed to fill out."

As I stood by her desk, the telephone rang. After a game that might have been called "It's Not *My* Turn to Get It," the Kabuki-secretary punched a button and answered. After she'd hung up, she announced to the rest of us: "This kid in the Poconos was chasing a girl and he ran through a door. A *glass* door. He got two hundred stitches." She said this as if the stitches had been a well-deserved punishment. "Good thing it wasn't the girl," she went on. "With a boy, scars don't matter." Her voice didn't allow a chance in the world that it wasn't his fault. He was young, he was male, so he must have been a hooligan.

Maybe this was true. But wasn't it possible that he and the girl had been playing the sort of game adolescents play with each other because it lets them touch, then run off again, pretending the brush of hand against breast or muscular thigh was only an accident? Maybe, as a joke, the girl had stepped lightly out of the way, while the boy, running faster, unable to slow his clumsy momentum, had crashed through the glass.

"Save it for Jack Noble. It's his territory. He's stopping by later to pick up his cases." This came from a woman veiled in blue smoke. She held her cigarette in a hand that was cocked like the hands of the mannequins in Ruthie's display. "Jack's always glad to go to the Poconos. Gives him the chance to stop off and see his tootsie in Scranton."

"Tootsie!" sniffed the woman who had taken the call. "That's a nice way to put it."

How could they know that Mr. Noble liked to visit a prostitute in Scranton? Not that I doubted for a moment he did. Not that I cared. Paying a prostitute, like joining the Navy, fighting for a union or digging for coal, seemed to me then to be one of the great transactions that made an ordinary man a part of something larger, something with weight. Besides, they sounded so cruel that I had to defend him. I imagined the prostitute sprawled on her bed, fleshy and white against red velvet sheets. "Jackie, don't go. When will you visit your Tootsie again?" And his wife at home, waiting. All these women, waiting, tied to their Dictaphones, their kitchens, their beds. I would never be a woman who sat around, waiting. I would take what I wanted and leave, just like Jack.

Miss Givens returned with my application. I hadn't yet memorized my number from the government so I copied it from the card in my purse. As I filled in the blanks, I felt I had registered as a grown-up at last.

• • •

I met Mr. Noble as he came up the stairs. We seemed to be standing in the chute to a mine. I could even smell coal, though that must have been cigarette smoke clinging to his skin.

"Dianne," he said. "So?" His eyebrows went up.

His using my first name gave me a jolt. "So I got it," I said.

"You got it." He smiled. The gap between his teeth made him look young. "I guess we'll be seeing a lot of each other."

Silence choked the stairway like heavy black dust.

"There's a case in the Poconos," I said to him finally. "A kid ran through some glass."

"Damn it," he said. "There goes my weekend. That's a four-hour drive each way."

"You can always stop and visit your girlfriend in Scranton." I said this in a voice that I didn't know I had—husky, a woman's voice, wounded and coy. Nothing would have followed that summer if I hadn't said those words in that tone.

He drew back, surprised. "I thought I'd have an ally! You haven't worked there a day and . . . Ahh, they're just jealous."

I believed this was true.

"They don't understand how a man . . . Never mind. The fact is I don't know anyone in Scranton. Not anymore. And it gets lonely driving. How'd you like to come along? I can teach you the ropes."

I saw all those women tied to their Dictaphones. I saw Mr. Noble holding a rope, the reins to a horse. These seemed to be the only options I had.

"So, how about it?" He pulled out his Pall Malls ("Wherever Particular People Congregate" it said on the pack) and lit a cigarette as casually as though such an invitation were an everyday thing. I pretended the same. We were planning a trip like the one our class was taking to Gettysburg next month. As we drove through the Poconos he would *teach* me *the ropes*.

"Sure. I don't mind."

"Good," he said, flicking the match to the floor. "Is there somewhere I can meet you on my way out of town in the morning?"

It surprised me how little thought this required. "How about the spillway out by the reservoir?" I would have to get there early, so he wouldn't catch me riding my bike, like a child.

He nodded. "That's fine. Be there at seven. And after we're done I'll treat you to dinner. I know a great little roadhouse." I must have looked nervous.

"Don't worry," he said, "I'll get you back before bedtime." He held out his hand. "So, welcome aboard."

The touch of his palm—warm, dry, the flesh hardened beneath—made me understand, finally, the force that my parents so feared because it could swipe away order, make a mockery of plans. I was dizzy, and hot. My knees felt too spongy to hold up my legs.

"See you bright and early." He jogged up the steps, whistling "Lips That Touch Liquor Will Never Touch Mine."

I tried to walk home, but I only got as far as the bench near the bank. I watched people park their cars, feed coins to the meters. The men bought their papers and ducked in for haircuts, the women picked up their newly heeled shoes, came out of the bakery with waxed-paper bags of rye bread and rolls. Most of these people were as solemn as though completing such chores had been their whole purpose in reaching this age. But a few men and women, among them a close friend of my father, seemed skittish, distracted, kept glancing around and stopping to remember what to do next, and it struck me these errands might only be a cover for their real, secret lives.

. . .

I went with Jack Noble to the Poconos that Saturday. We didn't sleep together that night, or that summer, but eventually we did.

One afternoon the following August we were lying in a cabin on a lake in the Poconos and Jack swore he remembered every word I had said, every caress. He seemed to regard our affair as a great historical event he was proud to live through. He said that he hadn't felt this alive since his time in the Navy, as humble as though I had done him a kindness, like the major who had stopped by his bed in the hospital and asked how he felt. As he said this, he slipped his hand down my breast and cradled my waist with a gratitude and tenderness I couldn't have predicted a grown man would show.

"What I'm doing is wrong. Don't you think I know that?" he said. "It's like in the Navy. You get all caught up in . . . You don't think how serious . . . And then you get hurt, or you hurt someone else. I *have* to stop," he said. "You can't understand. . . . I'm just the first man you'll be with. Already you're thinking how I'll compare to the boys you'll meet in college, the professors you'll have. For me, you're the last. After you, I'll spend thirty, forty years remembering back."

To make him feel better I stroked his scarred chest, the skin there as puckered as the elastic on the dress I had worn to my interview. I envied how Jack had gotten those scars. That's how little I loved him. That's how young I still was.

. . .

Both of us knew our affair couldn't go on. But we thought we could end it whenever we chose. That wasn't the case. Toward the end of the second summer I worked at Colonial Conn, the secretary with the lacquered black hair told Jack that she had punched the wrong button on her telephone and heard what he'd said to me earlier that day. Jane Givens wouldn't believe her, but finally she had to. Jane had worked in that office for twenty-eight years, but she never had suspected that people really did the terrible things that she heard through her earphones. The revelation that they did made her even more sparse and pale than before. (A few summers later, on a visit to my parents, I saw her on the street and I ducked in a store. Why had I been so eager to squander the gifts she had given me, her faith and good will? Did I think that I'd always have so much of these to spare?)

Jack, being so much older than I was, had much more to lose. His wife wouldn't divorce him, but their twins, Matt and Erin, ran away from home. They came back, of course—they were only thirteen—but they never forgave him for their mother's shame, or their own. Mr. Seiken, the principal, let him go quietly, but Jack was afraid to apply for a job in some other school. He eventually became the assistant claims manager for an office in Pittsburgh. The one time he wrote, he said he missed teaching more than he ever could have guessed that he would.

The scandal took a terrible toll on my parents, but they never blamed me. They acted as though I had been injured, the victim of an accident beyond my control. It took me many years to convince them that such "accidents" befell me too often to be random bad luck.

I got to go to college and, as Jack had predicted, to love other men. Because I was young, my actions barely mattered. A terrible mistake could still be atoned for, a wrong path retraced. Only later in my life did my errors bring sorrow that couldn't be recalled: when I slept with the friend of a man that I loved and he called off our wedding; when I screamed at my father what I had been wanting to scream for so many years—that I really was no better than the slatternly wives who tried to convince him to steal a few minutes from his route in their beds—then wished that I hadn't, he would never forgive me.

Maybe it was right that I wasn't held responsible for anything that happened. I was only fifteen. Jack was my teacher. He should have known better. But the facts of the incident, like the words on a Dictaphone or the documents I studied for my history degree—can be construed many ways. And sometimes I think that I used Jack to learn what I wanted to know, and then I moved on. Jack loved me much more than I ever loved him. He lost everything he had.

All this came later. The first week I worked at Colonial Conn I was asked to type the settlement in the case the other women had taken to calling "Hwang's Missing Hand." An accident that serious could have dragged on for years. But, for some reason, Hwang accepted a sum far below what the company might have paid if he had claimed that he could no longer cook. Lee and his wife ran away suddenly. As I typed this, I wondered if she had ever loved Hwang, or if she had only gone in that pantry to learn what she'd missed those long years in China, so pure and alone.

With his check from our company Hwang bought a restaurant on the outskirts of town. Last week I was driving to a history conference in upstate New York and I detoured through Paradise. I had no one to eat with—my father is dead and my mother in a nursing home, where she stares out a window, kneading thin air. I stopped in Hwang's restaurant, and I had to fight the impulse to go in the kitchen and watch him chop vegetables or bone a fish with one hand. I wanted to ask if he still kept his other hand—I imagined it mummified, soft as a glove—in a velvet-lined box, a memento of his passion, all he had risked and lost.

12

Sexual Harassment

Gaining Respect and Equality

Risa L. Lieberwitz

The protagonists in the stories, Caroline Moore, Wendy, and Dianne Rothman, all experienced inappropriate sexual conduct from men who wielded power over them at work. In "Plato, Again," Bill Densk, the chief of information technology, questions Caroline about her breast cancer. He then touches her chest, feeling the skin grown over the mastectomy. But Bill doesn't stop there. He continues to target Caroline with humiliating treatment—demoting her from being a full-time codirector of information technology to an administrative assistant.

In "Be Who You Are," Chuck, Wendy's supervisor at the car wash, exploits her vulnerability as a worker in a low-wage, dead-end job. He uses his managerial power—though rather than taking her down a notch, Chuck capitalizes on her marginal position at the bottom of the workforce. Discovering that Wendy has been stealing trinkets from the cars she washes, Chuck realizes that he can fire her for this. And he lets Wendy know she owes him her job. Chuck then uses this power to extort sexual favors from her.

Meanwhile, Dianne, the high school student in "Hwang's Missing Hand," becomes involved with her history teacher, Jack Noble, after he recommended her for a summer job as a secretary in an insurance office where he works as a claims adjuster. Dianne sought the relationship. She admired her teacher. She found him sexually attractive. And looking back, Dianne does not see this as sexual harassment, then or now. But should this be central to deciding whether it is sexual harassment? Or should Title VII of the Civil Rights Act stop Jack from taking advantage of his power to pursue their sexual relationship?

The Courts Prohibit Sexual Harassment—At Last

It was not until 1986 that the U.S. Supreme Court recognized sexual harassment as unlawful discrimination.[1] What took so long? Part of the explanation lies in how prevalent sexual harassment was. "Boys will be boys" is how the first charges of sexual harassment were met in the lower federal courts. Sexual harassment, in other words, was a "natural" outgrowth of putting men and women together.[2]

It was feminist scholars, most notably Catharine MacKinnon, who influenced the courts to turn sexual harassment into a legal claim. MacKinnon, through her scholarly work and legal advocacy, debunked the idea that men's sexualized conduct toward women simply reflected their personal desire.[3] To her, sexual harassment "forms an integral part of the social stereotyping of all women as sexual objects."[4] She associated a woman's sexual subordination with her economic subordination. More likely to be secretaries, nurses, domestic "help," librarians, and teachers—all low-paid positions—their usually powerful male bosses already had them in vulnerable and economically precarious positions.[5] As a result, the Supreme Court agreed that sexual harassment denied women's workplace equality. What used to be considered treating women "normally," the Court held in 1986, represented unequal treatment.[6]

Once this dam broke, thousands of sexual harassment charges came flooding into the Equal Employment Opportunity Commission (EEOC). At present, this enforcement and regulatory agency receives 12,000 claims per year, with women filing almost 85 percent of these.[7] In 2006, these charges composed about one-quarter of all Title VII charges filed with the EEOC.[8] Even this large number does not tell the full story. Many individuals do not report incidents of sexual harassment.[9]

Defining Harassment: Will We Know It When We See It?

Wendy's situation, in "Be Who You Are," is a "classic" case of what has been called the "lust paradigm" of sexual harassment.[10] Chuck used his supervisory authority to convince Wendy that she must have sex with him to keep her job. He overlooks that Wendy is "stealing" from the cars as long as she sexually "services" him. From Wendy's perspective: "Now she can see no end, no punishment, no result. Chuck calls her to the office almost every day and she steals more and more and more . . . Chuck takes her silk-cleanser hand and puts it on his trousers."

Wendy could charge her employer Wash Plus with sexual harassment. Chuck made sex a condition of her employment—if Wendy wanted to keep her job, she must have sex with him. This is called *quid pro quo* (something for something) sexual harassment. In quid pro quo cases, a supervisor might threaten an employee with discharge or other negative consequences for refusing to comply with sexual demands. Or the supervisor might promise to reward the employee for sexual favors.[11]

Chuck might assert that Wendy voluntarily had sex with him. In its watershed 1986 sexual harassment decision, the Supreme Court made it clear that a "voluntary" relationship could still be sexual harassment.[12] "The correct inquiry," the Court explained, "is whether . . . the alleged sexual advances were unwelcome."[13]

Were Chuck's advances "unwelcome"? Wendy views Chuck with mixed emotions. Sometimes, she sees herself as his "paramour." But she also feels trapped and is relieved that Chuck has not demanded full sexual service—"She's a little pleased that she's never had to open her legs for that." Yet, Wendy admits to herself, "there's something exciting about him. Maybe it's his rage." Given Chuck's ongoing use of his supervisory power over Wendy, a court could deem her actions "voluntary," but it's clear she did not welcome the sexual relationship.

Chuck's conduct would also be sexual harassment if he created a "hostile environment" through his "unwelcome sexual advances" or "other verbal or physical conduct of a sexual nature."[14] Wendy would have to prove that Chuck's actions were "sufficiently severe or pervasive" in a way that unreasonably interfered with her work or created "an intimidating, hostile, or offensive working environment."[15]

Certainly Wendy can show that Chuck made sexual advances. She can probably prove that they were unwelcome. Can she prove that Chuck's conduct was "severe or pervasive"? The Supreme Court has defined this as a two-part test. First is an objective test. Wendy must prove that a "reasonable person in [her] position" would find the conduct severe or pervasive. Wendy need not show that a reasonable person would have suffered "tangible psychological injury." But, at the same time, "merely offensive comments" or even "sporadic use of abusive language, gender-related jokes, and occasional teasing" will not create a hostile environment.[16] Title VII, the Court has said, is not a "civility code" for the "hypersensitive employee."[17] It should stop harassment.

A subjective test follows this objective one. Wendy must show that she, personally, found that the conduct created an abusive working environment. Again, Wendy did not have to suffer economic or psychological harm. ". . . Title VII comes into play," Justice Sandra Day O'Connor wrote, "before the harassing conduct leads to a nervous breakdown."[18] But Wendy must prove that the harassing conduct altered her working conditions in some way.

Wendy could probably prove both the objective and subjective aspects of a hostile environment. A reasonable person would find that Chuck's constant sexual comments and demands created a severe or pervasive working environment. And Wendy personally thought Chuck created an abusive workplace. While on the job, she had to cope and be clever. She sought ways of keeping her job despite the threats and sexual demands. Finally, though, frustrated by her powerlessness, Wendy escapes, running away from work "under the blue prison sky."

Has "Severe *or* Pervasive" Become "Severe *and* Pervasive"?

Was Caroline, in "Plato, Again," sexually harassed? She was the target of questions and physical contact by her supervisor, Bill, about her breast cancer treatment. Upon Caroline's return to work, Bill interrogates her, while staring at her chest, about her mastectomy and the likelihood of a second mastectomy. He even "touched her just there, where her breast had been. With his index finger. Tapped at the loose fabric." In this same meeting, Bill informs Caroline that she will work on a payroll project, as an administrative assistant, while he reviews her job as codirector of information technology. Immediately after her second mastectomy, Bill demotes Caroline permanently to administrative assistant, having already hired a replacement in her former managerial position. As a clerical employee, Caroline reports to Lori Gustafson, "a junior college accountant" who finds fault with all of Caroline's work.

Caroline has a good chance—though not a certainty—of winning a hostile environment claim. She can prove that she found Bill's conduct unwelcome and subjectively—or personally—abusive. After all, she told him to stop. Caroline felt humiliated by Bill's intrusive questions, his offensive touching, and by her demotion. Bill's actions may or may not have been motivated by sexual desire. But this is not legally relevant. Sexual harassment may result from speech and conduct that is hostile to women, even without sexual content.[19] But, the question remains—would a reasonable person find Bill's conduct so severe or pervasive that it would change her work conditions?[20]

What many lower courts have done, explains one legal scholar, is treat the definition of a "severe *or* pervasive" hostile environment as if it means "severe *and* pervasive" harassment.[21] Only in extreme cases do these courts find a hostile environment. For example, one federal appeals court defined sexual harassment as "conduct so egregious as to alter the conditions of employment and destroy [women's] equal opportunity in the workplace."[22] A federal trial court in Illinois concluded that a senior vice president's conduct was too isolated to be severe or pervasive. Yet, what this vice president had done was lock his office door, push his female colleague against a wall, attempt to kiss her, touch her breasts, and then put his hands under her dress.[23]

Meanwhile, another federal district court found that while one female employee had proved her supervisor's severe and pervasive behavior, she did not show that her working conditions changed. This woman withstood fifty incidents, including ones where her supervisor rubbed his genitals on her, stared at her breasts, and touched various parts of her body in a sexual manner. Yet she continued doing competent work "except to the extent the harassment distracted [her] and kept her from maintaining [her] focus."[24] The court nonetheless ruled that this was not enough. She had not shown that these fifty incidents had "undermined the victim's workplace competence, discouraged her from remaining on the job, or kept her from advancing in her career."[25] This judge's attitude represents a far cry from Supreme Court Justice Ginsburg's view that a woman need only show that the harassment made it "more difficult to do the job."[26]

Placing Caroline's experience within this context, Bill's one-time incident, even as offensive as his statements and conduct were, might not be enough. To be sure, some federal courts have created a lower threshold for what constitutes severe or pervasive behavior. These courts have found that a multitude of sexual comments in the course of one meeting, repeated derogatory statements about women, or a single incident of physical contact foster a hostile environment.[27] Yet, an empirical study of hostile environment cases over an eleven-year period reveals that the federal courts dismissed more than half of all cases because of inadequate evidence of severe or pervasive conduct.[28] This leaves someone like Caroline in a state of uncertainty about her case's potential outcome. She could not necessarily convince a court that a "reasonable person in [her] position" would have found the conduct abusive.

Who is this reasonable person? Prior to jury trials under the 1991 Civil Rights Act, judges decided what constitutes harassment. Since most judges are men, their workplace experiences may lead them to underestimate the impact on women of sexual harassment. A jury brings in more women's perspectives, but also increases the number of viewpoints of how a "reasonable person" would react. The EEOC emphasizes that "[t]he reasonable person standard should consider the victim's perspective and not stereotyped notions of acceptable behavior."[29] This approach gives meaning to the Supreme Court's description of the "reasonable person" in the position of the employee, "considering all the circumstances." It makes judges and juries empathize, taking into account the frequency or severity of conduct, as well as the impact the harassing conduct had on the woman's work performance."[30] This is important for both male-female and same-sex harassment cases. Even so, the "reasonable person" leaves judges and juries leeway. Their own biases and preconceptions—including sexism and homophobia—creep in.[31]

Treating Men and Women Differently

Sexual harassment is unlawful only if it is considered sexual discrimination. "The critical issue," the Supreme Court emphasized, is whether the harasser treats men and women differently.[32] The so-called equal opportunity harasser, who creates an abusive environment for men and women, has not engaged in sex discrimination.[33]

In cases of male-female harassment, as in Wendy's situation, most judges assume that the man would not have aimed sexual conduct at male employees. Same-sex harassment may also violate Title VII, but the Supreme Court does not find it as "easy to draw" an inference that the harasser's conduct was discriminatory.[34] The employee alleging same-sex harassment must prove that the harasser would not have targeted someone of the opposite sex. For example, the employee could show that the harasser was homosexual or bring in other evidence that the harasser treated men and women differently.[35] The Court's approach to proving same-sex harassment reveals its view of heterosexuality as the norm. The Court did acknowledge, though, that hostile environment harassment is not always motivated by sexual desire. Some federal courts have found that male supervisors harassed men for not fulfilling their gender stereotype. Supposedly, they were not "masculine" enough for a position.[36]

Race, religion, disability, or age also motivates harassers. Did Bill target Caroline, in "Plato, Again," because of her sex, her disability, her race, or some combination—or "intersection"—of these factors? As discussed in chapter 8, Caroline would find that courts differ in their openness to such intersectional claims. Some judges would require that Caroline prove separate sex, race, and disability hostile environment claims. Other courts would allow her to prove that Bill was motivated by all three of these reasons combined. For example, an African American woman was able to bring a suit involving sexual *and* racial harassment. She claimed that her supervisor had touched her and made racial slurs.[37]

Understanding Sexual Harassment as Sex Discrimination

Sexual harassment fits into the rubric of sex discrimination as a whole. It is no coincidence that sexual harassment cases include other Title VII violations, as in Caroline's situation, where she was demoted at the same time that Bill interrogated her and touched her. Discovering the connection between harassment and other discriminatory conduct shows that the former is not just "sexual desire run amok."[38] It's part of the deeper societal problem of women's social and economic inequality.

Feminist legal scholars underscore that sexual harassment reinforces sexual stereotypes and "gender norms" that define men's and women's roles in society. Vicki Schultz emphasizes the demeaning message of sexual harassment. The harasser's disrespectful conduct toward women in subordinate positions relays the message that women are not competent to hold jobs with higher wages, status, and responsibility.[39] As Katherine Franke observes, women who do enter these nontraditional jobs are harassed "as a way of putting them in their 'proper place.'"[40] Kathryn Abrams describes sexual harassment "as a practice that preserves male control or entrenches masculine norms in the specific setting of the workplace."[41] Understanding this means that the law should protect both men and women who are harassed when they do not conform to gender stereotypes.[42]

These insights reveal the scope of harm suffered by Caroline in "Plato, Again," and Wendy in "Be Who You Are." Bill's and Chuck's actions were sexual in content, but they also kept Caroline and Wendy "in their place." Bill humiliated Caroline by demoting her from a managerial position as codirector of information technology. Far from using her graduate degree in computer science, Bill placed Caroline into a clerical position that reported to a nitpicking "number cruncher." The fact that this new supervisor was female and obviously taking her cues from Bill reinforced the office hierarchy.

Meanwhile, Chuck takes advantage of how vulnerable Wendy is. Working in a car wash, she's stuck in a low-wage, dead-end job. But Wendy needs this job. With no prospects for a higher paid or higher status position, Chuck's sexual advances keep Wendy compliant. Indeed, Chuck knows that Wendy is "stealing" from the cars she cleans, and he uses this, conscious of how much power it gives him over her. In this quid pro quo, Chuck overlooks this as long as she satisfies him sexually.

Other "real life" situations reinforce the link between sexual harassment and keeping women out of better paid, higher status "men's" jobs. Brenda Berkman worked as a New York City firefighter after winning her long Title VII litigation battle over the fire department's discriminatory exclusion of women. Yet her supervisors and coworkers created an ongoing hostile environment.[43] Women miners at Eveleth Taconite Co. in northern Minnesota faced brutal sexual harassment by male supervisors and co-workers who sought to maintain their monopoly over well-paid jobs. These women brought the first class action sexual harassment lawsuit in the United States.[44] Their story became a widely distributed Hollywood movie called *North Country*.[45]

In the white-collar financial securities industry, men sexually harassed their female colleagues, driving them out of the best-paid jobs on Wall Street. In *Tales from the Boom-Boom Room,* Susan Antilla describes how Wall Street male brokers set up a party room. The level of hostile and offensive sexist behavior within the "boom-boom room" was seemingly limitless. This partying, moreover, was only part of the systematic sex discrimination in the banking investment division—which also included disparate treatment of women in salaries and promotions.[46]

What About Women's Choices?

Dianne's situation, in "Hwang's Missing Hand," raises different issues from Caroline's and Wendy's experiences. Dianne tells her story from the vantage point of an adult looking back on her experiences as an adolescent. As a successful university history professor, the adult Dianne benefited from changes in the 1980s, as women began to enter occupations held almost exclusively by men. As a high school student in the early 1970s, though, when women had only begun questioning these gender stereotypes, Dianne was left with a confusing set of choices. She had little guidance about the meaning of genuine equality. At the age of fifteen, more than thirty years ago, Dianne saw only male professional role models. All the women she knew fit into stereotypical roles of wife and mother at home and secretary at work. As Dianne realizes when she arrives for her summer job interview at Colonial Connecticut Insurance, the secretaries' power "only extended to young girls like me." Jack Noble, who recognizes Dianne's superior intellect, has contradictory views of women. Dianne understands that "in Mr. Noble's mind a woman was either a virgin, a wife, or a good-hearted whore, and he couldn't understand where I fit in this scheme."

Although it was Jack's age and his position as her high school teacher and summer job supervisor that seduced her, Dianne never considered him a sexual predator, either at the time of their affair or later, as an adult recalling her past. She wanted the relationship. Dianne recalled what she said when Jack invited her out of town: " 'You can always stop and visit your girlfriend in Scranton.' I said this in a voice, wounded and coy. Nothing would have followed that summer if I hadn't said those words in that tone." Dianne acknowledges that their relationship was consensual. Or in legal terms, Dianne "welcomed" their sexual relationship. Put in feminist theory terms, this choice meant Dianne exercised her own "agency."

Acknowledging this agency, however, does not mean that Dianne made good choices. Nor does it relieve Jack from his responsibility for the relationship. Disagreeing with her parents that she was "the victim of an accident beyond [her] control," Dianne engages in honest and painful self-analysis. She takes responsibility for her own choices, even as she also recognizes that Jack took advantage of his position. Dianne understands that, even as an adolescent, she possessed a significant amount of power. To her, this was a short-term relationship, like the summer job. She was going to college and eventually a professional career far away from her small hometown.

Dianne's story helps us understand fault and responsibility in sexual harassment cases. Dianne did not experience sexual harassment, as Jack's conduct was not unwelcome. Nor did it create an abusive environment. Still, their relationship caused harm. Jack lost his profession. He hurt his family. And Dianne wonders how this relationship influenced her ongoing problems in establishing intimate relationships. But these are not legal harms. Title VII provides an inappropriate—and perhaps, too crude—an instrument to remedy the personal costs of bad choices.

Dianne's experience reminds us about the difference between workplace romance and sexual harassment. Yet, the courts have sometimes interpreted the issue of choice or agency in ways that reinforce sexist stereotypes. For instance, the Supreme Court ruled that a woman's outfit may constitute evidence that she welcomes harassment.[47] Lower federal courts have also discounted the harm women face in sexualized and hostile workplaces. Nonetheless, the courts should not "outlaw" consensual sexual relationships or encourage employers to prohibit romantic relationships between employees.

Demands for women's equality are not demands for sterile or humorless workplaces. As Schultz argues, Title VII should protect employees from harassing conduct and encourage employers to educate supervisors and employees about respectful conduct. But Title VII should not prohibit flirting, joking, and romance—which bring some humanity to the workplace.[48] And with this humanity, of course, comes some risk. Workplace romances that include sexual bantering and even sexual relationships will sometimes end badly.

Consensual sexual relationships can even lead to hostile workplace environments for other employees. For instance, the California Supreme Court upheld employees' claim that preferential treatment of coworkers who are in a sexual relationship with a supervisor creates a hostile environment. The widespread sexual favoritism resulting from such sexual relationships, the court ruled, may convey a "demeaning message . . . to female employees that they are viewed by management as 'sexual playthings'" or that women can advance at work only by having sex with their supervisors.[49] Although based in California state law, this decision received nationwide attention.[50] Some commentators predict that employers will now be more inclined to monitor workplace relationships or to adopt rules prohibiting all workplace romances to avoid potential lawsuits.[51]

Privatizing Sexual Harassment: Have the Courts "Opted Out"?

In 1998, the Supreme Court made it more difficult for employees to win a Title VII charge of hostile environment sexual harassment. The Court created a special defense for employers. All an employer must do is demonstrate (1) that he or she took "reasonable measures" to prevent or remedy the hostile environment and (2) that the employee claiming harassment was unreasonable in not taking full advantage of these measures.[52]

Where this defense ends, however, is when the sexual harassment produces a "tangible employment action," such as a discharge or demotion. An employer remains automatically liable if a sexual harassment victim proves that he or she faced "a significant change in employment status." The employer should have stopped the supervisor from unlawfully using his or her authority.[53] Caroline, in "Plato, Again," can argue that Bill demoted her as part of his pattern of harassment. This demotion represents a tangible employment action, changing her workplace status. Such an employment action makes her employer, Grandville College, liable for Bill's sexual harassment regardless of any grievance process it may have. If Caroline wins her court case, she will receive remedies for intentional discrimination, including reinstatement to her former managerial position and monetary damages.

What about Wendy in "Be Who You Are?" Wendy quit her job—probably in response to Chuck's sexual harassment. If her employer, Wash Plus, has an internal complaint process, it would contend that she acted unreasonably by quitting rather than filing a grievance. Wash Plus might win the case, unless Wendy could prove that she quit because of a tangible action resulting from the sexual harassment—such as a humiliating demotion.[54] If she can show this, her quitting will be treated as a discharge, making Wash Plus liable for Chuck's harassment. She could not necessarily argue that his harassment—as offensive and coercive as it was—caused a tangible employment action. Chuck had not followed through with his threats of firing her if she refused his sexual advances.

Why did the Court create this defense for employers, a defense unique to sexual harassment cases? By so doing, it encourages employers to adopt educational programs and internal complaint processes to investigate and remedy sexual harassment problems. These reasons—prevention and deterrence—are worthy goals. But empirical studies have found that many employers use these processes as "window dressing."[55] Instead of preventing sexual harassment, the internal grievance defense can cultivate "file cabinet compliance."[56] What is more, judges often dismiss cases if an internal grievance procedure exists.[57]

Judges treat hostile environments that coworkers create differently than suits involving supervisors. Here, employers are liable only if harassed employees prove the employer knew, or should have known, about the harassing employee's conduct and did not remedy it.[58] Employers learn about coworker harassment, for example, when victims file internal grievances or if they observe the harassment.

The Privatizing Continues: The Role of Arbitration

Another Supreme Court decision could well make it harder for women to prove sexual harassment. In 2001, the Court ruled that employers can require employees to enter into private arbitration agreements. Under these agreements, private arbitrators decide all employment disputes, including Title VII claims such as sexual harassment.[59] Employers may present these "mandatory pre-dispute arbitration agreements" to prospective employees as a condition of employment. If you want the job, you must waive your right to enter a courthouse about an employment dispute. This means if a woman encounters sexual harassment—whether because of a quid pro quo situation or a hostile work environment—an outside arbitrator, not a judge or jury, decides the case.[60]

Many legal scholars criticize the use of mandatory arbitration agreements for some of the same reasons they dismiss the internal grievance process defense: Employment discrimination shifts from the public view to a private process.[61] To be sure, this "privatization" trend provides employees benefits. They can resolve disputes quickly, quietly, without the high costs of litigation. But such positive results depend on a sound internal employer grievance process structure. Private arbitration proceedings must also work well.[62]

Effective private arbitration proceedings must give thorough consideration of the evidence, the employee's legal rights, and full remedies. One of the remedies that came up short in the securities industry was damages. Damages in meritorious cases can be as low as three hundred dollars.[63] As a result, many attorneys "advise their client not to bother with arbitration at all. Instead they urge women to take modest settlements and walk away."[64]

With the greater use of mandatory arbitration agreements, courts police them to ensure fair hearings. These protections include the employee's right to participate in choosing the arbitrator, to have an attorney, and to have a full hearing where the arbitrator can award full remedies.[65] Some courts also require that the employer pay the arbitrator's fee.[66] Faced with these developments, some employers have abandoned mandatory arbitration agreements. Instead, they now require employees to sign agreements to waive their right to have a jury in court.[67]

Where Do Women Stand?

Overall, how much have women gained from the development of sexual harassment law? Has the amount of attention given to sexual harassment significantly advanced gender equality at the workplace? To Schultz, sexual harassment litigation has not achieved its aim. It has diverted us from the fundamental goal of achieving women's social and economic equality.[68] If women received equal pay; if jobs held primarily by women paid comparably to jobs held mostly by men; if all occupations had equal numbers of men and women at all levels of the workplace hierarchy—all this would go a long way toward eliminating sexual harassment.

Moving toward gender and racial equality requires active social movements. The harm from gender and race discrimination, including harassment, as legal scholar Marion Crain argues, is a collective one. As a result, all collective institutions, including social movements and labor unions, should have a great stake in fighting these forms of discrimination.[69] By recognizing the collective interest in an agenda for gender and racial equality, unions, in alliance with the women's movement and civil rights organizations, can work toward fundamental social change. The question is—will they?

HIDDEN OBSTACLES

13

ARTIFACT

Catherine Lewis

We dubbed our first ambulance Ezekiel's Flaming Chariot because a design flaw—low-lying twin gas tanks—made it prone to explosion. Those days, though, we never contemplated our mortality except with dark humor as sparks trailed behind us on the slope leading to the Hoyt projects. Tailpipe as match. Slope as strike plate. We entered the projects where we had been dispatched with emergency speed to find a toothache, or some guy with drip dick of untreated gonorrhea.

"This is not a goddamn taxi service." Martin would slam the door and light a cigarette. "Being made a crispy critter for the likes of that, shit." We kept on wailing ahead into the night for that one possible exception. Ubiquitous wail. Whoop-whoop. Phaser. After thirteen years I am partially deaf.

For the first ten years Martin was my partner. He trained me in C-collars, crashes, cardiac arrest. Blunt force trauma. There wasn't anything he couldn't do with his hands.

"You wait," he said. "We get wasted on another bullshit call like this and clear across our zone some guy will be dying of a heart attack."

I fastened my seat belt. Felt the adrenaline drain out of me.

"I know what you're thinking," he said.

He knew. My thoughts like my hands were still lily white with hope. I can't remember when it happened—maybe that day on the railroad tracks— a subtle transformation that begins to calcify the heart and squeeze off the flow of feeling. Shootings, stabbings, suicide brains on the ceiling. You pull out all the tricks in your black bag and a child still dies in front of you. Just like that. But your hands keep on working. They have found a life of their own.

. . .

We worked the afternoon shift from 4:00 until 2:00 a.m. Two days a week I'd drive the Chariot to the university to pick up Martin. Parking around the campus was nonexistent, and the days Martin had off work he rode a bicycle to class. I imagined him surrounded by shallow youth and suntans, one of the few truly interested students. Tuition rose like new buildings in this town, but these things didn't stop him from enrolling year after year. One, maybe two classes a semester, Martin was the proverbial turtle slowly working toward a degree that would lead to yet another low-paying job. I didn't understand it. Being a medic at least gave you an occasional rush.

To say I wasn't jealous of those bronze sorority girls who made their way into Martin's bed would be a lie. Often before I fell asleep or when I first woke, images of sex between us flickered in my mind but I pushed them away along with limbs and other body parts. Perhaps all the times our minds and hands acted as one, no greater intimacy seemed possible. Other days we fought, sometimes shoved each other, and in those heated exchanges it was hard not to grab on and let fury force desire.

. . .

Martin came to work with a book crammed in his back pocket so regularly that it seemed a part of his uniform. Tight ass with rectangle. He read in snatches. At the gas pumps. In between calls. Over coffee. I remember a sultry May. A dog-eared copy of *The Red Badge of Courage*. Railroad tracks. I remember that late afternoon which brought no relief from the heat.

We burned the red dust of back roads to get to the crossing where schoolboys had been jumping the boxcars. One of them had gotten dragged underneath. We found him on the tracks, and Martin, who was charging this call, ran straight to the boy—trauma kit in one hand, portable oxygen in the other. "Find those legs," he yelled. "Bag'em in sterile saline and gauze."

Mounds of kudzu and brush were everywhere. We'd never find a clearing for a chopper.

"Now Goddamnit. Move."

I slid down the rocky slope that bordered the tracks. The first leg was lying in a blackberry patch. I picked it up. Sock and tennis shoe attached.

Laces still tied in double knots. I was frozen for a moment in some Dali painting. Frozen for a moment. Frozen. Then sprung free. I scrambled up the hill to the Chariot.

"It's going to be okay, Jimmy." Martin's hands were a whirling blur. Tightly wrapping stubs. I bagged the first leg then stopped to ask if he needed help. "Just find those goddamn legs."

I crossed the tracks. Caught the toe of my boot on a loose spike and tumbled. In the settling dust I saw a dog rooting in the kudzu, the tip of a tennis shoe in his mouth. "Scat. Get." I threw my radio at him and he beat a hasty retreat. Scoop and run. I was off with the second leg. I was thinking with my hands the way Martin was doing, the way he was counting on me to. But the boy died anyway, just as we were lifting him onto the stretcher. Martin beat his fists against the ambulance door. Dented it good. In the truck I let the tears come. Martin cursed me for it. I cursed him back. On days like that—our white shirts covered in blood, our T-shirts soaked in sweat—it was hard not to turn tail and run.

. . .

At first I wasn't sure if it was liquor I smelled on Martin's breath. We'd been partners for several years by then. I knew him better than anyone, even his daddy who fished with him in good weather.

We'd just had another Baker Sam—radio code for a bullshit call—at the Hoyt projects. Martin's mood swung oddly to the merry side. "I ever tell you the leaves up the wajumba story? I get a call out here," he says. "A woman tells me she's got leaves up the wajumba. 'Excuse me, ma'am,' I say, 'You got what?' 'Leaves,' she says. 'I got leaves up the wajumba.' She's sitting on the couch in her living room when she lifts her dress and points. I see a small strand of green vine growing out of her vagina. It's sprouting tiny leaves."

I roll my eyes. Now who's full of it.

"This is gospel, girl. I swear it. Turns out she shoved a quarter potato up there for birth control. I tell you it cleared the entire ER when that speculum went in. Security had to put fans in the doorway."

"Liar."

"Lay plenty but never lie." He turned the corner and pulled into the parking space of our station. He crossed the white line, helping himself to two spaces. I popped the seat belt, held the strap in my hand.

"Alright then, Mr. Honest. Did you dine with Jack Daniels?" I knew he drank off duty, like everyone in this pleasure palace. Off duty. Only.

Martin cut the engine, stepped out onto the pavement, and lit a cigarette.

Later that month he came to work and passed out on the stretcher. I drove the ambulance. Persuaded patients to get a neighbor or a friend to transport them to the hospital. Save a bundle. We beat the odds of no life-threatening calls that night. When our shift ended I kicked the stretcher. "You come to work this way again, you can find yourself a new partner."

Spring came and the Chariot was retired. Our new truck was wide and low to the ground. It slithered over the roads like a bright fat lizard. I picked Martin up at the university and we drove to Skeeters for fish sandwiches. Six-inch brim with head and tail poking out of two slices of white bread. I could get myself to eat the crispy fin but not the head. Jesus Christ, I'd sooner pick up fingers at the Publix deli than watch Martin suck out the brains. Today his sandwich lay on the dash as he read *Mrs. Dalloway*. Martin, who could never cry for legless boys or old women, cried over Woolf's passage about the ambulance and how it was one of the triumphs of civilization.

I tore off the fish head and handed it to him.

. . .

In August we drove to the outskirts of our zone, away from the lights and traffic and pavement which held heat like an electric blanket.

We rolled down the windows and listened to the crickets. Between the seats was a narrow passageway. Martin climbed through it into the back and lay on the stretcher reading. I sat at the driver's consul, the day's crossword puzzle on my lap. It was a slow night, people driving slow, moving slow, thinking slowly in the heat. Around midnight when it cooled off, calls would pick up.

A seven-letter word for atonement. That's what I was thinking when a small paper plane drifted lazily through the cab. Dash landing. I opened it and read the message. Martin's words were few. His handwriting consisted of straight block printing, a skill he had acquired in a high school drafting class. Whenever he wrote a report, the most chaotic scene imaginable seemed orderly. The ordinary power of his handwriting made me think we could do it, that everything would stay in its place, like letters in a crossword box.

In the back he lay on the stretcher, his uniform shirt open, the hairs on his chest matted beneath his T-shirt.

I sat down on the bench across from him, waved the paper plane. "Why now?" I held my breath like a kid passing a cemetery. Keep the inevitable at bay. It scared the hell out of me.

"Why not? You got something better to do?" He looked up at me, a crooked grin cutting across the right side of his face.

"You sure you don't have me confused with Smitty?"

He grabbed the back of my boot, slid his hand up my pant leg and lightly massaged my calf. "Maybe *you'd* rather I be Smitty."

Laura Smitts was a good-looking nurse who had started working in the ER about six months earlier. We both looked at her with interest whenever our paths crossed. Martin added: "We could both be Smitty, or pretend she's here."

I thought about that for a moment. Us and our yin-yang halves, Smitty and Smitty's girlfriend—a snotty x-ray tech with braces. The ambulance suddenly seemed crowded. Then Martin's fingertip grazed the hollow behind my knee. It was, after all, Martin who was making me itch like poison ivy.

We unloaded our radios, shoulder mikes, belts, keys. There was no hurry. We had waited so long, a few minutes more meant nothing. Our boots fell on top of the radio. Its static squelches of protest became mere background noise like the crickets. I closed my eyes. An arm floated by, its jagged tissue gray around the edges. To shake the image, I grabbed Martin's T-shirt at the v neck. It tore.

"What are you doing?"

"I want a memento," I said. I reached for the cardiac monitor. I yanked open the EKG gel pads, stuck one below each clavicle, the third below the heart.

He propped himself up on an elbow. "I knew you'd be weird about this."

I snapped on the leads, connected the cord to the monitor, and turned it on. I watched the small green screen, Martin's heart beating a normal sinus rhythm.

He lay back down then propped himself up again. "What if I throw some PVCs?"

I laughed. Premature ventricular contractions. "Then they'll be forever recorded on my strip."

Laughter faded when our palms touched. Our fingers interlocked. I watched the monitor, felt Martin's pulse rise. His chest began to sweat and the highly sensitive leads made a meaningless scribble.

"What about your shirt?" He tugged at the buttons.

"I'm leaving it on," I said and climbed on the stretcher, Martin beneath me. My knees on either side of his hips, I leaned forward and ran my hands along his chest. I traced around the gel pads like they were tiny nipples. Goose bumps formed on his skin. Nonsensical in this heat until a low growl in his throat wreaked havoc with my breathing.

I leaned forward, pressing toward him. The monitor lying by his head crashed onto the floor and neither of us cared that it cost three grand. We tore the sheets loose from our narrow bed, knocked the oxygen hose from the side wall. A steady hissing from the O2 line filled the cabin.

I could feel Martin's hands under my shirt and a slow undulation move through my body like the gentle Gulf waves. In this imagining floated a child's leg, a cluster of fingers like frightened minnows, and eel-like eviscerated intestines.

Martin sat up and tried to trade places but I pushed him back down like I did the images. Band-Aids, sprays, and gauze fell out of their containers. Neat little compartments of my life all mixed together. Martin struggled once more to move me.

"Try again and I'm out of here."

"You serious?" he groaned.

"As a heart attack." The weight of one more person would suffocate me.

A six-inch paper strip rolled out of the monitor. It was all "artifact," a no-sense cardiac rhythm. I plucked one of the gel pads out of his hair. Another had crawled up under his chin. "Sweat hog. I should have smeared you in Benzoin first."

The dispatcher's voice came over the radio.

"Shit," said Martin. "Hand me my pants." He sounded like the radio had eyes.

We hurriedly dressed in silence. I didn't know how I felt, wasn't sure I wanted to go to that place inside and find out either. Seal it now and label it hazardous to your health. We cut our way through the heat and darkness of another Panhandle night. In the glow of the dash Martin's hands seemed almost phosphorescent. A pair of mime gloves caught in the spotlight. I'd seen him clamp off a bleeding vein in a heartbeat, clear an airway passage in a face smashed beyond recognition, pull traction with confidence when I would have been afraid to.

My turn to charge. We arrive at a duplex. Sandy lawn littered with bright plastic toys. A woman wearing an abaya opens the door. Small children cling to her legs. Swaying kelp in the blue folds of fabric. "My husband," she says.

We follow her into the living room. He's laid out on the couch, diaphoretic, and shivering beneath a wool blanket.

"Hello," I say. "Where do you hurt?" He turns his head away. I set down my bag, reach for his wrist to get a pulse. He recoils. "It's okay. I'm just going to take your pulse."

"Please not to touch him," says the wife.

"But I'm wearing gloves."

"No, it's better for the other." She points to Martin.

"Look here," I say.

"Please. Let the man help him."

"I got it," says Martin.

I peel off my gloves and leave them on the floor. On my way out the door I hear his litany of complaints in perfect English. I'm in the truck when Martin radios me to bring the stretcher. We load him onto our pleasure mattress and drive off. In the back I hear him wince, and I know Martin has just stuck him good with an IV needle. Too bad. I'm a gentler stick.

The glass doors of the ER whoosh open and we push the stretcher into the hands of the female resident on call. Our shift is over. The moment limp. We go our separate ways for the night.

. . .

It cost a considerable sum to repair the damaged cardiac monitor for which we both received written reprimands. But by the end of summer we were back to some semblance of our earlier selves and again we continued to move lazily over the roads in the Lizard, listening to the stereo and sucking up sweet tea through straws. Things unspoken from that night occasionally floated to the surface and formed hot words, but mostly little was said. I was like an accident victim. Full of slow bleeders. Clamp off one vein and another starts oozing.

Early in autumn Martin had begun checking in the truck, going down the long list and inventorying supplies. It was a routine part of the job I hadn't minded doing but Martin welcomed the distraction. One night, when windows were full of grinning pumpkins, glass shattered in the back of the ambulance.

I climbed into the rear of the truck. On the floor was a broken vial of Demerol from the narcotics box. "What happened?"

He shrugged his shoulders, held his palms out like the risen Christ. "Call me Martin Butterfingers."

Controlled substances wasted in the field had to be reported and I signed off as witness. There was no liquid with the broken glass. I said nothing.

Around that same time we transported a woman with a tib-fib fracture. Martin had radioed for narcotic orders and drawn up more than the required dose, a mistake totally alien to the way he worked.

Thoughts about these things set up an intermittent buzz in my head. Persistent mosquito. Then, small items began to disappear. A pair of gold stud earrings I'd put in my change purse. A ten-dollar bill from my wallet. Much later, door speakers from the Lizard. I invented excuses. Maybe I misplaced the earrings. Maybe I spent the money elsewhere. Often we left the truck unlocked at the station, an open invitation for anyone.

Thanksgiving came and went. Mistletoe hung in the dispatch office. The only thing I wanted to kiss was Martin's face with my aluminum clipboard.

He insisted on taking charge of all the trauma calls where narcotics were likely to be given. "I'll take this one," he'd say.

On Christmas Eve I finally said "No you won't."

"It's cardiac. You hate cardiac," he said.

"I don't care. I'll charge, you drive."

"No."

On scene, I climbed into the back of the truck and sat there waiting for him to push drugs into the man's sweaty arm. "I'm not driving until you do."

He injected the morphine, and I rushed through to the cab and took off with a wail. We delivered our patient to the hospital where Martin disappeared. I cleaned the back, changed the sheets on the stretcher, and went looking for him. He was standing outside the snack shop eating an egg sandwich and complaining to Smitty what a rotten partner I'd turned into.

I sat in the ambulance and waited, cursing the missing stereo speakers. When he came back, I said "Get yourself a new partner if you're so damn unhappy."

"I'm getting the hell out, period."

"Don't let the door hit ya where the good Lord split ya."

"Kiss my ass."

We shouted until words didn't work. He shoved me and I shoved him back. I was crying, but not Martin. What did it matter, I was doing it for both of us and couldn't stop—weeks, months, years stored up like grain in King David's dream. I blew my nose on a gauze bandage because nothing else was handy. "You need help, Martin."

"I am the help," he said, "remember?"

Then, like the drinking, this too ended abruptly. He called in sick for three days. He returned to work, a little pale but otherwise the same. I went back to checking in the narcotics each shift. Martin put new speakers in the Lizard—Jansen, with superb woofers and tweeters. For my birthday he gave me a gold necklace with an emerald birthstone. A pricey buy-back that wasn't even my style.

A period of calm followed but I was afraid to let myself relax, afraid of the pattern I had begun to see emerging, afraid of what might come next.

• • •

On a day so humid that the Freon gave out, I drove to the university with the windows down and picked up Martin. He was across the street from the south entrance, leaning against the wrought iron fence which circled the city's oldest cemetery. He climbed into the truck and slapped his knee. "That," he said "was my last class."

"What do you mean your last class?"

"I'm graduating. Gonna blow this one-horse town." A college in New York had hired him to teach composition.

"What?" Anger sucked my breath away. "You never even told me."

"Told you? You think I've been going through all this for nothing?"

I opened the door, jumped two feet to the ground, then slammed it behind me. My boots smacked hard against the sidewalk.

"Hey, come back here. Where the hell you going?"

When I reached the cemetery gate I went inside. Members of the LaFayette family were buried here. Side by side with horse thieves. I weaved through the tombstones like an obstacle course, cursing Martin, not caring that I walked on the dead. Then I cursed myself. He'd been working toward this for years—an obvious vital sign I had failed to register.

Martin caught up with me, spun me around by my shoulders. "You don't need me anymore. You're a crack medic. Anyway," he smiled, "it's time you had a change of face."

I flung off his hands. "Don't give me that shit, Martin. I don't want to work with anyone but you. I hate everyone else."

Martin laughed and tried to grab my shoulder again.

I pushed his hand off.

"Come on. Let's go to Skeeters and celebrate. I'm buying."

"Bastard. Celebrate yourself." I walked back to the ambulance and started the engine. Martin remained in the cemetery, leaning against a large granite obelisk. I tooted the horn. "Step on it. We got a call."

The dry smell of Marlboro filled the cab when Martin shut the passenger door.

"I can't do this anymore," he said.

"Oh bullshit. You drank. You did some drugs. It's over. Forget it." I pulled away from the curb, en route to another Baker Sam.

"It's beyond that. Way far beyond. You've no idea how fried I am."

I mashed the brakes and the ambulance rocked to a halt. "We're all burnt toast," I said. "You think quitting will change what runs in your veins? Don't do it Martin. Take time off, but don't quit." I stuck my arm out the window and waved for the cars behind me to pass. Even as I said these things I struggled to believe them. Flesh sagged beneath his eyes like dark curtains. Why hadn't I noticed that before? What other vital signs was I missing because I was too close? His gray eyes moved slowly back and forth hunting for something in the empty air between us. "We had something once," he said.

"Is that what this is about?" Another car pulled up behind us and honked. I accelerated slowly.

"I don't know. Maybe."

I turned down a narrow brick-lined side street, slithering from left to right to avoid the parked cars. Most of the houses were off-grade wooden shacks. Shotgun houses. Fire through the front door and buckshot flies out the back.

"Martin, take a vacation. Take your daddy jug fishing somewhere. Lay in the boat. Snooze in the sun."

"That's your solution. Pretend nothing ever happened."

That made me mad, and I slapped the visor down in front of me blocking the sun. "If I have to pretend, then I pretend. I pretend I'm working in the stockroom of Dillard's. I pretend I'm wrapping up mannequin limbs for shipment to another store. It's just merchandise. Period."

"That's not what bothers me."

"Then what?"

"Just this," said Martin. "People suffering. I've begun to enjoy it."

. . .

At his going away party, my cinder block house ballooned with paramedics and hospital employees. Cops and firefighters. Latex gloves filled with helium dangled from the ceiling. Little fingers like stalactites. We drank and laughed. We sang "For He's a Jolly Good Fellow." And then, Martin was gone.

In the morning I shuffled around the living room in Tweety Bird slippers. I opened the windows and let out the stale smoke. I emptied ashtrays, collected beer bottles, poking my finger down the long necks. Down here no one ever leaves home. Like apples on the same tree. Shake us and we fall, but never very far. The way it's supposed to be. Has to be, in a world of sudden horror. Apples on my tree. Martin in my orchard.

On Monday afternoon I found myself with a new partner. A stringy blond with plenty of upholstery on her bones was sitting in Martin's seat. I started the engine without looking at her.

"My name is Mayl—"

"Shut up," I said, and turned on the radio.

She was fresh out of paramedic school, full of energy and mistakes. She was polite to people and I watched her like some forgotten part of myself. We had been reassigned to a different zone and our first call put us on the porch of an antebellum home, white columns surrounding the joint. A housekeeper led us up the grand staircase and into the master bedroom where an elderly woman could barely contain her surprise. "They let two women work together?"

"It's the men's day off," I said.

Maylene charged the call. The woman had broken her hip some weeks ago and it wasn't healing properly. When I returned with the stretcher, I saw that the housekeeper had packed an overnight bag. She led the way down the stairs.

The old woman grabbed the rails of the stretcher. "Are you going to be able to lift this?"

Maylene patted her hand. "Don't worry. We won't drop you."

She looked up at us, her pale eyes shifting from Maylene to me, then she squeezed them shut. I pictured the stretcher whizzing down the stairs like a toboggan.

. . .

A few weeks later I got a postcard from Martin with a picture of a New York standpipe. Said he didn't miss those project calls. Didn't miss anything about being a medic except our meal breaks. He'd been eating at a place called Sylvia's because the food was like back home. Said he'd taken up the hobby of spitting on the subway tracks like the city's finest citizens.

I wrote him a dozen times but he never answered me. A writing teacher all day with words, who would feel like it. Two years passed with only Christmas cards until one late spring morning I was out mowing the lawn. Green stains around bare ankles, soot on my face from burning oil. I'd gone inside for Gatorade and was standing in front of the open fridge sucking in the cold air when the phone rang. There was no answer on the other end. Just quiet baby breathing. Martin half asleep next to me while I drove the dark streets. "I know it's you," I said. "Where are you?" The stove clock ticked through a sixty-second cycle. A minute of silence for the dead. Or maybe for something never born. I heard the receiver on the other end quietly settle into its cradle.

That tiny click woke a black bear of anger that was hibernating in me. Anger at Martin for coasting out of my life. Anger that he never wrote back. Anger that he couldn't even say Boo into the goddamn telephone. Anger that maybe just maybe my life was much better without him. And if it was, what did that mean about all the years gone by? My drink grew warm on the counter. The mower stood in the middle of a half-cut lawn. Either drink and shoot darts at Quarters or go to the beach. I grabbed my bathing suit, a change of clothes, a mystery. Two hundred pages later I was skipping flat stones into the ocean.

Martin sightings followed. Those who had seen or thought they had seen him in town. Most recently Smitty's girlfriend. I felt sick with unease. Sooner or later, like a night bat, Martin would land and draw blood.

Rumors circulated at the hospital. Martin had been in to see the personnel director, had seen him twice, wanting his old job back.

"You think it's true?" In the cab, Maylene brushed the wispy bangs off her forehead and looked at me. Months of street experience had begun to turn her into a decent medic although she still worried too much.

I shrugged. News came on the radio about the hurricane down south. Its wake was a disaster—our kind of party for sure. The county was sending a truck and two medics to help out. We volunteered to go, wanted to go, but the captain had already picked two guys. Fresh fish at that, then jammed us when we called him on it.

I turned off the news. "Still disappointed?"

"How could he say that?"

"We's just two womens with no stamina."

She tried not to smile. "Shut up. It's not funny. We're more experienced and better and everything."

"So write your damn memo and see where that gets you."

"Well maybe I will."

The light changed. "Waiting for a pleasanter shade of green?"

She accelerated and we drove a few blocks in silence. I wondered if I would be going to the ball if Martin and I were still partners. I looked over at Maylene. Her forehead was all scrunched. "Now what?"

"You want to go back to him—I mean, be his partner again?"

She dropped one hand from the steering wheel onto her chunky thigh. Beneath her was the pillow she always sat on so she could see over the dash when driving.

"It's natural," she said. "Ten years, that's a history together."

"You and I have a history now too." Maylene. A shoe that doesn't pinch my foot. Maybe something more. I wasn't sure.

I wouldn't call her attitude contagious, but people at work were beginning to speak to me. Housekeeping with their big stainless steel carts. The blue-haired volunteers that ran the gift shop. Nurses in the hallways. Without my ice twin, I was losing my reputation as a cold, hard-edged lady who couldn't be bothered. But still, those days with Martin flying over gravel roads and stirring up a storm of words clung like dust to the present.

· · ·

Thump of boots. Martin landed on my porch in the middle of an August night. I pulled on a pair of jeans, felt my way into the darkness of the living room, and flipped on the porch light.

"It's me," Martin said. "Open up." Then I heard him hit the wooden planks.

I slid the chain back and opened the door, put my arm under his and helped him to his feet. Already, moths had begun to swirl around the yellow porch light, knocking softly against the glass.

"Hey," he said.

"Hey yourself. What the hell are you doing here?" Three in the morning, reeking of alcohol and perfume so strong it overpowered the tea olive bushes blooming along the railing.

"Needed to see you."

I looked at Martin's face and wondered what I had stashed in the medicine cabinet that could help.

"Yeah. There's a phone to arrange that. You dial and do more than breathe when the other person answers."

Inside, I moved him toward the couch, my bare feet dancing around the heavy shovel of his steps. "Lean your head back." I examined the cornea and sclera, then the surrounding tissue.

"A dandy hematoma you got there, Martin." Besides the eye, there were cuts on his face, none serious, but they needed cleaning.

He groaned.

"A door take a swing at your face?" All the domestics we'd responded to. Doors suddenly responsible for damage not to be believed. Cats and dogs to trip you up and break your nose. Never a mention of the frying pan with wings, or the fist hungry to connect with flesh and bone.

His head rested against the back of the couch, a position that relaxed his jaw slightly enough to reveal a chipped incisor. I wondered when that had happened.

"You got a cigarette?"

"Screw you Martin. You know I don't smoke. Or have you forgotten that?"

He patted his pockets. "I got one here somewhere." I followed his gaze as it landed on the saucer I'd lifted from the hospital cafeteria. Sitting under a feeble cactus plant on the windowsill. Martin's ashtray whenever he came over.

"How many fingers do you see?"

"Two."

"You'll survive." Two weeks in town and this is all I get. Son of a bitch.

"I shouldn't have left." He raised his hands then let them drop onto the couch. I wasn't sure if this gesture was part of his sadness or resignation at not finding a cigarette.

"Yeah, well, you did." From the top shelf of the hall closet I grabbed a pillow and sheet and threw them in his direction. Maybe I'd just leave Martin there and walk out the door. Then I thought that it was my house, and I should stay.

"I don't blame you for being mad, it's just—"

"Just what? You think you can waltz back in here and pick up like nothing ever happened? If you weren't so drunk I'd kick your sorry ass out right now."

Martin leaned forward and for a moment I thought he was going to be sick on my floor, then something much worse—that he was going to cry. "I didn't know I needed anyone."

"Oh Christ, Martin." But he was off babbling in a stupor about partners. Batman and Robin. Lone Ranger and Tonto. Ren and Stimpy. Oatmeal-like vomitus followed the words, trailing down his shirt and onto the floor.

I let him soak in his own bodily fluids while I cleaned up around him. Two soiled towels into a plastic pail. A pine-scented candle to clear the odor. Then carefully, I undid his shirt, watching as his chest hairs sprang up from beneath each tiny white button. Dark hairs were mixed with gray and I slid my fingers through them and tugged gently, as if this could comfort me.

Martin's head rested on my shoulder while I pulled one sleeve, then the other over his arms. Remove the shirt, toss it in the pail. I leaned him back against the couch. His chin dropped onto his chest. I am dressing a mannequin for a window display. I repeated this even as I rooted through the closet and medicine cabinet scooping supplies into my arms: washcloth, soap, water, cotton balls, ice pack, Band-Aids, peroxide.

I soaked the washcloth in the basin of warm water and began to clean Martin's face. Things I had forgotten—like the small cluster of freckles that loosely resembled a clover—and new things—deeper lines at the edges of his eyes—pulled me toward him and would be a painful Braille-encoded memory, my fingers touching and remembering touch. I put a butterfly Band-Aid high over Martin's left cheekbone, pulling together the split flesh. Washing the cuts on his temple, his jaw, his lips, I circled the wounds, somehow afraid of hurting him yet wanting to hurt him, to dig my nails deep into his flesh. I remembered the story I had been told. About how I was born with lean fingers and long nails, scratching my face until the nurses put tiny white socks over my balled-up fists.

Outside, the distant wail of an ambulance pierced the silence. Even off duty, a low jolt of electricity coursed through my veins and made my heart skip a beat. Something deep inside of Martin heard this call too, and his eyes briefly fluttered open. "Wouldn't take me back," he mumbled.

I stared at the basin while tiny swirls of blood circled in on themselves like a universe.

"Don't want me anymore at the hospital."

For a panicked moment I wondered who I could talk to for him, who I could convince.

"What do I do now?"

Anger overrode my anxiety. Go back to grading your goddamn essays, I thought. But still. Martin in the neighborhood, sitting on my porch in the dark slapping at mosquitoes and drinking beer, the glow of his cigarette the only light.

"Go to Quincy." Quincy where the medics are white and the folk black except during tomato picking season when the town swells with Mexicans. In hot summer fights some get sliced open as easily as the plump red fruit. "There's plenty of action there."

"Maybe . . ." And then he was asleep, his right hand tucked halfway below his belt. I threw the sheet over him and it fluttered slowly down, but for a moment on the way it caught in the draft of the air conditioning and was magically suspended. Aladdin's carpet. A healing shroud. I didn't know what, but something.

In bed, I lay awake listening to the final spin cycle of the washing machine, and afterward a much fainter sound—the cool swoosh and hum common to all overburdened air conditioners. Around dawn, when pale gray lines showed through the vertical blinds, I heard the sound of the front door opening and pictured Martin quietly carrying his boots in hand. Minutes later the sound of his car engine faded into the distance and I lay there a long time before getting up and walking into the empty living room. With my hand I traced the indentations in the leather couch. Shallow compressions like those left by a deer in a field. Then I brought the sheet to my face and inhaled. The perfume that had clung to him had faded, but the strong familiar scent of Martin had not, and I began to wonder if it ever would.

I wore the sheet around my shoulders like a shawl, walking from room to room, until I had opened all the windows. Back on the couch I hugged my knees and waited. A humid breeze rattled through the front screens, and then drops, heavy like nickels, fell on the tin roof of the porch. On days like this—such beautiful rainy days—we would have been so busy.

14

FINAL CUT

Kristen Iversen

Dana heard his car before it turned into the parking lot. The lot was fenced with chain link, eight feet high, and she had pulled the heavy gate open just moments before. She glanced at the digital clock on her desk. *Let it not be him*, she thought. *Not yet.*

It was. Despite the gray sky, he had the top down on his Mercedes and he whipped it neatly through the gate and into a parking spot. The one right in front, reserved for him. He glanced up at Dana's office window—she dipped her head as if she hadn't seen him—and she heard him jangle his keys noisily at the front door. The lock relented and he stomped up the stairs.

"Mr. James." She looked up from her desk. "I didn't hear you come in."

"Morning," he said. He glanced around her office. "Where is everyone?" There was a sharp look to his face that made her shrink. Slightly. She was learning to deal with it.

"It's only 7:30," she said. "Most of the staff doesn't come in until 8."

"Did you make coffee?"

"Yes." She looked down at the manuscript on her desk. "You might have to make a new pot. I've been here since six."

The statement failed to register. He turned and opened his office door, directly across from hers. Each evening he left a clean desk, every pen and pencil in place, and closed the door behind him. "Where's Jodie?" he asked.

"What?" She looked up.

"Jodie. Jodie. Where's Jodie?" He was a good-looking man—tall, lean—but she thought there was something a little forced about his features. A certain strut to the jaw.

"Most people don't come in at six, Mr. James."

"I need to make some calls," he muttered. "Let me know when she gets here."

Dana glanced down at her telephone. No word yet from Jodie, which was good. She'd already taken a sick day this month.

. . .

This was the summer of hail. Hailstones the size of peas, the size of gumballs, the size of golf balls if the conditions were right. Just last week Dana had stood at her office window and watched hailstones pummel the roof of her Toyota, covering it with dimples like tiny thumbprints. Storms blew in with little warning. Branches fell across the road and power lines went down. Dana wore rubber boots with her skirts and changed into heels in the office.

She finished marking the manuscript. She had taken her time—she liked the rhythm of her blue pencil hovering over each line, deleting commas, adding paragraph breaks, tidying up the world one sentence at a time. As senior editor she didn't have to do this, but she liked the idea of saving Jodie a little time and effort, and no one ever edited a manuscript to her satisfaction anyway.

Max came in, dragging a wet umbrella. Like Dana, his title was a little inflated: art manager. He managed no one but himself. Jodie said Max had a wife undergoing chemo, but Max never talked about his home life. He stayed an hour late each evening without complaint to finish typesetting the day's galleys.

"Jodie here yet?"

"No." Dana noticed Max's hands, the short fingers and thick palms. He looked like the kind of guy who might work in a machine shop. But here he was, designing book covers and laying out page design, tinkering with fonts as delicate as lace.

"Let me know when she gets here, okay?"

Dana nodded. Jodie fit in, oddly. Even Max liked her. The last girl, Dorothy, had quit without notice. It was hard to do two jobs, half-assistant to Dana and half-assistant to Mr. James. Part of Jodie's day was spent proofreading and talking to authors, and the rest of the time she placed phone calls for Mr. James and kept his coffee cup filled. You had to get a girl who wanted to be a writer, who thought she could write and was looking for a good stepping stone. A girl looking for a place to start. A girl willing to pay her dues, as Mr. James said.

Jodie had few delusions. She could write, sure. But she wasn't about to bank her literary future on writing book jacket copy for some cookbook company. Jodie referred to *How to Thrill with Your Grill*, their latest regional bestseller, as *Why I Need a Pill*. The manuscript they were working on now, *The Busy Baker*, she called *The Busy Banker*. In lieu of employee raises, Mr. James was taking his family to Italy for Christmas.

In the six months since Jodie had arrived, the office had taken on a more domestic look. With her own money she bought small potted plants to balance in the window sills and hung an old string of white Christmas lights around the door to the warehouse. Jodie rearranged the worn couch and coffee table where authors and potential authors waited to hear their fate, and carefully displayed the company's latest titles in an attempt to inspire more hope than the spartan look of the building as a whole might immediately arouse.

Tom came in. His overcoat reached to his knees and he wore a furry cap with ear covers, as if he were about to set off on a hunting trip in frigid weather. He nodded to Dana and banged through the warehouse door. In a moment she would hear his radio, tuned to a conservative talk show at full volume. She wasn't sure if he agreed or disagreed with the host. "It just gets my blood up in the morning," Tom said. "Gets me going." Tom had a graduate degree in biology and had spent the last ten years of his life in the warehouse dock, packing boxes of books.

Still no sign of Jodie. Dana rose, poured a fresh cup of coffee, and set it on Jodie's desk. Just in case Mr. James came out.

· · ·

At her apartment, there was nothing for Jodie to do but wait.

It would be easier when Sammie started full-day kindergarten. But that was next fall—months and months away, which might as well be years. Preschool started at nine and ended at noon, and Jodie spent a good deal of energy each day worrying about seven to nine and noon to five. There was daycare, sure, but it was expensive—more than half her salary, in fact—and it never seemed to work out. Jodie was not opposed to the idea like some mothers were. She liked the idea of Sammie getting to know other children, learning her letters, or just providing her mother with a little time to think about something other than Legos and peanut butter sandwiches. Yesterday she had arrived at the daycare center at six minutes past five. The director, a portly woman with an authoritative air, met her at the door to inform her that she would be charged two dollars a minute for being late. "Where *is* Sammie?" Jodie asked, irritated, when she didn't see her daughter in the small group of leftover children sitting in the playroom.

"She was fussy," piped up one of the teachers, a teenage girl wearing a tight T-shirt that stopped just above her belly button. "So I put her in a crib in the back."

The back room was dark but Jodie could hear her daughter snuffling. Sammie sat cross-legged in the crib and climbed to her feet when she saw her mother. Her forehead was burning.

"She's running a fever," Jodie called. "How long has she been like this?"

The teenage girl appeared. "I'm not sure." She frowned. "We thought you would be here any minute, so we weren't really paying attention."

Jodie felt a flash of rage. She could have slapped her. "An hour? Two? This fever feels pretty high."

The girl backed out. "Well, you're not supposed to bring them in if they're sick," she said.

Jodie wrapped the blanket around Sammie and gathered her up in her arms. "Tell the director—Mrs. what's-her-name—that we quit. That's it. We're not coming back."

"Shall I tell her to send you a bill?"

"You can tell her—." Jodie stopped. Sammie looked up at her mother's face. "You can tell her whatever you like," she said, and walked out.

At the clinic it turned out to be nothing serious, just a virus, and Sammie was prone to high fevers. But there was an after-hours charge and money for the prescriptions and then a night of no sleep, as Sammie couldn't breathe and couldn't eat and wanted to be rocked all night. And in the morning, a crisis. No daycare center or daycare mom would take a sick kid, especially one with a fever. She called Mary Woods, a retired secretary in the next apartment building who sometimes agreed to sit with Sammie for an hourly fee. "You need to pay me today," Mary said. "I'll do it, but only if you pay me today. Is there anything in your refrigerator?"

"I'll pay you today," Jodie said. "I promise. Can you come over now?" It was already seven thirty.

"I need time to get dressed." Mary was not a morning person. "Just hold your horses." Jodie could hear the television in the background.

"Please hurry," Jodie said. She thought about calling Dana at work, then changed her mind. Better just to drive fast.

· · ·

"We got to a point where, well, we had married so young." Dana leaned across the table toward Jodie, who sipped on her iced tea and rolled the paper sleeve of the straw into a ball between her fingertips. Jodie smiled faintly and nodded.

"At first we were in love. I suppose everyone feels that way."

It had been Jodie's first day. Dana's first gesture with every new hire was to take them to the delicatessen on the corner for matzo ball soup and convince them to give the job a chance.

This lunch was different, though. Jodie reminded Dana of herself, maybe a younger version of herself. Her hair was shorter and she hadn't finished college, but there was an earnestness about her, a kind of idealism, that appealed to Dana even though she barely knew the girl. And Jodie was tough. Dana could tell by the way she talked to Mr. James, right off the bat.

"David and I get along now, more or less. Mostly for the sake of the kids." She looked up to see Neil, behind the deli case in his white apron and paper cap, set their soup on the counter. "He wasn't a very committed husband, but he's trying to be a committed dad," Dana added. "My friends say I should be grateful for that."

Jodie leaned back in her chair, looking slightly put-off. Dana suddenly felt self-conscious. "I'm sure you don't want to hear about my divorce," she said. "For heaven's sake. I don't even know you. I have no idea why I'm talking like this." She stood, walked to the counter, and carried the bowls back to the table. She smiled. "I think you'll like the soup."

"Thank you." Jodie conscientiously examined her spoon, overly large and flecked with spots from the dishwasher. She dipped the spoon into the soup and raised it to her lips, cherry red with the brightest lipstick Dana had ever seen in her life.

"It sure has been raining a lot," Dana quipped.

"I can see that," Jodie said, as if she came from a different country and was just visiting.

"Very hot soup," Dana said, waving her fingers in the air.

"Yes."

It wasn't until they had finished their soup and placed the spoons and bowls in the plastic dishwasher tubs—Neil's Deli was informal at best—that Jodie turned to Dana with a questioning look. "How many children do you have?" she asked.

"Two."

"Boys or girls?"

"One boy, one girl."

"They're in school, right?"

"Fourth and fifth grade."

"They see their dad?"

"Every Thursday. Sometimes on the weekends."

The next day Dana tucked a slender box next to Jodie's telephone, a new fountain pen that had been a gift from an advertiser. The box was cherry and the pen looked expensive, although it probably wasn't. She added a sticky note written in block letters: "For surviving your first day."

She watched Jodie to see if she noticed the gift. Jodie opened the box, looked at it for a moment, and slipped it into her purse. She said nothing.

Later that evening Dana mentioned the new girl to Sarah and Ellen, the women she sometimes met after work for a beer on Thursdays.

"She won't last," Sarah said. "She sounds too smart to work at that place."

• • •

Ward James Jr. hadn't intended to become a publisher. Well, yes, a publisher of sorts, but when he was in graduate school he had imagined himself the publisher of great writers. Maybe not great writers, but good writers, writers who could represent his generation and tellingly reveal the cynicism he himself felt about growing up in the sixties in a spirit of optimism and change and ending up here, now, sitting behind a desk just as his father did, going home each night feeling like he'd been kicked in the stomach. He liked cookbooks well enough, he guessed. His wife had come up with the idea, back when they had only two kids and a mortgage and it was clear his career wasn't going anywhere. Not just cookbooks but cookbooks sponsored by advertisers—rather, companies that provided healthy endorsements of healthy ingredients—that appeared in page after page of ads in the back of each book.

Thanks to Amanda's marketing sense and a good collection of soup recipes, the first book caught on. And then the next one and the next. He hired a salesperson and a writer and a graphic designer, and then they started producing calendars as well as cookbooks—a brilliant marketing move on Amanda's part. Profits from calendars put their first daughter through college.

But Ward couldn't shake the faint sense of failure that seemed to dog him. He knew it was his father's voice; he could still hear that mild sense of surprise and displeasure on the other end of the line when he told his father how well the company was doing. "Cookbooks?" his dad growled, then laughed. Well. Ward's brother was a corporate attorney in Santa Barbara, and Cindy, his sister, had five kids, two grandkids by now. They thought his company was just fine. And their father was dead now, five years dead, although Ward still thought about him almost every day.

He looked out the window of his office to the fenced parking lot—still no sign of Jodie's car—and then down at his fingers on the desk, deliberate and steady. There was a cost to all this but he still wasn't sure what it was, how to quantify it, contain it, get it under control. He and Amanda lived separate lives. Perhaps it was his coolness that made her untangle herself from the business and turn to the children, managing their lives, orchestrating their success. But that hadn't turned out so well either. Arthur, Art, the baby, was sixteen now and didn't talk to either of them. He came home and stalked to his room, shut the door, turned up the music. He preferred to eat dinner alone in his room. Amanda hated an empty dinner table and she rarely ate anyway, going from diet to diet as she did. Sometimes Ward was so angry when he came into work in the morning he had to sit behind his desk for a few minutes to calm himself before he could call in Jodie to begin phoning authors and advertisers.

The Christmas trip to Italy would help. Not all four kids could make it, that was understandable, but Amanda and Art would be there and the three of them could see Florence, visit the museums, get a sense of place and culture and history. The things that mattered. He hadn't been to Europe since he was a college student thirty years ago, traveling around with a backpack and a train pass. He thought he might discover a part of that idealistic kid again.

•   •   •

Mary showed up on Jodie's doorstep in a flurry of scarves and a long overcoat that nearly touched the ground. She carried a bag of knitting.

"You're here!" Jodie said. She already had her coat on, keys in hand. "Sammie's watching *Sesame Street*."

"Well, I don't like such short notice."

"I have no one else to call," Jodie said. "You're a lifesaver."

Mary beamed. "I have grandchildren, you know. But I never get to see them." She stomped her boots on the rug. "I hate this wet weather." She shook her umbrella and closed it up tight. "Oh dear," she sighed. "I should have done that out on the stoop."

"There's fresh coffee in the kitchen," Jodie said. "And yogurt in the fridge if you want lunch." She took Mary's coat and hung it in the closet.

"Yogurt?" Mary opened the wide mouth of her purse and started digging around. "Better than nothing, I guess." She set her keys and a pack of Juicy Fruit on the coffee table.

"Sammie just gets soup today. Don't give her any gum."

"Gum don't hurt a child."

"She just swallows it, Mary." Thank god she doesn't choke, she silently added. "Her medicine is on the counter. One tablespoon after lunch."

Mary found what she was looking for and snapped her purse shut.

"Mary." Jodie paused. "Please don't smoke in the house."

"I do it out on the patio and Sammie can't even tell."

Yes she can, Jodie thought. I can smell it in the curtains. "Mary, really," she said.

"Don't go begging me to give up something I done every day of my life." Mary looked petulant. "My one real pleasure. You sound just like my daughter."

"It makes the house smell."

"I can't smell it. Not even in my own house."

Sammie toddled in from the living room, barefoot, her face flushed. The rubber band around her ponytail had slipped and her hair was bunched in a knot.

"Mom?"

"Has she had a bath this morning?" Mary asked.

"She just woke up."

"I don't do baths," Mary said. "Especially if they're sick."

"Mommy, are you going?" Sammie's voice started out as a whimper and rose. Her head was stuffed up and her breath raspy.

"Just for a little bit, sweetie. Mommy has to go to work."

Sammie howled.

"Go! Go!" Mary cried, and made a shooing motion with her hands. "You just make it worse." She gently pushed Jodie to the door. "We'll be fine."

. . .

Jodie was not like the other girls who had worked for Mr. James.

Some of them cried in Dana's office. How can you work with him? they asked. Once he threw a stack of address cards at a girl—Dorothy, was it?—and she didn't even bother to complain to Dana, she just walked out. Stopped just long enough to pick up her coat and purse.

He wasn't unpredictable. Dana knew in the first five minutes whether Mr. James was having a good day or bad, and there were more good days than bad days.

But Jodie was different. She didn't seem to care what kind of day Mr. James was having. Each morning she greeted him evenly. Each evening she tidied her desk, left a to-do list for the next day under her telephone pad, and stopped in his office to say goodnight. She arrived promptly at eight, left at five, and never worked overtime. She wore black skirts and bright lipstick and terrified some of the cookbook authors who sat in the office, middle-aged blousy women who wanted to publish recipes for children or new Crock-Pot meals.

Dana suspected she'd had a brief fling with one of the photographers who came to shoot tomatoes for their new line of Italian cookbooks, but Jodie never said anything.

They started having lunch every Wednesday. It was a nice break in the week. After a few Wednesdays Jodie began to talk more. They both liked to travel and they talked about the places they'd been, the places they'd like to go. Jodie wanted to go to Greece. Dana was just hoping for New York. "There's a conference coming up," she said. "Four days, with printers and publishers from all over the country. I think I could talk Ward into letting me go." She called him Ward when he wasn't around.

"Who would take care of your kids?" Jodie asked, not unkindly. It wasn't an offer, Dana noted. Just a question.

"I don't know. Maybe David can take them for a few days. But he's not very reliable." She wondered if Jodie was married. She didn't wear a ring. Jodie's fingers were long and slender, pale, like her complexion. Dana had dark thick hair, impossible to comb, and her own hands were red as if she kept them plunged in a laundry tub all day.

"What time does school start for them?" Jodie asked.

This was the thing, Dana thought, that really rancored her about other women. She drove herself crazy trying to get into the office by eight when everyone else just breezed in, no problem. School didn't start until nine, so she rose at six to get the kids ready to take to Alice's, three blocks from the school. Alice gave them breakfast, walked them to school, picked them up at two to walk them back, and gave them an afternoon snack until Dana arrived at six. Or sometimes seven, depending on whether or not Mr. James was having a good day.

Alice was expensive. But that wasn't it, really. It was something else. Dana had never imagined herself the kind of mother who didn't walk her own kids to school.

"It's no big deal," Dana said. "I've got things worked out."

"That's good."

Dana flinched at the flippancy of the words. As if this girl knew any-thing. Dana imagined Jodie's apartment, clean and elegant. Like her clothes. Like her hair. Like her lipstick.

Still, she was a good proofreader and a half-decent editor. She kept Mr. James at bay.

After work the next day, Dana stopped at a stationer's store and bought Jodie a ceramic coffee mug, creamy white with a blue handle the color of sky. Blue, blue sky, Dana thought, like the kind they hadn't seen in weeks. In the morning she set it next to Jodie's phone before she came in. Once again, Jodie was wordless, but Dana noticed she used the cup faithfully each morning.

. . .

Jodie was halfway to work before she turned off at a freeway exit, turned left, then left again, and got back on the freeway.

She couldn't miss another day of work or she'd be fired. Or that's what Dana said, the words supposedly passed on from Mr. James himself. One sick day a month should be enough for anyone, she'd said. Company policy.

What did Dana do on the days her kids were sick? Her ex sounded like a flake but Dana was the type who probably lived with her mother or had a sister right down the street. That must be it. She probably had a sister, with kids.

Jodie had never seen or heard a hint of Dana's kids, except for the day Dana mentioned them in the deli. Mr. James kept a framed photo of his family on his desk. The kids were small—it must have been taken years ago on some kind of mountain vacation—and his wife was laughing. The kind of laugh that was hard to imagine around Mr. James, but it was that very laugh—the toothy smile, his wife's long hair blown back from her face—that made Jodie believe there was a side to Mr. James that few people saw.

The women knew better than to put a family photo on their desk. The kiss of death. All it took was a quip from a coworker or client that Ms. So-and-so was on the mommy track rather than the career track and suddenly you were looking for another job.

Jodie pulled into the parking lot of her apartment complex and noticed the blinds to her apartment were still closed. She furtively cut up the side of the lawn, or what passed for lawn, and tiptoed up the concrete steps. She stood outside her own door and could hear the television inside, turned up loud. She turned the key in the lock.

Mary sat at the kitchen table, a ring of smoke above her head. Sammie sat in front of the television. The station was switched to a soap.

"Turns out I don't have to go in after all, Mary," Jodie said. She attempted a smile.

"Oh!" Mary cried. "All right." She rose, stubbed out her cigarette, and glanced at her watch. "Well, that's twenty-two minutes worth, at least. Do you have a five?"

Jodie did.

"Don't hesitate to call me next time," Mary cooed as she bustled out the door. "I'm just a few doors down."

"Thanks, Mary." Jodie closed the door and looked at the clock. Eight forty-five. No time for a bath, but she could put Sammie in her jumper and tights and maybe still make it by nine fifteen.

. . .

Fortunately Sammie fell asleep in the car.

It was the cold medicine. Jodie would never go so far as to feed her children European chocolates filled with a thimbleful of brandy, which is what her friend Lydia did on long car rides, but a half-teaspoon of cold medicine was good for half an hour of sleep. Sammie snored.

Rush hour had ended and the freeway was blissfully free of traffic. Jodie pressed her car over the speed limit, then imagined how she would feel if she got in a wreck with Sammie in the car. She imagined Sammie dead. A sense of dread filled her chest and she slowed. Better to be poor than dead. Better she were dead than Sammie, but then who would take care of Sammie?

She drove into the fenced parking lot. Was that Mr. James at the window? Whatever face was there suddenly disappeared. She pulled into the end of the lot, where her car was virtually invisible. It struck her as odd—as it did every day—that a building that was supposed to be filled with creative people looked like an old cement barracks in some war-torn country.

She could see her little plants in the first-floor windows, straining for light. Pitiful, really.

She cracked the back windows and quietly locked Sammie inside, still sleeping. No one was in the front office so Jodie was able to slip up the stairs to her desk without notice. She turned on her computer. Someone had filled her mug with cold coffee.

She looked around for signs of distress but there were none. The door to Mr. James's office was closed. She snapped open her purse, checked her lipstick, and walked down the hall to Dana's office.

"There you are," Dana said, looking up from a manuscript.

"Yes, I've—"

"I told Mr. James you were in the warehouse with Tom, checking on a shipment."

"Good." Jodie looked grateful. Jodie was not, today, anything like the Jodie Dana had been thinking about just before she came in. The dark-stockinged, red-lipsticked blithe spirit that tripped around the office watering plants.

"Sit down for a minute." Dana stood and moved a stack of papers from the single chair in her office to the floor. She had a system of stacking manuscripts, proposals, books in progress, and books to be reviewed in a series of piles that stretched around the perimeter of her office.

"Okay." Jodie sat down on the edge of the chair, legs pressed together, hands between her knees. She looked distraught. Dana had never seen her this way. As if reaching for some distant gesture of civility Dana ventured, "How was your weekend?"

Small talk didn't seem to interest her.

"Is something wrong?" Dana laid down her blue pencil.

"No. Yes." Jodie paused. "I have something in my car."

For a moment Dana considered the fact that Jodie might be violent. She certainly seemed unglued.

Dana leaned back in her chair. "What do you have in your car, Jodie?" she asked calmly.

"I guess I should have told you about this earlier."

Had she stolen something? Did she have a drug habit? Dana couldn't possibly imagine what could make this girl so upset.

"It's my daughter. She's four." Jodie spoke rapidly but in a whisper. "I had no place to take her today because she's sick and I have her in my car."

"In your car?"

"In the backseat. She's asleep." Jodie glanced at the clock. "Probably not for long."

"How sick? Sick with what?"

"Sick enough that I can't get a sitter and I can't miss work because I'll get fired."

They both heard Mr. James open the door to his office. "Is that Jodie?" he called down the hall.

"It's just a virus. A cold. Nothing," Jodie whispered.

"She's right here," Dana said, loudly.

"Send her in." It sounded like it might be turning into a bad day. He closed his door.

"Go get her," Dana commanded. "She can stay in my office until you're done with Mr. James. I'll keep my door shut. Then she can stay with you. I'll tell everyone you're editing a manuscript and can't be disturbed."

"Thanks." Jodie stood. Dana noticed her hands shaking.

"It's almost lunchtime," Dana said. "I think we can pull it off."

• • •

Once she had brought Jason to the office.

Of course kids got sick all the time, and it was almost impossible to keep it all separate from work. When Jason and Kelly picked up pink-eye from the daycare center, Dana got it too. "Allergies," she told Mr. James. She tried to catch all those tell-tale dribbles on her blouses and skirts from spilled sippy-cups, runny noses, or, sometimes, tears. It got a little easier as the kids got older.

There were times when she couldn't get a sitter. Once she told Mr. James she had an urgent manuscript she had to get to press and couldn't concentrate with all the interruptions at the office. She then spent the afternoon at her kitchen table, manuscript pages spread everywhere, trying to concentrate with two kids with chicken pox. Perhaps Mr. James had figured this out; at any rate, he said he needed her in the office. "You're my right-hand person," he said. "I can't run the place without you." Other employees might come and go but "you stick with me," he said, "and you'll always have a job."

That meant something, when small publishing companies appeared and disappeared just as quickly, and one missed paycheck meant she would lose her apartment.

So when Jason had the flu and couldn't go to daycare because he had a fever, Dana brought him into work and set him up in the stairwell with his blocks and large-print books while she met with an advertiser in her office. Jason promised to be quiet; she thought he might fall asleep on his blanket. The client, an ad agency exec who couldn't be more than twenty-five, smiled and cooed at Jason as they walked down the hall to Dana's office. "Your boss must be great," she said.

An hour later, Mr. James came in from lunch. "What the hell do you think this is?" he barked. "A nursery?" He slammed his door.

Dana waited long enough to restore some sense of dignity and then scooped Jason up in her arms and took him home, wondering if she'd still have a job the next morning.

She did. Nothing was ever said about the incident.

• • •

Sammie didn't like to be corralled. Dana explained that sitting under her desk was like playing house. Sammie didn't buy it. "Let's pretend we're in a tent in the woods," Dana said. "There are lions and bears out there, and we're hiding in here to be safe." She was a little embarrassed about the analogy—could a pulp fiction writer be any more obvious?—but it was lost on the child, who scurried out from under the desk every time Dana answered the phone. She couldn't be too sick, Dana thought. In fact she seemed hyperactive.

"Please be quiet," she begged. "Please please please."

Sammie squealed. Dana tried to pick her up to rock her, but the girl squirmed out of her arms. So much for the silk blouse, Dana thought.

Finally she heard Mr. James's door open and close. She peeked out. The coast was clear. She wrestled Sammie into her arms and trotted down to Jodie's office. "Keep her under the desk," Dana said. "I'll watch your door." Their desks were large, gray, and metallic with a distinct government feel. Sammie clung to her mother's stockinged calves.

"I think she's feeling better," Jodie said.

Dana nodded.

"Should I lock the door?" Jodie asked.

"No, that would seem odd. We don't want anyone to notice anything going on."

"Right."

"I'll shut the door behind me and keep an eye on it from my office."

"Okay."

An hour passed. Then another. Dana went downstairs for fresh coffee and returned, and Jodie's door was still safely shut. The room was quiet. Sammie must have fallen asleep, she thought.

. . .

This was the dilemma. Mr. James liked to hire women, preferred it, in fact. Twice Dana had wanted to hire men as editorial assistants and Mr. James said no. He said he liked women because they worked harder and were more willing to work overtime. He was quite adamant about that. And they were less likely to complain. Rarely did he hire a woman over the age of twenty-five. He thought it was important to mold new employees into the company image.

But there were problems. Before Max there was Elizabeth, a graphic designer who had a flair for book design. Dana could still spot the covers Elizabeth had designed. But six months into her employment, Elizabeth announced she was pregnant. Mr. James called Dana privately into his office. How long had Dana known about this? Was this the plan right from the start? Maybe Elizabeth was just looking for a good health insurance policy. And now the company premiums would go up.

Max came in that same day, resume in hand. By the end of the week Max was setting up his art tools in the workroom—even though he required a higher salary—and Elizabeth was gone.

Dana tried to take all this in stride. She had a good job with a growing company. It was better than working for a temp pool. In a year or two, when the kids were a little older, she could begin to think about moving to New York and becoming a real editor at a real publishing house.

So she shouldn't have been surprised when Jodie's door opened and Mr. James came out. How long had he been in there? She couldn't tell, but his face and neck were crimson. He strode into Dana's office and didn't bother to close the door. "You can be the one to tell her she needn't show up in the morning," he said. He returned to his office and pulled the door shut.

Dana sat stunned. She rose and walked down the hall. Jodie stood with her purse in one hand, gripping Sammie's hand with the other. She looked defiant. "Don't bother," she said. "I heard."

"Jodie, I—"

"I had to tell him that you said it was okay," Jodie said. "I'm sorry about that. I thought he would understand."

"You thought he would understand?"

"He had been so nice to me," she said. "He gave me a pen. And a nice cup." Dana noticed Jodie had tucked the mug with the sky blue handle into her purse.

Dana felt like a lead weight had been dropped in her stomach. "Jodie, I— I'll call you. I know some places that are hiring—"

"That's okay," Jodie said. "Don't worry about it." She pressed past Dana and walked down the stairs, pulling Sammie after her.

Dana felt like she was slipping, like her whole life was slipping, skidding out of control. And there was nothing she could do about it.

• • •

Three months Dana went without an assistant and then it was almost Christmas. No one was ever hired at the end of the year. Costs had to be kept down until the print runs began again in February. A girl from the temp agency came every day to answer the phone and help Mr. James with his calls.

Tom stomped in from the warehouse, kicking the snow from his boots and complaining about the weather. He had a high school kid to help with packing in the afternoons, and the kid—Jake or Jack, Dana could never remember his name—kept the radio tuned to rock and roll. He wore thick gloves and a furry hat like Tom's and said the weather didn't bother him in the slightest.

"Seen Jodie?" Tom asked. Dana shook her head. It was a common question. No one knew where Jodie had gone. There had been no word. Dana thought she might have filed for unemployment but that was tricky if you hadn't technically been laid off.

"I bet she got married," Tom said. "Pretty girl like that."

"I bet not." Max laughed. They were sitting around a table in what served as the lunch room, eating from plastic containers warmed in the microwave. "I bet she's president of a bank by now."

Dana often thought about writing Jodie a letter. If ever there was a girl who could write, who wanted to write and maybe even had the talent, Jodie was it. Had anybody told her that? Had anyone bothered to notice?

Mr. James walked in. He was civil and businesslike. Firm, calm, not unkind. He said he was busy, and went up to his office and closed the door. Tom grinned. It was Christmas bonus time, everyone knew. The bonuses were small but still, it was something, and everyone had expenses at Christmas.

At four o'clock that afternoon it took Dana a moment to realize that the extra check that had been laid on her desk was a severance check, not a bonus check. With a start she realized Mr. James had been waiting all along; waiting until he could close out his year-end and pull that last cook-book off press. Soon enough he'd be back from his Italian vacation and he'd hire a new girl—a girl who would work at half Dana's salary. A girl willing to pay her dues.

She thought of tearing it up, or stalking into Mr. James's office and lay-ing it on his desk. Or maybe throwing it. That would be a satisfying thing to do. With justice, too. But finally she simply stood and tucked the check in her purse. There was nothing in her office she needed to take. She said goodnight to the temp girl—"You're leaving early?" she inquired—and Dana walked out to the parking lot, where her car was covered with a new film of snow.

15

Vacation Days

Alice Elliott Dark

Diane wakes up abruptly and looks at the alarm clock. 5:45. Her stomach clenches. She'd set it for half an hour earlier, she always got up at 5:15, that was the latest she could afford to wake up and still make it from Brooklyn to New Jersey by 9 a.m. What had gone wrong? She couldn't afford a new clock, that is her first thought. She fills with anxiety at the thought of having to buy anything at all right now, when she is faced with letters nearly every day threatening her with terrible things if she doesn't pay her medical bill. She runs her fingers over the back of the clock and discovers that she forgot to pull the buzzer out. That's a small relief; it isn't broken. But she will be late for work.

She gets out of bed, puts her feet in her slippers and pulls on her robe, and goes out her door and down the hall to the communal bathroom to pee and shower. She is in luck; it is empty. The minute she is under the warm water, however, there is pounding on the door and she washes quickly and leaves. The man waiting leers at her as she brushes past him. She senses his hand reaching for her but she ducks away and runs back down the hall. When she reaches her apartment she is wheezing. She had pneumonia in the winter and fainted on the street, so someone called an ambulance. She told the people there as soon as she was conscious that she couldn't pay and the Indian doctor told her not to worry about it, but still the letters come. She has been trying to pay ten dollars every week but it isn't enough to make the letters stop. She is frightened the people will report her to the

INS. She had a weekend job at a supermarket near her apartment cleaning and sweeping but she missed a weekend because of her shoulder and she was fired. Her shoulder still hurts. It had hurt so much in the night that she woke up every time she moved. She has been taking Motrin but it doesn't help.

A woman who goes to the park where she brings the children she watches is a physical therapist. She is a mother, not a babysitter. She noticed Diane's trouble with her shoulder and told her the only way it would get better would be to stop using it for a few weeks. Diane thanked her. There was nothing more to say. The children were six, two, and nine months. She had one of them in her arms or on her lap at nearly all times. Rest her shoulder?

The woman saw her face. "Do your best not to use it," she said, "and try this."

She put her hand in her purse and swished it around, as if she were washing clothes in the sink. After a moment she came up with the bottle of Motrin.

"Okay," Diane said, "thank you." She'd become used to taking the things offered her. She couldn't afford not to.

She opens the pill bottle; only two left. She'll have to buy more. The thought churns in her stomach. It is Friday, though. She will be paid. When she spends money on Friday, when her purse is full of cash, it doesn't feel as much like she can't afford whatever it is she buys. She knows the truth, but she likes the feeling of buying something, of being like all the other people around her where she works that buy things every day.

She dresses quickly and leaves the house. It is a pretty day, but it will be hot. She doesn't mind. It is very hot where she comes from, so this kind of weather feels familiar to her. In winter she is always freezing and homesick. Most of all she hates cold rain that soaks through her shoes.

She runs to the subway and swipes her Metrocard through the turnstile. The cost of her commute is $15.30 a day. She has friends in the playground whose employers pay their transportation, but she has never worked for a lady who has offered. The lady now, Mrs. Gwen, pays her eight dollars an hour for a ten-hour day, so she makes $400 a week. Her room costs $700 a month, her transportation to work $306, her cell phone $49, and she sends home $100 a month to her mother to help pay for the two children she left behind in Jamaica. At the end of the month she has no money. That was true even before the medical bill.

She still sends the money home; she wants her children to go to college. One day she hopes to go to college herself. Some of the employers pay for college, but Mrs. Gwen hasn't suggested it. She isn't ready anyway. How could she study when she is so exhausted by the time she gets home that she can only watch TV? She is hungry, too. She tries to eat enough at work to last her through the night, but it is difficult to stuff herself. She has cut back on buying food to pay the medical bill. At the Port Authority she waits. The bus is running behind, as it often is. She gets up her nerve and calls Mrs. Gwen to tell her she'll be a little late.

"How late?"

"I don't know, I think half an hour."

There is a silence.

"I have a thousand things to do this morning!"

"I'm sorry, Mrs. Gwen."

"I know, I know. These things happen. But I really can't wait to pick you up, I have a lot of errands to do today. Can you walk?"

Usually Mrs. Gwen met her at the bus. The walk to her house was another half an hour.

"Yes, I'll walk."

"You can do laundry until we get home."

Diane doesn't mind; she, after all, is late. Then it gets worse; there is a car accident in the Lincoln Tunnel. It is nearly eleven by the time Diane arrives at the house. Mrs. Gwen is at home, in the kitchen with the children. She must have finished her errands fast, Diane thinks. When she enters the kitchen, the children run to her, and the baby, in his mother's arms, pumps his strong legs. She smiles at them and feels her heart swell. These are wonderful children, they help her forget her own. She cares for them with all her might, and thinks it shows because they love her. Mrs. Gwen smiles.

"They've been waiting for you."

Diane doesn't know what to say. Some of the mothers are jealous. She hasn't seen this in Mrs. Gwen, but she doesn't want to risk it. It happened to her once, and she had to leave that job.

The baby reaches his arms towards Diane. Mrs. Gwen jostles him. "I'll watch them for another minute while you put the laundry in."

Diane carries the heavy basket down to the basement. Her shoulder is on fire. She has to put the clothing in the machine nearly piece by piece. A slow process.

"Diane? Where are you?"

She throws the rest in at once and winces, then lumbers back up the stairs. Mrs. Gwen keeps the house cold, too cold for her. She feels sorry for the children, thinks they are freezing, but she doesn't say anything about it.

"I'm going out to tennis, then lunch," Mrs. Gwen says. "They should eat indoors today, it's too hot to go out."

"Yes, okay." This makes no sense to Diane, though. There is a beautiful patio in the back, with a table shaded by an umbrella. It is much better out there for the children. Diane's mother got pneumonia from cleaning rooms in a hotel, and the doctor there told her it was from the frigid air conditioning that the tourists insisted on. Her country was so breezy, too, a good climate. She never understood why people would come to a tropical island and want to be cold there.

When she'd gotten pneumonia herself, she wondered if her lungs were weak from going to work with her mother when she was a girl.

Mrs. Gwen hands her the baby—her shoulder shrieks—and she takes him and the other children into the playroom. Within half an hour the baby and the two-year-old need changing. They both squirm on the changing table; they think it is a game. Usually she doesn't mind this, but now she has less patience because her shoulder is so sore. "Hold still," she says sharply, and three pairs of eyes widen and search her face. "Diane is sorry," she says immediately. "You are very good." They relax again. She takes pride in her ability to relax them, to keep them even and calm all day.

She makes their lunch and they eat it at the kitchen table. Diane is tempted to open the window but the six-year-old might tell her mother; she will take approval wherever she can get it. She listens when Diane talks to the other babysitters, so Diane has to be careful now. Anyway, it's difficult to open the window with her bad shoulder. Today her shoulder hurts more than it ever has. She thinks when she gets paid this afternoon she should go to the Immedicenter to find out if anything is really wrong. That will be fifty dollars, though, and she cannot afford it. Most likely the doctor will tell her the same thing as the woman in the park—rest it. She can tell herself that, but it can't happen.

She eats with the children and wraps their leftovers in a piece of plastic and puts the bundle in her purse. This will be her dinner. She will save money. On the weekend she can eat pizza, one whole pie lasts for two days.

After lunch she puts them all down for naps and does the rest of the laundry. She is in so much pain she cries. It's actually a relief to cry in the basement where no one can hear her. She cries for a long time, thinking of home. She doesn't want to go back, but she misses the feel of the place, the flavors and aromas that are as familiar as her own hands. This new country is stimulating and she loves many things here, but she cannot shake off the feeling of strangeness.

She carries the baskets upstairs and puts the clothes away. Mrs. Gwen showed her where everything went on the first day, but she couldn't remember it all. She spent a few days after that, during nap time, studying Mrs. Gwen's organization. She takes pride in keeping the house as neat as a museum. It makes her feel like a light feminine spirit whose touch is noticed but unidentified. She doesn't need credit; Jesus knows.

She gets the children up and changed and dressed for the park. She wants to spend the rest of the day outside in spite of the heat. For some reason Mrs. Gwen accepts the park, but not her own back yard.

Diane packs eight water bottles and some snacks and wipes into a cooler and carries it alongside the stroller. The six-year-old likes to push the stroller, which is a help, although it would be even better if the child could hoist the cooler. They manage, though. She winces a few times, and the children notice, but they're too young to focus for long on the pain of another person. She doesn't want them to see, anyway. She wants them to feel safe with her, not as though she is in their care.

She does this well enough that when they arrive in the playground they run off to the swings and sliding board. She follows the toddler around while holding the baby. The toddler is likely to fall, but he is tough and doesn't mind unless he is really hurt. If that happened, she knew what to do. She'd asked Mrs. Gwen in her interview about emergencies, which had impressed Mrs. Gwen very much. A friend of hers was fired from a job for not taking the child to a doctor after a bad fall. The child had gotten a concussion and ended up in the hospital. Diane is prepared, though; she wouldn't make a mistake. She has her cell phone and knows where the hospital and the doctor's office are, and she has the numbers programmed in of the taxi service and Mrs. Gwen's friends. She feels very responsible because of this precaution.

At five o'clock she takes the tired children home. Mrs. Gwen is in the kitchen. She asks Diane to bathe them before she leaves. This is more painful than anything she has done all day. She is so desperate that she opens the medicine cabinet and looks for Motrin. She is in luck. The bottle is full, too. She is tempted to put several in her pocket, but she does not. Two are all right, she decides, but more would be stealing, and Jesus watches her closely, she has felt that since she was small. Leftover food is one thing, because Mrs. Gwen will throw it out. The medicine isn't hers and she must leave it alone. She leans over the sink and takes the pills with water cupped in her hand.

When the children are clean—smelling of baby shampoo—and in their pajamas, she leads them back down downstairs. Now they run to Mrs. Gwen. After she nuzzles them she straightens up, opens her purse, and hands Diane her weekly pay. Diane is relieved to have it in cash. Sometimes Mrs. Gwen doesn't get to the bank and gives her a check instead. Diane has to take it to the check cashing service on Saturday, which is always bad. They take a few dollars out for the service, and beggars stand outside asking for a handout. Diane feels obliged to give them something because Jesus would want her to. But then she is even more strapped, more nervous.

"Diane, I want to discuss vacation with you."

"Okay."

Last summer she'd worked for another family who'd taken her with them to the beach for two weeks. Then they hired an au pair, who was cheaper, so Diane took this job. She hoped to move to the town so her commute wouldn't be so bad, but the apartments here required first and last month's rent and she hadn't been able to save it yet.

"We're going away on August 1 for three weeks so we won't be needing you. But—I spoke to my husband and we have decided to give you one full week's pay, even though you won't be working."

Mrs. Gwen smiles. Diane tries to smile back, but she is thinking about the two weeks' pay she won't be receiving. What is she going to do?

"It will be a nice break for you. You can rest up."

"I need to work," she said flatly.

"But you deserve a vacation, Diane."

She says nothing. She is afraid she will cry if she speaks.

"Well I want you to stay with us," Mrs. Gwen says. "Maybe one of my friends could use you while we're gone. Would you like that?"

"Okay, Mrs. Gwen."

"I'll make some calls, all right?"

"Thank you."

. . .

Gwen Hastings puts her fragrant children in the car, turns on the air conditioning, and drives Diane to the bus. They arrive just as one is pulling away, but she honks loudly and the bus stops and waits for Diane to clamber on. The children wave goodbye. On the way home Gwen thinks about what she has just promised. She wants to find Diane something; she doesn't want to lose her. She has her flaws—she is a slow mover, lumbers like an elephant—but the children are happy with her, and that's the most important thing. She can think of a few friends who might want some coverage for August. She'll have to make them promise they won't pay more than she does. She doesn't want Diane spirited away.

16

It's All in the Numbers

The Toll Discrimination Takes

Risa L. Lieberwitz

The stories in this section raise questions about work requirements and family responsibilities that block women's professional advancement. In "Artifact," the unnamed female narrator, an emergency medical technician (EMT), enters a male-dominated occupation, marked by a sort of "cowboy" or macho ethos. The narrator in the story must show that she is tough enough to handle the job, all the while knowing that her male colleague Martin has trouble coping with the stress. She has become "a crack medic," even professionally and personally stronger than Martin. Motivated by their personal relationship, she helps cover Martin's growing drug problem—until she confronts him. The narrator is concerned for Martin but, as importantly, for the welfare of the patients. Yet the women EMTs hear comments from clients who doubt they can do the work. Supervisors still question whether experienced women EMTs have the stamina to do the job without a male partner.

What do women need to do to work in dangerous jobs, such as being an EMT, a firefighter, or a police officer? Will women's physical differences from men prevent them from doing the job? The narrator in "Artifact" can physically do the work, maybe even better than her male partner, but what if she had children? As discussed in the introduction, women still carry the primary load for family caretaking. Without family responsibilities, the narrator can be on call for her EMT duties at any time of day or night. With children—and probably primary care duties—could she still fulfill these job requirements? Should an employer be obligated to change a job to match the realities of women's lives?

"Final Cut" and "Vacation Days" both deal with work and family, although the women in the stories are affected in different ways. Jodie, in "Final Cut," is a single working mother panicking. How can she find adequate day care for her child? Beginning a new job, she goes to enormous lengths to hide from her employer that caring for her sick daughter is what accounts for her tardiness as well as her absences from work. Working women with children, like Jodie, face a dilemma. They try to balance and reconcile contradictory societal institutions—work and family. But the "normal" work day demands that women arrive early and stay into the early evening. An infant's or a small child's needs cannot be met with this schedule. Neither day care centers nor schools take sick children or children on snow days and bank holidays. So, how can this dilemma be resolved?

Gwen Hastings, in "Vacation Days," is a wealthy suburban wife and mother who hires Diane to clean her house and watch her three children. If Gwen decides to get a job, she is in a different position from Jodie in "Final Cut." Gwen can make her family life fit with her work schedule by increasing Diane's work hours. But is it optimal for wealthy women like her to succeed by shifting their family duties to low-wage women workers? How does this cut across racial lines? How often do white middle-class women hire women of color for domestic labor? Diane does her best to survive without a visa for work in the United States. She has children too—who must stay in Jamaica while she works in the United States. What is more, without a work visa and living in poverty, Diane is completely dependent on women like Gwen.

The women in these stories face workplace problems that did not occur because of an employer's intentional discrimination. But does this mean that there was no sex discrimination? What happens when a company, an industry, or a whole profession facilitates sexism and racism? What happens when the rules of the game behind institutional sexism and racism are so clear that patterns begin to emerge? And what happens when hiring and promotion practices become so deeply imbedded in an institution that no one can point fingers, but the negative effects of the practice on women and people of color can be documented and quantified?

Going Beyond Intent: The Unlawful Effects
of Employment Practices

Finding the "smoking gun" or other strong proof of an employer's discriminatory intent is hard. Nonetheless, there is a second means of proving employment discrimination called "disparate impact" theory. Put simply, this theory eliminates the element of intent. It challenges job requirements that employers use on a daily basis that exclude women.[1] Without considering an employer's intent, this approach opens the door to eliminating institutional or systemic discrimination against women and other protected groups. Federal courts scrutinize the impact of an employer's practices, not the employer's intent behind these practices.

On first glance some job requirements reflect "common sense." For example the employer in "Artifact" might require a weight-lifting test for the EMT drivers. But Title VII requires that an employer go further, proving that these requirements are necessary. A weight-lifting test unlawfully discriminates if it disproportionately excludes women—that is, unless an employer proves its necessity for the job. Undoubtedly, the EMT company could show that the drivers require a certain level of physical strength to lift and move bodies and equipment in emergencies. But even if this employer demonstrates that strength is a "business necessity," a woman protesting discrimination could win by showing that alternative practices do not exclude women. For example, since two EMTs always work together as partners and can assist each other, a single EMT need not lift the full weight.

If courts scrutinize the uneven effects of employer practices, will this help restructure the workplace and achieve greater substantive equality for women as well as other protected groups? Could Title VII eliminate employment practices that the Supreme Court has described as "built-in headwinds" of discrimination?[2]

The Supreme Court Considers the Impact of Employers' Actions

The Supreme Court created the legal theory of "disparate impact." These words do not appear in the words of Title VII as enacted in 1964. In its landmark 1971 decision of *Griggs v. Duke Power Co.*, the Court concluded that eliminating job requirements with a discriminatory effect advances the Title VII goal of achieving "equality of employment opportunities."[3] Ironically, the Court adopted this approach in a case with strong evidence that the employer intended to discriminate on the basis of race. Duke Power Company had a long history of overt racism prior to passage of the Civil Rights Act of 1964.[4]

After Title VII was enacted, Duke Power no longer openly discriminated. Rather, this company started using job requirements that caused racial segregation. All hires and transfers into jobs other than the low-paid jobs in the labor department now had to have a high school diploma and pass two written aptitude tests measuring reading comprehension skills.[5]

Instead of relying on evidence of Duke Power's intentional discrimination, the Court examined the effects of the employer's actions. Justice Warren E. Burger, writing for a unanimous Court, found that the job requirements "operate[d] to 'freeze' the status quo of prior discriminatory employment practices."[6] On the surface, Duke Power seemed to treat all job applicants equally by requiring everyone to have a high school degree and to pass the two tests. But in reality, the job requirements kept African Americans out of the better jobs at a significantly higher rate than white applicants. African Americans were far less likely to graduate from high school than whites and passed the two written tests at a much lower rate.[7]

The Court attributed these uneven results to the disadvantages African Americans had faced in racially segregated schools. This history created a current reality that the employer's neutrally stated job requirements excluded African American employees from the more desirable jobs at Duke Power. The employer's intent was irrelevant. What matters most was that practices deeply imbedded into the workplace created discriminatory exclusions as effectively as intentional discrimination. "[G]ood intent or absence of discriminatory intent," wrote Chief Justice Burger, "does not redeem employment procedures or testing mechanisms that operate as 'built-in headwinds' for minority groups and are unrelated to measuring job capability."[8]

But how is discrimination proved without examining an employer's intent? First, a woman or a person of color must show that a "neutral" employment practice has a disproportionately negative impact on the protected group. In some cases, like *Griggs*, the effects are so great that the discriminatory result is obvious. In less clear cases, most courts use a mathematical 80 percent "rule of thumb" to compare different groups' success rates in meeting the job requirements. For example, what if the EMT company in "Artifact" required that all EMT applicants be able to lift one hundred pounds? Women charging sex discrimination would need to show that women passed the required test at a rate of less than 80 percent of the pass rate of men. If so, the court would likely find that the weight-lifting test had a disproportionately negative impact on women.[9]

Next, employers must defend themselves by justifying their use of a particular employment practice. The key is that the employer must prove that the job requirement—such as the high school diploma in *Griggs*—is needed to do the job. In Justice Burger's words, the "touchstone is business necessity."[10] Duke Power's vice president testified that the requirements would "improve the overall quality of the workforce."[11] But, this statement came nowhere close to proving a "demonstrable relationship" between the requirements and "successful performance of the jobs."[12] In fact, employees already on the job who had not completed high school nor taken the tests stayed in their positions and continued to perform competently.[13]

Similarly, the EMT company in "Artifact" could not rely on generalizations that EMTs should be strong enough to lift a hundred pounds. Such assumptions may lead to the discriminatory exclusion of women. The narrator and her female partner have run into the stereotype that women are too weak for the job. A patient asks them if they are strong enough to carry her stretcher down the stairs. Their supervisor assigns two men—who are less competent—to go out on a post-hurricane disaster call.

The EMT employer, though, would have a better defense than Duke Power. The narrator and her partner Martin performed difficult jobs such as pulling bodies from under trains and carrying people on stretchers and heavy equipment. But their employer would need to show more than this to defend the hundred-pound weight-lifting test. The EMT company must prove that the test accurately measures the job requirements. Did the EMTs really need to lift one hundred pounds? Was this an important part of the job? Did the weight-lifting test simulate the manner in which EMTs actually lift heavy objects or people?

Even if the employer justifies its weight-lifting test, women protesting discrimination could still win by showing that an acceptable alternative practice exists that does not disproportionately exclude women.[14] As noted earlier, they could show that EMTs rarely lift such weight individually because they work together.

Workplace Practices With Significant Effects on Women

Looking at the effects of employment practices opens a wide range of them to judicial scrutiny. The federal courts could now question whether objective requirements such as educational degrees and written or physical tests or even subjective interview processes were discriminatory. Some types of employment practices greatly disadvantage women. Physical ability tests, seniority systems, leave policies, work day scheduling, subjective hiring criteria, and word-of-mouth recruiting constitute some of the most prevalent practices.[15]

Physical Ability Tests

Women can claim that physical ability tests for jobs such as firefighter or police officer have a negative impact on them. But they face an uphill battle in winning their cases. One exception is found where employers use objective and well-defined physical qualifications. For example, in 1977, the Supreme Court concluded that women successfully challenged the minimum 5'2" height and 120 pound weight requirement that kept many of them from becoming state prison guards. Given their average height and weight compared to men, these criteria excluded over 40 percent of the U.S. female population but less than 1 percent of the male population.[16] The height and weight standards, Justice Potter Stewart concluded, were not job-related nor a business necessity. Although the employer asserted that these requirements could be correlated with a guard's strength, the Court ruled that employers could measure this directly on a case-by-case basis.[17]

Other cases challenging physical ability tests present greater obstacles for employees and job applicants. Like the narrator EMT in "Artifact," women's entry into public safety jobs, such as firefighter and police officer, has been difficult. Applicants for these jobs have had to pass physical examinations that are much more complex than the example of a hundred-pound weight-lifting requirement. In a well-publicized case, Brenda Berkman and other women won a class action suit against the New York Fire Department. These women contested the physical test portion of the exam for entry-level firefighter positions. Berkman and the other women in the class action proved their case with evidence that no women passed the physical exam, compared to 46 percent of the men. Both the federal trial court and appeals court judges rejected the employer's defense that the test physically replicated the actual duties of firefighters.[18] These judges found, for example, that the "dummy test" inaccurately assessed the way firefighters rescue people from buildings. The physical ability test also emphasized characteristics such as strength and agility by requiring the applicants to engage in activities, such as an obstacle course, that had little to do with an actual firefighter's duties.[19]

Berkman and the other class action members won this lawsuit challenging the firefighters' entrance exam. But for them, the lawsuit's aftermath could be described as anything but smooth. While Berkman and the other women became firefighters after they passed a revised interim test, they faced years of hostile environment sexual harassment from fellow firefighters who resented their presence.[20]

Still Berkman, herself, persisted in fighting for gender equality. She filed yet another legal challenge to a new firefighter physical test for job applicants. And although Berkman won this case at trial, she lost on appeal.[21] The judges on the federal appellate court first rejected her argument that the test overemphasized speed and strength—two attributes not necessarily needed for firefighting—but attributes that are correlated with more male applicants than women. And second, the judges spurned Berkman's argument that the test underemphasized aerobic stamina and pacing, two attributes that women generally have more than men.[22]

More often than not, judges defer to employers' decisions to use physical ability tests, especially concerning public safety. At least one federal appellate court, however, scrutinized some of these tests more closely.[23] This court rejected the state employer's defense that police officers in Philadelphia must run 1.5 miles in under twelve minutes. Fifty-six percent of men passed, compared to 7 percent of the women applicants. Applying a stringent standard, the appellate judges demanded that the employer prove that this exact cutoff score measured "the minimum qualifications necessary for successful performance of the job."[24]

Work/Family Issues

Employer policies about work day scheduling, part-time work, temporary leaves, or light-duty assignments hinder women first because they bear children; and second, because women are more likely than their spouses or partners to shoulder most of the family responsibilities. A "neutral" employer policy that denies paid leaves to employees thus has a greater negative impact on women than men. The Family Medical Leave Act (FMLA) of 1993 mandates that employees can have up to twelve weeks per year of unpaid leave for childbirth or serious illness of a family member as long as he or she works for a company with fifty or more employees.[25] This provision, however, is far from adequate. Most employees cannot afford unpaid time off from work.

Jodie, in "Final Cut," faced the untenable choice of staying home with a sick child, thereby placing her job in jeopardy, or going to work while leaving her sick daughter with an untrustworthy sitter. Ward James declared that his "company policy" of one sick day per month "should be enough for anyone." And Dana tells Jodie that "Mr. James" will fire her if she takes more sick days. This "neutral" policy may apply to everyone, but it is harder on women than men. Women like Dana and Jodie are the primary caretakers at home. They cannot fulfill their family responsibilities and their work schedules on one sick day per month. Even the "normal" work day schedule presents a hardship for them. The preschool and elementary school schedules run into Dana's and Jodie's work days. "Preschool started at nine and ended at noon, and Jodie spent a good deal of energy each day worrying about seven to nine and noon to five. There was daycare, sure, but it was expensive—more than half her salary, in fact—and it never seemed to work out." Dana "drove herself crazy trying to get into the office by eight when everyone else just breezed in, no problem. School didn't start until nine, so she rose at six to get the kids ready to take to Alice's, three blocks from the school." Mr. James counts on his wife to take care of these needs, while Jodie and Dana struggle to shape their family lives to fit their work.

Even without the problem of a sick child, employers often ignore how work schedules conflict with daycare or school hours. These so-called neutral policies create serious obstacles for women that can be compounded if a job requires long or unpredictable hours, or much travel. Clearly, the narrator in "Artifact" would not fit the workplace culture of EMT drivers if she had family duties that prevented her from fulfilling basic working conditions of unpredictable hours. Dana, in "Final Cut," has put her career aspirations on hold until her children get older. Jodie wonders how Dana can even manage to go to a publishing conference. Who will take care of her children?

Further, employers with limited leave policies disadvantage working women who seek maternity leave beyond the period for childbirth prescribed by the FMLA. Only fourteen years after the passage of this law, the EEOC did finally recognize some of the problems associated with balancing work and family. As a result, this federal agency issued a new "enforcement guidance" in 2007 that can help employers and employees evaluate their workplace policies and practices. The EEOC's document underscores how employers can avoid policies and practices that intentionally discriminate against women or harm pregnant employees and mothers responsible for taking care of their families' child care duties.[26] This said, the EEOC did not observe that an employer's scheduling and leave policies necessarily have discriminatory effects on women. What accounts for this omission? One explanation is that most of the legal challenges to these policies that negatively affect, but do not intend to single out women, have rarely succeeded in the federal courts.[27]

Feminist legal theorists argue that the federal courts should use Title VII to address these common employment policies that hinder working women. Rather than forcing women to fit into the workplace schedule, they contend that institutional practices should accommodate the reality of women's lives. As long as women carry the primary caretaking role in their families, workplace scheduling, travel, and leave policies will adversely affect them.[28] Most federal court judges, however, take a deferential attitude toward employers' business needs. They do not require employers to make such structural changes under Title VII or any other civil rights law. These judges defend the workplace status quo.[29]

But given the status quo, most women find themselves in Jodie's predicament. They must adjust their family lives to accommodate their employer's prerogative over job requirements. While Dana, like Jodie in "Final Cut," juggles work and family needs, her higher salary means that she can hire someone to pick up her children from school. Dana can employ child care workers, shifting her so-called responsibility to other women. Diane in "Vacation Days," by contrast, constitutes a good example of this inequity since she leaves her children behind in Jamaica. Who is taking care of her children? Why must she make a choice between working or caring for her children? The failure of employers or governmental policies to alter the workplace in ways that ease a woman's entry causes a chain reaction of shifting "private responsibilities" from one woman to another.

Seniority Systems

A seniority system by definition means that the employees who have put in the greatest number of years in a workplace receive advantages in promotions and wages. More senior employees are the last to be laid off, and the first to be recalled to work if there are general layoffs. In turn, employees with the least amount of seniority will be laid off first. For women who enter occupations that have been historically male dominated, like the women EMTs in "Artifact," this means that seniority systems perpetuate exclusions. Yet, it is particularly difficult for women and people of color to prevail in legal challenges to the discriminatory effects of seniority systems.

Congress recognized the dilemma between long-standing employment practices and Title VII. The legislators' way of resolving this dilemma, however, came not from undoing seniority systems because they are inherently discriminatory. Rather, Congress wrote a provision into Title VII that allows employers to use the seniority system as long as they did not institute it as a means of discriminating against women or people of color.[30] Despite the fact that seniority systems have a clear negative impact on women and other persons in protected groups, in other words, Congress did not challenge them as "built-in headwinds" to equal status.[31]

Uphill Battles in Challenging Discriminatory Effects

Women and other individuals protesting discrimination have had difficulty winning cases that rely on proof of the discriminatory effects of employment practices. Legal expert Michael Selmi's study of cases between 1983 and 2002 confirms this, showing a low success rate for women and people of color, who won only 25.1 percent of their cases of discriminatory impact in federal trial courts and only 19.2 percent on appeal.[32] These rates are even lower than the general 35 percent success rate for women and people of color who encounter discrimination in all employment discrimination cases.[33]

Why do women and people of color seeking relief from discrimination lose their cases so often? One possibility is that federal judges are ambivalent about finding that employers violated Title VII without evidence that they intentionally discriminated against job applicants or employees. Selmi argues that this absence of "blame" may make the courts less willing to find employer liability based on the discriminatory effects of employment practices.[34]

By the late 1980s, even the Supreme Court started showing its ambivalence about cases dealing with the effects of employer actions. In early cases the Court raised some women's and people of color's expectations by setting a high bar for employers to prove that a job requirement was a business necessity.[35] Later decisions diminished this hope. The Supreme Court steadily raised the evidentiary burden on individuals bringing Title VII claims, while lowering it on the defense. In one case the Court did both. It gave people protesting discrimination a broader scope of claims while simultaneously making the allegations more difficult to prove. Clara Watson, an African American woman, had applied several times for promotions in the bank where she worked as a teller. Each time, the promotion went to a white employee on the basis of subjective judgments made by the bank supervisors, all of whom were white. The Court concluded that Watson could challenge subjective employment practices, like interviews, that could be carried out with a disproportionately negative effect on women or people of color.[36]

At the same time, though, the Court made it harder for Watson to prove her case.[37] It required her to identify "the specific employment practice that is challenged" and prove that it "caused the exclusion of applicants for jobs or promotions because of their membership in a protected group."[38] This can be very difficult to show.[39] In "Artifact," the narrator and her new partner Maylene volunteered to be the EMT team sent to work on hurricane disaster relief. Yet their supervisor passed them over to send a team of men who were not as competent or experienced. If the supervisor continues to exclude the women from the more challenging assignments, could the narrator and Maylene argue that this is sex discrimination? Could they successfully identify the supervisor's decision-making process as a "specific employment practice"? Or has the supervisor simply used discretion that is part of his managerial authority?

A Title VII case from 2000 shows the continued difficulty of proving discrimination based on effects of employment practices. A famous Miami restaurant, Joe's Stone Crab, had a "near-total forty year ban on hiring female servers."[40] The women who brought the suit claimed that the restaurant's tradition of hiring only male "tuxedo-clad" servers to promote its "Old World atmosphere," its word of mouth recruiting practice, and its subjective hiring criteria had a disproportionately negative effect on women.[41] The women lost their case, though, when a federal appeals court held that they did not prove that the "Old World atmosphere" was a specific hiring practice.[42] The judges concluded, further, that these women failed to demonstrate that Joe's Stone Crab's practices of recruiting through word of mouth and its subjective hiring criteria caused the disproportionate effects on them.[43] Finding that the women did adequately learn about job openings, the court decided that they had simply chosen not to apply.[44]

Selmi concludes that over time, judges have made it more difficult to win cases that rely on proof of the discriminatory effects of employer actions.[45] His study reports that since the Civil Rights Act of 1991, there have been fewer than twelve cases with "any substantial doctrinal discussion" by federal judges of charges of discrimination based on the discriminatory impact of employment practices.[46] This trend is significant. The 1991 amendments added provisions explicitly prohibiting employment practices that have discriminatory effects on the basis of race, sex, national origin, or religion.[47] Unlike advocates and commentators seeking to reinvigorate litigation against employment policies with discriminatory effects, Selmi proposes refocusing on employer intentional discrimination. He urges greater attention be paid to pattern or practice cases, where statistical imbalances in hiring patterns can show an employer's discriminatory intent.[48]

Explaining Sex-Based Occupational Segregation: Meritocracy or Discrimination?

Why are so many occupations still segregated on the basis of gender? Do the same reasons explain the low percentage of women in physically demanding jobs as in high-status professional jobs? Are these questions related to the differences between intentional sex discrimination and discrimination based on the effects of employer actions? Would women gain equality at work if judges rigorously applied both Title VII definitions of discrimination? Would all workers—male and female—benefit from greater fairness for women?

As discussed in earlier chapters, societal and governmental institutions—including courts, employers, and schools—have relied on gender differences to explain where women and men belong. Judges, bosses, and teachers justify women's primary caretaking role in the family as natural to women's biological differences in reproduction. They tell women that they are innately suited for jobs that emphasize skills of care, nurturing, and support, such as secretary, nurse, or elementary school teacher. Employers exclude women from jobs as police officer, firefighter, or construction worker based on their physical differences in size and strength.

Sex-based occupational segregation seems like a rational outcome if employers genuinely make decisions based on employees' qualifications and merit. Through this lens, women and men choose jobs and careers that best match their innate abilities and priorities. Since men and women have different interests and skills, employers will hire them for jobs where they will excel.

But is the workplace a meritocracy? Do employers hire and promote the most qualified individual for the job? As discussed in chapter 4, employers often use gender role stereotypes about women's and men's abilities. They rely on sex-based generalizations, not individual merit, to exclude women from well-paid and high-status jobs. In "Artifact," the narrator learns the ropes of being an EMT from Martin. And she surpasses him. She becomes a "crack medic" who handles the job stress better than Martin. She even covers for his drinking and drug use. Yet her supervisor still makes assumptions about women not being up to the hard knocks of being a paramedic.

The women employees in "Final Cut" "knew better than to put a family photo on their desk. The kiss of death. All it took was a quip from a co-worker or client that Ms. So-and-so was on the mommy track rather than the career track and suddenly you were looking for another job." Mr. James replaces a talented female graphic designer with a man when he learns that she is pregnant.

If ability, interests, and merit do not explain historic and current sex-based occupational segregation, then what does? Conscious and deliberate intentional discrimination by employers tells only part of the story, as gender stereotypes are so deep-seated that they function at an unconscious level. The Supreme Court recognizes, moreover, that sex and race discrimination is systemic. Judges and juries can infer intentional discrimination based on an employer's long-term hiring pattern of excluding women or people of color.

Scrutinizing employers' actions, regardless of their intent, represents the next step toward explaining discrimination as a systemic phenomenon. Many job qualifications that seem ordinary or "normal" exclude women or other people of color from certain types of occupations. Employers may have consciously set minimum height and weight standards to exclude women from jobs such as prison guard or firefighter. Or they may have chosen these criteria based on stereotypes about what a prison guard or a firefighter should look like—which also results in excluding women. What matters, though, is that height and weight requirements *do* exclude women, that employers should prove these criteria are necessary to do the job, and employers should use alternative practices that could also meet business needs without negatively impacting women.

Systemic discrimination reveals the cracks in the ideal of a workplace meritocracy.[49] Certainly, an employer who purposefully discriminates against an individual woman ignores her qualifications for the job. An employer who intentionally discriminates against women as a class violates the merit principle at a broader and deeper level. Similarly, employers who take actions with discriminatory effects fail to follow the merit principle. For example, the Supreme Court concluded that a state employer incorrectly assumed that large physical stature was required for a prison guard position. Instead, the employer should have evaluated job applicants more accurately by directly testing for the required degree of strength.[50] In other words, hiring applicants on the basis of actual qualifications, rather than assumed abilities, advances a meritocracy. Both women and men benefit from analyzing how job requirements actually function. Employers now have an incentive to choose job practices that genuinely measure success for actual job duties.

In theory, eliminating both intentional discrimination and the discriminatory impact of employer policies will move the workplace closer to a reality rather than only an ideal of a meritocracy. As we've seen, though, the courts have applied these two definitions of discrimination in ways that fail to fully realize the egalitarian potential of Title VII. As Selmi has noted, it is even possible that excessive attention to the effects of employer actions harms the cause of achieving equal rights. He argues that focusing on effects rather than on employer motives creates a false impression that intentional discrimination is a thing of the past.[51]

Selmi makes a good point. At the same time, eliminating working conditions with a discriminatory impact addresses systemic workplace discrimination. Put more positively, employers should take social responsibility to adopt business practices that are evenhanded as written and as applied. Employers would contribute toward a vision of substantive equality by reforming job criteria and employment policies in the context of actual experience.[52] Testing of job applicants should be carefully calibrated to measure ability—to enable both men and women to demonstrate skills that are essential to being a firefighter, a police officer—or an EMT, as in "Artifact." Work schedules and leave policies should enable men and women to compete on an even playing field. Everyone knew that Jodie, in "Final Cut," was an excellent writer and editor. Yet she was fired because she could not comply with a "neutral" policy that disproportionately harmed women.

Will Title VII alone achieve substantive equality for women? The answer is a resounding "no." Congress did not require employers to make fundamental changes to the workplace. Judges defer to employers' managerial control over most job criteria and scheduling. The best parts of employment discrimination law, though, provide some ideas for making progress. Group-based Title VII lawsuits hold the promise to remedy systemic discrimination. But women and people of color need other means of achieving equality—in particular, through social movements. Members of political organizations and unions have autonomy to set their own priorities and agendas for change. Through social, labor, and political movements, women can find commonalities with each other and with men who seek a more egalitarian society.

Dana and Jodie, in "Final Cut," have common needs, but they could not find a way to join together to gain family leave or flexible schedules to care for their children. In the end, they both lost their jobs. In "Artifact," after Martin left the EMT job, the narrator realizes that she can find common ground with her new female ambulance partner and other employees. Her growing relationship with her colleagues may ultimately bring her greater satisfaction in her job. Diane, in "Vacation Days," faces the hardest situation of all. As a domestic employee in a private home, Diane is isolated from other workers, unable to join with other people in the same circumstances. She is not even protected by Title VII, which covers only employers with at least fifteen employees. As an undocumented worker in the United States—without a work visa—Diane faces constant fear of deportation. Diane's situation reminds us that the women's movement agenda must expand beyond middle-class women to include the needs of poor and working-class women in all countries.

Notes

Foreword

1. The UCLA Civil Rights Project conducted the study, http://www.civilrightsproject.ucla.edu/research/metro/discrimination_boston.php.

2. *Betty Dukes v. Wal-Mart Stores, Inc.*, 222 F.R.D. 137 (N.D. 2004).

Introduction

1. *Title VII of the Civil Rights Act of 1964*, Public Law 88-352, *U.S. Code* 42 (1964), sec. 2000e et seq. Title VII prohibits employment discrimination based on race, color, religion, sex, and national origin.

2. Betty Friedan, *The Feminine Mystique*, 4th ed. (New York: W. W. Norton, 1997; first published 1963).

3. Martha Weinman Lear, "The Second Feminist Wave," *New York Times*, March 10, 1968. See Eleanor Flexner, *A Century of Struggle: The Women's Rights Movement in the United States* (Cambridge, MA: Harvard University Press, 1959). Also see Martha Fineman, *The Illusion of Equality: The Rhetoric and Reality of Divorce Reform* (Chicago: University of Chicago Press, 1991); Jill Norgren, "In Search of a National Child Care Policy: Background and Prospects," *Western Political Quarterly* 34 (1981): 127–42, for excellent overviews of the problems associated with divorce laws and the absence of a national child care policy.

4. See Judith Warner, *Perfect Madness: Motherhood in the Age of Anxiety* (New York: Penguin, 2005); Miriam Peskowtiz, *The Truth Behind the Mommy Wars: Who Decides What Makes a Good Mother?* (Emeryville, CA: Seal Press, 2005); Caitlin Flanagan, "How Serfdom Saved the Women's Movement: Dispatches from the Nanny Wars," *Atlantic Monthly* (March 2004), http://www.theatlantic.com/doc/prem/200403/flanagan; Leslie

Morgan Steiner, *Mommy Wars: Stay-at-Home and Career Moms Face Off on Their Choices* (New York: Random House, 2007). Also see Susan Douglas, *The Mommy Myth: The Idealization of Motherhood and How it Has Undermined All Women* (New York: Free Press, 2004).

5. Kristin Luker, *Abortion and the Politics of Motherhood* (Berkeley: University of California Press, 1985); Faye D. Ginsburg, *Contested Lives: The Abortion Debate in an American Community* (Berkeley: University of California Press, 1998); Eileen McDonagh, *Breaking the Abortion Deadlock: From Choice to Consent* (New York: Oxford University Press, 1996); Rickie Solinger, *Abortion Wars: A Half Century of Struggle, 1950–2000* (Berkeley: University of California Press, 1998); Rickie Solinger, *Pregnancy and Power: A Short History of Reproductive Politics in America* (New York: New York University Press, 2005); Mark Graber, *Rethinking Abortion: Equal Choice, the Constitution, and Reproductive Politics* (Princeton: Princeton University Press, 1996).

6. See Arvonne Fraser, "Becoming Human: The Origins and Development of Women's Human Rights," *Human Rights Quarterly* 21 (1999): 853–906; Leila Abolfazli, "Violence against Women Act (VAWA)," *Georgetown Journal of Gender and the Law* 7 (2006): 863–81; Rachel Johnson, "Feminist Influences on the United Nations Human Rights Treaty Bodies," *Human Rights Quarterly* 28 (2006): 148–85.

7. Rachel Arnow-Richman, "Accommodation Subverted: The Future of Work/Family Initiatives in a 'Me, Inc.' World," *Texas Journal of Women and the Law* 12 (2003): 345–417.

8. See Richard Delgado, "Storytelling for Oppositionists and Others: A Plea for Narrative," *Michigan Law Review* 87 (1989): 2411; Laura Gardner Webster, "Telling Stories: The Spoken Narrative Tradition in Criminal Defense Discourse," *Mercer Law Review* 42 (1991): 553–58; Kathryn Abrams, "Hearing the Call of Stories," *California Law Review* 79 (1991): 971–76. Abrams suggests that unlike research that relies on scientific rationality, this narrative methodology does not make claims about universal truths or that there is only one way of "knowing about the world."

9. In scholarship, however, academics argue that women's voices have not been heard. Nowhere is this more the case than with supposedly sensitive, emotionally loaded topics such as rape, domestic violence, and abortion. It was not a dearth of material or evidence that kept these issues off the scholarship screen for decades. Rather, it was their "uncomfortable" nature. Some powerfully written books about these topics relying wholly or partially on narrative, however, broke through, finding readers. In "Hearing the Call of Stories," 976, 995, and 1001–3, Kathryn Abrams explores feminist legal narrative by analyzing, first, Susan Estrich's article on rape, which she calls "courageous and controversial," though her autobiographical narrative is short and only introduces the argument. Second, Martha Mahoney's "Legal Images of Battered Women: Redefining the Issue of Separation," uses stories that "inspire and punctuate." Like Estrich, Mahoney does not make the fiction construct her argument. Third, Abrams lauds the work of Patricia Williams, who relies on narratives to create a new conceptualization of civil rights. And finally, she views Marie Ashe's work on reproduction as too radical since it is not representative of most women's experiences or choices.

10. Susan Antilla, *Tales from the Boom-Boom Room* (Princeton, NJ: Bloomberg Press, 2002).

11. Instead of interpreting stories with a few exceptions, I commissioned short story writers to construct them. It is an active, not a passive, literary act. The intentionality of the storytelling, moreover, represents a "taking back" since, as Kate Millett maintains, "women have not been free to use their own power to name themselves. When a system of power is thoroughly in command, it has scarcely a need to speak itself aloud; when its workings are exposed and questioned, it becomes not only subject to discussion, but even to change." Fetterley, *The Resisting Reader,* xix, quoting Kate Millett, 58.

12. It was Derrick Bell and Patricia Williams who, among others, created the legal storytelling genre to underscore the moral reasoning underlying civil rights and to help understand and explain the persistence of racism in the 1980s despite legal protections. They condemned racism along moral grounds. They illustrated how every African American—even

well-known law professors—experienced racism. See Derrick Bell, *Faces at the Bottom of the Well: The Permanence of Racism* (New York: Basic Books, 1992); Derrick Bell, *And We Are Not Saved: The Elusive Quest for Racial Justice* (New York: Basic Books, 1987); Patricia J. Williams, *Alchemy of Race and Rights* (Cambridge, MA: Harvard University Press, 1992).

13. Critical race and feminist legal storytelling are not the only methodologies that inform this book. It is also undergirded by narrative theory within the field of law and literature and moral philosophy. Narrative knowledge, as Martha Nussbaum and Wayne Booth argue, provides "moral reasoning": "That is to say, the telling of narratives itself becomes a moral action that has the potential to shape the lives of both the teller and the listener, leading to a form of culture-wide knowledge that ultimately determines how human beings rediscover and recreate their individual selves over a lifetime." See Rita Charon, "What Narrative Competence *Is* For," *ajob* 1 (2001): 63; Martha Nussbaum, *Love's Knowledge: Essays on Philosophy and Literature* (New York: Oxford University Press, 1990); Wayne C. Booth, *The Rhetoric of Fiction,* 2nd ed. (Chicago: University of Chicago Press, 1983). James Phelan, "Narrative Theory 1966–2006: A Narrative," manuscript used with permission from the author, offers an excellent overview.

14. Abrams, "Hearing the Call of Stories," 976, 1003. The narratives in this book fulfill what Abrams calls an "experiential epistemology." In other words, it is "the way they claim to know what they know." The stories themselves put forth a theory of knowledge. It is both their *form*—the storytelling and the listening or sharing—and their *content*—what the characters feel and think when facing discrimination—that helps us understand sexism. We know what we know by sharing our experiences.

15. Nancy L. Cook, "Symposium on Law, Literature, and the Humanities: Outside the Tradition: Literature as Legal Scholarship: The Call to Stories: Speaking In and About Stories," *University of Cincinnati Law Review* 63 (1994): 96, 99.

16. Narratives "embolden the hearer, who may have had the same thoughts and experience the storyteller describes" writes Abrams, "but hesitated to give them voice." Delgado, "Storytelling for Oppositionists and Others," 24–37.

17. Nan Maglin-Bauer, introduction to *Cut Loose: (Mostly) Older Women Talk about the End of (Mostly) Long-Term Relationships,* ed. Nan Maglin-Bauer (New Brunswick, NJ: Rutgers University Press, 2006), 4.

18. The ethic underlying these stories reveals that the choice for the novelist is not whether to use rhetoric but rather which type to use. In 1986, Robert Scholes's *Textual Power* became an instant classic by showing how a text's formal features could be linked with the study of texts as ideological instruments. Seeing a book from this perspective put the reader in the position of no longer being a passive recipient of an ideological message. Rather, s/he became an active evaluator of that message. The feminist legal storytellers concur. "The narrative is a means of making connections between readers and authors whose stories are similar," writes legal narrative theorist Nancy Cook, "yet the same concrete detail that allows the reader to connect with the writer also gives the story—and its author—individuality." Cook, "Outside the Tradition: Literature as Legal Scholarship," 95–114.

19. Anne Lamott, *Bird by Bird: Some Instructions on Writing and Life* (New York: Anchor Books, 1994), 105, 108, 109.

20. Narrative theory underscores that people have subjective experiences and thereby bring their own bias into writing and reading. This theory puts the writer and the reader in a position of knowing their roles in history, embracing the idea that "literature is political." See Judith Fetterley, *The Resisting Reader: A Feminist Approach to American Fiction* (Purdue: Indiana University Press Midland Books, no. 247, 1981), xi–xii.

21. Heather S. Dixon, "National Daycare: A Necessary Precursor to Gender Equality with Newfound Promise for Success," *Columbia Human Rights Law Review* 36 (2005): 561–70.

22. Jeff Madrick, *The Case for Big Government* (Princeton: Princeton University Press, forthcoming), see part 2, point 2.

23. Cornelia Dean, "Women in Science: The Battle Moves to the Trenches," *New York Times*, December 19, 2006. Top-tiered institutions report that only about 15 percent of full professors in social, behavioral, or the life sciences are women.

24. Stephen Rose and Heidi Hartmann, "Quick Takes: Women's Earnings and Income," http://www.catalystwomen.org/files/quicktakes/Quick%20Takes%20-%20Women%20Earnings%20and%20Income.pdf. For historical perspectives see Alice Kessler-Harris, *A Woman's Wage, Historical Meanings and Social Consequences* (Lexington: University Press of Kentucky, 1990); Vivien Hart, *Bound by Our Constitution: Women, Workers, and the Minimum Wage* (Princeton: Princeton University Press, 1994); Alice Kessler-Harris, *In Pursuit of Equity: Women, Men, and the Quest for Economic Citizenship in the Twentieth-Century America* (New York: Oxford University Press, 2001). For a good perspective about the women's movement, wages, and unionization, see Dorothy Sue Cobble, *The Other Women's Movement: Workplace Justice and Social Rights in Modern America* (Princeton: Princeton University Press, 2003).

25. Tamar Lewin, "At Colleges, Women Are Leaving Men in the Dust," *New York Times*, July 9, 2006. The U.S. Department of Education statistics show that men, whatever their race or socioeconomic group, are less likely than women to get bachelor's degrees.

26. Quoted from James Wolcott, "Caution: Women Seething," *Vanity Fair*, June 2005, 92–94. Jeanne Whalen and Sharon Begley wrote the article.

27. Women own 38 percent of all businesses (although most are small and struggling in the service sector). Approximately 86 percent of the Fortune 500 companies have at least one woman on their boards. Susan Faludi, *Backlash: The Undeclared War against American Women*, 15th anniversary ed. (Three Rivers, MI: Three Rivers Press, 2006), xi.

28. Dean, "Women in Science," F1.

29. Sacha Pfeiffer, "The Inside Scoop from Women at Top Firms," *Boston Globe*, December 17, 2006.

30. Stephen Rose and Heidi Hartmann, "Quick Takes: Women's Earnings and Income," http://www.catalystwomen.org/files/quicktakes/Quick%20Takes%20-%20Women%20Earnings%20and%20Income.pdf.

31. Andrew A. Beverage, a demographer, conducted a study that showed twenty-one to thirty-year-old women of all educational levels making 117% of men's wages in New York City and 120 percent in Dallas. See Sam Roberts and Christian Maldanado contributing, "For Young Earners in Big City Gap Shifts in Women's Favor," *New York Times*, August 3, 2007.

32. See Arlie Hochschild with Anne Machung, *The Second Shift: Working Parents and the Revolution at Home* (London: Penguin, 1989); Arlie Hochschild, *The Time Bind: When Work Becomes Home and Home Becomes Work* (New York: Metropolitan Books, 1997).

33. Dixon, "National Daycare: A Necessary Precursor to Gender Equality 561–70. In Sweden, 86 percent of mothers with children under three are in the workforce. There is a correlation, moreover, between this figure and pay equity. Indeed, the gap between men's and women's pay is smaller in France than in the United States, where they have free public nursery school and government-sponsored recreation programs after school and during school vacations.

34. Linda Tarr-Whelan, "Long Way to Go in Gender Gap; Attitude Shift Needed to Fully Capitalize on Women's Talents," *Newsday*, August 24, 2006, A43.

35. In addition to Faludi, Joan Williams, *Unbending Gender* (New York: Oxford University Press, 2000) also writes about "choice rhetoric."

36. See Ulrike Liebert, "Degendering and Engendering Freedom: Social Welfare in the European Union," in *Women in Welfare: Theory and Practice in the United States and Europe,* ed. Ulrike Liebert and Nancy J. Hirschmann (New Brunswick, NJ: Rutgers University Press, 2000); Kimberly J. Morgan, "Child Care and the Liberal Welfare Regime: A Review Essay," *Review of Policy Research* 20 (2003): 743–48 (good review of books comparing the United States, Canada, and Australia with references to Europe).

37. Letizia Mencarini questioned more than 3,000 mothers from five different cities

across Italy in an effort to find out what would persuade them to have more children. http://www.doki.net/tarsasag/novedelem/upload/novedelem/document/birth_rate_in_Italy.htm.

38. See Kimberly J. Morgan and Kathrin Zippel, "Paid to Care: The Origins and Effects of Care Leave Policies in Western Europe," *Social Politics: International Studies in Gender, State and Society* 10 (2003): 49–85. Also see Seth Koven and Sonya Michel, "Womanly Duties: Maternalist Politics and the Origins of Welfare States in France, Germany, Great Britain and the United States, 1880–1920," *American Historical Review* 95 (1990): 1076–108.

39. See Eileen Boris and S. J. Kleinberg, "Mothers and Other Workers, (Re)Conceiving Labor, Maternalism, and the State," *Journal of Women's History* 15 (2003): 90–117. Also see Gretchen Ritter, *The Constitution as Social Design: Gender and Civic Membership in the American Constitutional Order* (Palo Alto: Stanford University Press, 2006) for a wide-ranging historical explanation of how the American state created a "gendered" interpretation of the constitution.

40. Statistics from a "Statement of Heidi Hartmann, President, Institute for Women's Policy Research Introduction of the Healthy Families Act, June 15, 2004." She cites the Institue for Women's Policy Research (IWPR) study that took an employee benefits survey, an annual sample survey of establishments regarding a wide variety of benefits available to workers, for the years 1996, 1997, and 1998.

41. Faludi, *Backlash,* "Preface to the Fifteenth Anniversary Edition."

42. Ibid., ix.

43. Kathie A. Smith, "Status Quo Shattered in 'Year of the Woman,'" *Modesto Bee,* November 5, 1992, 1.

44. Faludi, *Backlash*, xiii.

45. Readers may recall Quayle's protesting television character Murphy Brown's "mocking the importance of the father." Ibid., xi.

46. Ibid., x.

47. See Elizabeth Fox-Genovese, *Feminism without Illusions: A Critique of Individualism* (Chapel Hill: University of North Carolina, 1992); Christina Hoff Sommers, *Who Stole Feminism? How Women Betrayed Women* (New York: Simon & Schuster, 1995); Katie Roiphe, *The Morning After: Sex, Fear, and Feminism* (New York: Back Bay Books, 1994).

48. Faludi, *Backlash*, xv.

49. Lisa Belkin, "The Opt-Out Revolution," *New York Times Magazine,* October 26, 2003.

50. Ibid.

51. Quoted from Faludi, *Backlash*, xv.

52. Cathy Young, "Opting Out: The Press Discovers the Mommy Wars, Again," *Reason,* June 2004, http://www.reason.com/news/show/29157.html. A scholarly article exploring this issue shows that 72 percent of a sample of highly educated, highly paid professional women explained that it was their children who were the key factor in their decision to leave the workforce. See Pamela Stone and Meg Lovejoy, "Fast-Track Women and the 'Choice' to Stay Home," *Annals, AAPSS* 596 (2004): 66, 72. Similarly, in her review of *Perfect Madness* Judith Shulevitz wrote, "As soon as I began bearing children I hit, not a glass ceiling, but a brick wall. . . . After God knows how many thousands of books, articles and talk shows on the rapid-aging process human resources professionals politely call 'the work-life balance,' we have had about as much as we can stomach on the subject. We are not zesty, pie-eyed, would-be superwomen. We acknowledge life's limitations and the needs of our children and adjust our ambitions accordingly." Judith Shulevitz, "The Mommy Trap," review of *Perfect Madness: Motherhood in the Age of Anxiety* by Judith Warner," *New York Times,* February 20, 2005, sec. 7, p. 1.

53. Rose and Hartmann (see note 22 above). This statistic is up from 17 percent in 1987.

54. Flanagan, "How Serfdom Saved the Women's Movement."

55. Fittingly, one of the follow-up pieces about this revolution traced how many women attending Ivy League colleges plan on dropping out once they have children. Sociologists have observed that women's liberation has meant more socioeconomic parity among partners. The

lawyer does not marry the secretary; the doctor no longer marries the nurse. This Ivy League story of female student plans for dropping out too is a variation on a traditional theme. Today, a woman might earn the B.A. rather than drop out to get married as her grandmother did, but this does not stop her from snagging an Ivy League–educated husband. Louise Story, "Many Women at Elite Colleges Set Career Path to Motherhood," *New York Times*, September 20, 2005.

56. Linda Gordon, Pitied But Not Entitled: Single Mothers and the History of Welfare (New York: Free Press, 1994). For a historical perspective, see Gwendolyn Mink, The Wages of Motherhood: Inequality in the Welfare State, 1917–1942 (Ithaca: Cornell University Press, 1995).

57. The Deficit Reduction Act of 2005 (PL 109-171) reauthorized the 1996 Personal Responsibility and Work Opportunity Reconciliation Act (PRWOR) (PL 104-193).

58. Belkin, "Family Needs in the Legal Balance." A study done at Hastings College of Law discovered a new use for Title VII called "family responsibilities discrimination" (FRD). Here, the plaintiffs, primarily women, are caring for spouses or parents, not children, and claiming discrimination at work because they are giving care at home. While the first FRD case was tried in 1971, only eight other cases followed during that same decade. From 1996 to 2005, there were 481 cases filed. Like so many evolving subsets in law, FRD cases are not a part of the Civil Rights Act, but the federal courts have responded to this new argument. "Discrimination based on care-giving is not an expressed category," writes the study's author Joan Williams. "It's a reflection of the creativity of lawyers who have set up a new subcategory of litigation within existing workplace discrimination laws" (sec. 1, p. 1).

59. Smith's amendment did not catch either the Kennedy or the Johnson administration off-guard. Attorney General Nicholas Kazenbach, who as the Kennedy and later the Johnson administration's legal craftsman, warned supporters about Smith's legislative maneuvering. To the civil rights advocates, the bigger question was why any southern Democrats supported this legislation? Was it just a clever divide and conquer legislative strategy? For Smith it was complicated. First, he sought civil rights for women only in the workplace under Title VII. And second, Smith was a "sincere feminist egalitarian" when it came to work. Since 1945, he had endorsed the equal rights amendment (ERA). Representative Martha Griffith, the first woman to join the House Ways and Means Committee, threw her backing to Smith. Characterized as a woman warrior, Griffith said "a vote against this amendment today by a white man is a vote against his wife, or his widow, or his daughter, or his sister." "You are going to have white men in one bracket," she added, "you are going to try to take colored men and colored women and give them equal employment rights, and down at the bottom of this list is going to be a white woman with no rights at all." Hugh Davis Graham, *The Civil Rights Era: Origins and Development of National Policy* (Oxford: Oxford University Press, 1990), 133, 136–37.

60. Ibid.

61. Ibid., 133.

62. Ibid.

63. Ibid., 212. Without the authority to coerce employers, moreover, the EEOC had to cultivate a cooperative atmosphere between employers and employees. The EEOC did not dare offend Congress since it depended on it for both funding and authority.

64. See Richard T. Seymour and Barbara Berish Brown, "Equal Employment Law Update," *American Bar Association Section Labor and Employment* (1998), part L, vi–vii.

65. John J. Donohue III and Peter Siegelman, "The Changing Nature of Employment Discrimination Litigation," *Stanford Law Review* 43 (1991): 983–85.

66. Thomas C. Kohler, "The Employment Relation and Its Ordering at Century's End: Reflections on Emerging Trends in the United States," *Boston College Law Review* 41 (1991): 103, 107, and Kevin M. Clermont and Stewart J. Schwab, "How Employment Discrimination Plaintiffs Fare in Federal Court," *Journal of Empirical Legal Studies* 1 (2004): 429.

67. Ibid., 108. Most of the cases that passed the summary judgment dismissal hurdle, moreover, favored the employees protesting workplace discrimination. A 1992 study about

California showed that there were 20,000 on court dockets. If a jury heard the case, about 70 percent of the time, the employees won, with juries awarding the employees anywhere from 300,000 to 500,000 dollar judgments.

68. Ibid., 109. By 1990, the Age Discrimination and Employment Act and the Americans with Disabilities Act passed Congress and were signed by the President, creating two more categories for protection from discrimination—those over forty years old and those with disabilities.

69. *Griggs v. Duke Power Co.*, 401 U.S. 424 (1971).

70. Quoted from the House Report, quoted from Daniel F. Piar, "The Uncertain Future of Title VII Class Actions after the Civil Rights Act of 1991," *Brigham Young University Law Review 2001* (2001): 305. Congress strengthened the disparate impact analysis developed in *Griggs*—offsetting the conservative Supreme Court case making it more difficult for women to prove that they had been adversely affected by an employer's recruiting practices or job requirements.

71. David G. Savage, "Justices Define Employer Reprisal Liberally," *Los Angeles Times,* June 23, 2006, 11.

72. Representative Carolyn Malony, a Democrat from New York, responded to this decision by announcing her intent to introduce legislation in the Democratic Congress that would specifically change the 180-day statute of limitations so that it began the moment a woman or person of color discovered discriminatory pay scales. Martha Burk, "High Court vs. Working Women," *Tom Paine, Common Sense,* June 8, 2007. New York Senator Hillary Clinton also concurred: "It is my hope that Congress can remove the technical hurdles that will prevent individuals from receiving what is rightfully theirs." Along with Rosa DeLauro, a Democrat from Connecticut, Clinton introduced the Paycheck Fairness Act to better enforce equal-pay mandates. Juliette Terzieff, "Maloney and Ginsberg Parry High Court Ruling Run Date" *Women's Enews,* June 1, 2007.

73. *Ledbetter v. Goodyear Rubber Co.*, 127 S. Ct. 2162, 2007.

74. Joanna Grossman and Pamela Brakeman offer astute analysis in "The Failure of Title VII as a Rights-Claiming System" (manuscript presented at the Law and Society Conference, Berlin, Germany, July 2007).

4. Gender Roles

1. See *Equal Pay Act of 1963*, Public Law 88-38, *U.S. Statutes at Large* 77 (1963): 56, codified at *U.S. Code* 29 (1963), sec. 206(d). *Title VII of the Civil Rights Act of 1964*, Public Law 88-352, *U.S. Statutes at Large* 78 (1964): 241, codified at *U.S. Code* 42 (1964), sec. 2000e et seq.

2. Amy Joyce, "Wal-Mart Suit May Force Wider Look at Pay Gap Between Sexes," *Washington Post,* June 24, 2004, E01.

3. David Leonhardt, "Scant Progress in Closing Gap in Women's Pay," *New York Times,* December 24, 2006, sec. 1, p. 1.

4. Jane Waldfogel, "The Family Gap for Young Women in the United States and Britain: Can Maternity Leave Make a Difference?" *Journal of Labor Economics* 16 (1998): 505; Jane Waldfogel, "Understanding the 'Family Gap' for Women With Children," *Journal of Economic Perspectives* 12 (1998): 137; Jane Waldfogel, "Family-Friendly Policies for Families with Young Children," *Employee Rights and Employment Policy Journal* 5 (2001): 273. See Michael Selmi, "Sex Discrimination in the Nineties, Seventies Style: Case Studies in the Preservation of Male Workplace Norms," *Employee Rights and Employment Policy Journal* 9 (2005): 28–29 (discussing these studies in relation to stereotypes about women with children).

5. E. J. Graff, "Too Pretty a Picture," *Washington Post,* November 13, 2005, B1. On the pay gap between traditional female and male occupations, see Selmi, "Sex Discrimination in the Nineties," 38 (citing Paula England et al., "The Effect of Sex Composition of Jobs

on Starting Wages in an Organization: Findings from the NLSY," *Demography* 33 [1996]: 520; Judith Fields and Edward N. Wolff, "Interindustry Wage Differentials and the Gender Wage Gap," *Industrial and Labor Relations Review* 49 [1995]: 116–18).

6. See Selmi, "Sex Discrimination in the Nineties," 32–33, and sources cited therein.

7. Graff, "Too Pretty a Picture," B1.

8. See Selmi, "Sex Discrimination in the Nineties," 32–33, and sources cited therein. Anne Lawton, "The Bad Apple Theory in Sexual Harassment Law," *George Mason Law Review* 13 (2006): 817 n. 129 (citing the EEOC's census data).

9. Lawton, "Bad Apple Theory in Sexual Harassment Law," n. 153 (discussing the "index of segregation" in Daphne Spain and Suzanne M. Bianchi, *Balancing Act: Motherhood, Marriage, and Employment Among American Women* [New York: Russell Sage Foundation, 1996], 94).

10. Francine D. Blau, Marianne A. Ferber, and Anne E. Winkler, *The Economics of Women, Men, and Work,* 4th ed. (Upper Saddle River, NJ: Prentice Hall, 2002), 139.

11. There is a vast literature on the relationship between women's social identity as primary caretaker and their workplace identity in low-paid sex-segregated occupations. See Martha Albertson Fineman, *The Autonomy Myth: A Theory of Dependency* (New York: New Press, 2004); Alice Kessler-Harris, *In Pursuit of Equity: Women, Men, and the Quest for Economic Citizenship in Twentieth Century America* (New York: Oxford University Press, 2001); Joan Williams, *Unbending Gender* (New York: Oxford University Press 2000); Selmi, "Sex Discrimination in the Nineties," 28–29.

12. Risa L. Lieberwitz, "Contingent Labor: Ideology in Practice," in *Feminism Confronts Homo Economicus: Gender, Law, and Society,* ed. Martha Albertson Fineman and Terence Dougherty (Ithaca: Cornell University Press, 2005), 324, 328.

13. *Nevada Department of Human Resources v. Hibbs,* 538 U.S. 721 (2003), 738, in which the Supreme Court held that state public employees may sue their government employers for money damages under the federal Family and Medical Leave Act, *U.S. Code* 29 (1993), sec. 2612(a)(1)(C).

14. See Fineman, *Autonomy Myth,* 55–70; Joan C. Williams, "Deconstructing Gender," *Michigan Law Review* 87 (1989): 797; Katherine M. Franke, "The Central Mistake of Sex Discrimination Law: The Disaggregation of Sex from Gender," *University of Pennsylvania Law Review* 144 (1995): 1.

15. Betty Friedan, *The Feminine Mystique* (New York: Norton, 1963).

16. Blau, Ferber, and Winkler, *Economics of Women, Men, and Work,* 84–85.

17. Legal scholar and Title VII expert Michael Selmi recounts three such polls, including "[a] 2000 survey conducted by the firm International Communications Research report[ing] that 69 percent of eighteen- to thirty-year-olds and 80 percent of forty-five- to sixty-year-olds agreed with the statement: 'It may be necessary for mothers to be working because the family needs money, but it would be better if she could stay home and take care of the house and children.'" Selmi, "Sex Discrimination in the Nineties," 39–40.

18. Regarding the threat that men feel when women enter male-dominated occupations, see Susan T. Fiske and Peter Glick, "Ambivalence and Stereotypes Cause Sexual Harassment: A Theory with Implications for Organizational Change," *Journal of Social Issues* 51 (1995): 97 (discussed in Selmi, "Sex Discrimination in the Nineties," 38–39).

19. "Sandra Day O'Connor," Supreme Court Historical Society, http://www.supremecourthistory.org/myweb/justice/o'connor.htm; and Nina Totenberg, "Sandra Day O'Connor's Supreme Legacy: First Female High Court Justice Reflects on 22 Years on Bench," http://www.npr.org/templates/story/story.php?storyId=1261400.

20. *Price Waterhouse v. Hopkins,* 490 U.S. 228 (1989), 235.

21. Ibid., 251.

22. See Blau, Ferber, and Winkler, *Economics of Women, Men, and Work,* 24, 86.

23. Kimberlé Crenshaw, "Demarginalizing the Intersection of Race and Sex," *University of Chicago Legal Forum* 1989 (1989): 139; Angela Harris, "Race and Essentialism in Feminist Legal Theory," *Stanford Law Review* 42 (1990): 581; bell hooks, *Feminist Theory: From Margin to Center* (Boston: South End Press, 1984).

24. See Dorothy E. Roberts, "Spiritual and Menial Housework," *Yale Journal of Law and Feminism* 9 (1997): 51 (analyzing "the relationship between the spiritual/menial dichotomy [of domestic labor] and the racialized structure of women's work"); Evelyn Nakano Glenn "Cleaning Up/Kept Down: A Historical Perspective on Racial Inequality in 'Women's Work,'" *Stanford Law Review* 43 (1991): 1333.

25. Evelyn Nakano Glenn, "Servitude to Service Work: Historical Continuities in the Racial; Division of Paid Reproduction Labor," in *The Second Signs Reader*, ed. Ruth-Ellen B. Joeres and Barbara Laslett (Chicago: University of Chicago Press, 1996).

26. See Julie A. Seaman, "Form and (Dys)Function in Sexual Harassment Law: Biology, Culture, and the Spandrels of Title VII," *Arizona State Law Journal* 37 (2005): 353–61 (describing and comparing the range of biological and social construction approaches).

27. Williams, "Deconstructing Gender," 801 (describing a social construction approach and critiquing the biological determinism of difference feminists as "encourage[ing] women to 'choose' economic marginalization and celebrate that choice as a badge of virtue"). Also see Franke, "The Central Mistake of Sex Discrimination Law," *University of Pennsylvania Law Review* 144 (1995): 1 (arguing that "equality jurisprudence must abandon its reliance upon a biological definition of sexual identity and sex discrimination and instead should adopt a more behavioral or performative conception of sex. The wrong of sex discrimination must be understood to include all gender role stereotypes whether imposed upon men, women, or both men and women in a particular workplace.")

28. See Selmi, "Sex Discrimination in the Nineties," 34, discussing the tendency to explain sex-segregated occupations as a "natural" result of women's primary childcare responsibilities (citing Robin J. Ely and Debra E. Meyerson, "Theories of Gender: A New Approach to Organizational Analysis and Change," *Research in Organizational Behavior* 22 [2000]: 129).

29. Williams, "Deconstructing Gender," 842–43.

30. See Franke, "The Central Mistake of Sex Discrimination Law."

31. See Richard A. Epstein, *Forbidden Grounds* (Cambridge, MA: Harvard University Press, 1992), 367, 372–75, who argues that "the persistence in differences in employment patterns is that they are desired by employees and employers alike."

32. *EEOC v. Sears, Roebuck & Co.*, 839 F.2d 302 (1988).

33. For commentary on the *Sears* case, including the expert testimony, see Sanford Levinson and Thomas Haskell, "Academic Freedom and Expert Witnessing: Historians and the Sears Case," *Texas Law Review* 66 (1988): 1629; Mary Joe Frug, "Sexual Equality and Sexual Difference in American Law," *New England Law Review* 26 (1992): 665; Vicki Schultz, "Telling Stories About Women and Work: Judicial Interpretations of Sex Segregation in the Workplace in Title VII Cases Raising the Lack of Interest Argument," *Harvard Law Review* 103 (1990): 103; Williams, "Deconstructing Gender," 813–21 (arguing that "*Sears* provides a dramatic illustration of the power of relational feminism to provide a respectable academic language in which to dignify traditional stereotypes. . . . To relational feminists, the key point of domesticity may be women's higher morality; to Sears managers it was that women are weak and dependent, delicate and passive").

34. *EEOC v. Sears, Roebuck & Co.*, 361.

35. See Arlie Russell Hochschild with Anne Machung, *The Second Shift: Working Parents and the Revolution at Home* (London: Penguin Books, 1989).

36. Ibid. Also see Fineman, *Autonomy Myth*, 31–54.

8. Bad Intentions

1. *National Labor Relations Act*, U.S. Code 29 (1935), sec. 151–69.

2. See *Age Discrimination in Employment Act*, U.S. Code 29 (1967), sec. 621 et seq.; *Americans With Disabilities Act*, U.S. Code 42 (1990), sec. 12101 et seq.

3. See Arthur S. Leonard, "Twenty-First Annual Carl Warns Labour and Employment Institute: Sexual Minority Rights in the Workplace," *Brandeis Law Journal* 43 (2004/2005): 145.

4. Deborah A. Ballam, "Exploding the Original Myth Regarding Employment-At-Will: The True Origins of the Doctrine," *Berkeley Journal of Employment and Labor Law* 17 (1996): 92–98; Mack A. Player, *Federal Law of Employment Discrimination in a Nutshell*, 4th ed. (St. Paul, MN: Thomson/West, 2004), 1–11 (discussing employment-at-will and common law exceptions).

5. Kenneth A. Sprang, "Beware the Toothless Tiger: A Critique of the Model Employment Termination Act," *American University Law Review* 43 (1994): 855. Montana is the only U.S. state with a statute protecting employees from discharge without just cause. Wrongful Discharge From Employment Act, Mont. Code Ann. (2005), sec. 39-2-904.

6. In 2006, the unionization rate in the United States was at 12 percent, including public and private unionization. In the U.S. private sector, union membership is under 8 percent. Bureau of Labor Statistics, "Union Members Summary," http://www.bls.gov/news.release/union2.nr0.htm.

7. Since the 1970s, state courts have also made some inroads into employment-at-will by developing common law—or judicially created—exceptions to employment-at-will. These exceptions, such as finding "implied contracts" in employee handbooks, have been developed unevenly in the state courts and continue to provide only limited protection to employees. Sprang, "Beware the Toothless Tiger," 855.

8. Private and governmental employers with at least fifteen employees, labor organizations with at least fifteen members, and all employment agencies are covered under Title VII. *U.S. Code* 42 (1964), sec. 2000e. A labor organization, or union, could be charged for alleged actions against union members, or as an employer against its employees, if it employs at least fifteen employees.

9. The EEOC reports that in fiscal year 2006, it "received a total of 75,768 discrimination charges against private sector employers, the first increase in charge filings since 2002." Title VII charges comprised 45,785 of these. The EEOC also enforces the Equal Pay Act, the Age Discrimination in Employment Act, the Americans With Disabilities Act (titles I and V), sections 501 and 505 of the Rehabilitation Act of 1973, and the Civil Rights Act of 1991. The most frequent allegations in 2006, as in other years, were based on race, sex, and retaliation. EEOC chair Naomi C. Earp concluded, "These figures tell us that discrimination remains a persistent problem in the 21st century workplace" (http://www.eeoc.gov/press/2-1-07.html).

10. See Linda Hamilton Krieger and Susan T. Fiske, "Behavioral Realism in Employment Discrimination," *California Law Review* 94 (2006): 1053 (observing that "[t]he intent requirement itself is a judicial innovation").

11. *U.S. Code* 42 (1964), sec. 2000e-2(m), provides that disparate treatment may be proved with evidence that "race, color, religion, sex, or national origin was a motivating factor . . . , even though other factors also motivated the practice."

12. *Price Waterhouse v. Hopkins*, 490 U.S. 228 (1989), 235.

13. Ibid., 251.

14. Ibid., 249.

15. *Hopkins v. Price Waterhouse*, 737 F. Supp. 1202 (1990).

16. *Desert Palace v. Costa*, 539 U.S. 90 (2003).

17. These facts and further details are recounted in the decision of the Ninth Circuit Court of Appeals. *Costa v. Desert Palace*, 299 F.3d 838 (2002), 844–46.

18. Ibid.

19. The Civil Rights Act of 1991 amended Title VII to add section 706(g)(2)(B), providing that if a plaintiff proves that the defendant was unlawfully motivated under section 703(m), and if the defendant "demonstrates that [it] would have taken the same action in the absence of the impermissible motivating factor," the court "may grant declaratory relief, injunctive relief . . . and attorney's fees and costs demonstrated to be directly attributable only to the pursuit of a claim under [section 703(m)]." The provision also instructs that a court "shall not award damages or issue an order requiring any admission, reinstatement, hiring, promotion, or [back pay]."

20. The Civil Rights Act of 1991, section 102, amends *U.S. Code* 42 sec. 1981 to add pro-

visions for remedies for intentional discrimination claims under Title VII of the Civil Rights Act of 1964, the Americans With Disabilities Act, and the employment provisions of the Rehabilitation Act of 1973. Under Title VII, after the plaintiff proves that the employer was unlawfully motivated, but the employer fails to prove its affirmative defense, sec. 1981a provides for recovery of "compensatory damages," defined as "future pecuniary losses, emotional pain, suffering, inconvenience, mental anguish, loss of enjoyment of life, and other nonpecuniary losses."

21. The new *U.S. Code* 42, sec. 1981a, created by section 102 of the Civil Rights Act of 1991, provides for recovery of "punitive damages" (except against a governmental employer), where the plaintiff proves that the defendant's actions were made "with malice or reckless indifference to the federally protected rights of an aggrieved individual."

22. Section 102 of the Civil Rights Act of 1991 provides that the award of compensatory and punitive damages is made in addition to any back pay or front pay. The cap on compensatory and punitive damage amounts, therefore, does not affect the separate award of back pay or front pay.

23. The Civil Rights Act of 1991, section 102, states that the right to a jury trial does not apply in disparate impact cases, which do not require proof of discriminatory intent. Disparate impact discrimination will be discussed in chapter 16.

24. *Ledbetter v. Goodyear Tire & Rubber Co.*, 127 S. Ct. 2162, 550 U.S. __ (2007). The EEOC filing period is extended to 300 days in states where an individual can also file a claim with a state or local agency, *U.S. Code* 42, sec. 2000e-5(e).

25. Ibid., 2188. Justice Ginsburg was joined in her dissenting opinion by Justices Stevens, Souter, and Breyer.

26. *U.S. Code* 42, sec. 2000e-3(a).

27. *Burlington Northern & Santa Fe Railway Co. v. White*, 126 S. Ct. 2405, 548 U.S. ___ (2006), 2409.

28. Ibid., 2412, citing with approval, *Berry v. Stevinson Chevrolet*, 74 F.3d 980, 984 (1996).

29. *Burlington Northern & Santa Fe Railway Co. v. White*, 2409.

30. Judith A. Winston, "Mirror, Mirror on the Wall: Title VII, Section 1981, and the Intersection of Race and Gender in the Civil Rights Act of 1990," *California Law Review* 79 (1991): 779–80.

31. *Jefferies v. Harris Co. Community Action Assn.*, 615 F.2d 1025 (1980), 1032.

32. *Hicks v. Gates Rubber Co.*, 833 F.2d 1406 (1991).

33. *Arnett v. Aspin*, 846 F. Supp. 1234 (1994). See Nicole Buoncore Porter, "Sex Plus Age Discrimination: Protecting Older Women Workers," *Denver University Law Review* 81 (2003): 79.

34. *Degraffenreid v. General Motors Assembly Division*, 413 F. Supp. 142 (1976). Also see Tanya Kateri Hernandez, "A Critical Race Feminism Empirical Research Project: Sexual Harassment and the Internal Complaints Black Box," *University of California Davis Law Review* 39 (2006): 1269 (noting the "scarcity of intersectional analyses of sexual harassment issues"); Kimberlé Williams Crenshaw, "Demarginalizing the Intersection of Race and Sex: A Black Feminist Critique of Antidiscrimination Doctrine, Feminist Theory, and Antiracist Politics," *University of Chicago Legal Forum* 1989 (1989): 139.

35. *DeSantis v. Pacific Telephone & Telegraph Co.*, 608 F.2d 327 (1979).

36. Ibid.

37. See Anne Lawton, "The Meritocracy Myth and the Illusion of Equal Employment Opportunity," *Minnesota Law Review* 85 (2000): 590–91, 612–28.

38. Ibid.; Jeffrey A. Van Detta, " 'Le Roi Est Mort; Vive Le Roi': An Essay on the Quiet Demise of McDonnell Douglas and the Transformation of Every Title VII Case After *Desert Palace, Inc. v. Costa* Into a 'Mixed Motives' Case," *Drake Law Review* 52 (2003): 105–8 nn. 181–92 (discussing studies showing the high rate of summary judgments in Title VII circumstantial evidence cases decided under the Supreme Court's approach in *McDonnell Douglas Corp. v. Green*).

39. *McDonnell Douglas Corp. v. Green*, 411 U.S. 792 (1973).

40. Ibid., 802–3. See Player, *Federal Law of Employment Discrimination in a Nutshell*, 91–93.

41. *McDonnell Douglas Corp. v. Green*, 804–5; *St. Mary's Honor Center v. Hicks*, 509 U.S. 502 (1993).

42. Lawton, "The Meritocracy Myth," 661.

43. See Daniel P. Johnson, "Employment Law: *Desert Palace, Inc. v. Costa*: Returning to Title VII's Core Principles by Eliminating the Direct Evidence Requirement in Mixed-Motive Cases," *Oklahoma Law Review* 57 (2004): 415, 426 n.88.

44. *Desert Palace, Inc. v. Costa.*

45. At this point, the employer may try to lower its damages with its defense that it would have taken the same action anyway.

46. *Dare v. Wal-Mart Stores, Inc.*, 267 F. Supp. 2d 987 (2003) (decided by a federal district court in the Eighth Circuit). However, in *Griffith v. City of Des Moines*, 387 F.3d 733 (2004), the Eighth Circuit Court of Appeals held that the *McDonnell Douglas* pretext analysis still applies at the summary judgment stage. See William R. Corbett, "An Allegory of the Cave and the Desert Palace," *Houston Law Review* 41 (2005): 1549 n.72.

47. See *Rachid v. Jack in the Box*, 376 F.2d 309 (2004); *McGinest v. GTE Serv. Corp.*, 360 F.3d 1103 (2004); Corbett, "An Allegory of the Cave and the Desert Palace," 1565 n. 71.

48. *U.S. Code* 42, sec. 2000e-2(e)(1) (permitting job qualifications on the basis of "religion, sex, or national origin in those certain instances where religion, sex, or national origin is a bona fide occupational qualification reasonably necessary to the normal operation of that particular business or enterprise").

49. *Phillips v. Martin Marietta Corp.*, 400 U.S. 542 (1971).

50. *United Automobile Workers v. Johnson Controls, Inc.*, 499 U.S. 187 (1991): 211.

51. Ibid., 204.

52. Ibid., 207.

53. *U.S. Code* 42, sec. 2000e(k).

54. *United Automobile Workers v. Johnson Controls, Inc.*, 204.

55. *Jones v. Hinds General Hospital*, 666 F. Supp. 933 (1987) (catheterization procedures); *Torres v. Wisconsin Dept. of Health & Social Serv.*, 859 F.2d 1523 (1988) (searches of prisoners' body cavities).

56. 29 C.F.R. 1604.2, sec.(a)(1)(iii) (2002). Courts have been more deferential toward employer privacy arguments than authenticity defined in terms of having sexually attractive women in jobs such as waitresses. See Kimberly A. Yuracko, "Private Nurses and Playboy Bunnies: Explaining Permissible Sex Discrimination," *California Law Review* 92 (2004): 155–60.

57. *Dothard v. Rawlinson*, 433 U.S. 321 (1977), 336.

58. Ibid., 343 (quoting *Phillips v. Martin Marietta Corp.*, 545).

59. E. J. Graff, "Too Pretty a Picture," *Washington Post*, November 13, 2005, B1.

60. See Porus P. Cooper, "Gender Gap at Law Firms," *Philadelphia Inquirer*, July 4, 2005 (stating that women comprise more than 30% of lawyers in Philadelphia, but only 16% of managing partners). Also see Lisa M. Fairfax, "Women and the 'New' Corporate Governance: Clogs in the Pipeline: The Mixed Data on Women Directors and Continued Barriers to their Advancement," *Maryland Law Review* 65 (2006): 584–85. (In 2003, women held 16% of available seats on boards of directors of Fortune 100 firms, and 13.6% of available board seats in Fortune 500 companies; in 1995, women had held 9.5% of board seats in Fortune 500 firms; in 2003, women of color held 3% of board seats in Fortune 500 companies; in 1999, women of color held 2.5% of board seats in Fortune 500 companies.)

61. See *International Brotherhood of Teamsters v. United States*, 431 U.S. 324 (1977).

62. The Supreme Court's 2007 *Ledbetter* decision would not bar the women's claim that the employer's pay system discriminated on the basis of sex, even though they filed the claim more than 180 days after the initial pay structure was created. Each paycheck under a discriminatory system triggers a new period to file a charge. *Ledbetter v. Goodyear Tire & Rubber Co., Inc.*, 2172–74.

63. Michael Selmi, "Sex Discrimination in the Nineties, Seventies Style: Case Studies in

the Preservation of Male Workplace Norms," *Employee Rights and Employment Policy Journal* 9 (2005): 5.

64. Ibid.

65. On its website, Pricewaterhouse Coopers (the result of a 1998 merger between Pricewaterhouse and Coopers) acknowledges this problem, stating: "Women represent half of our global workforce at the recruitment level, but only 13 percent of the partnership. Although great progress has been made to help women climb the corporate ladder, we know we need to do more." "Women at Pricewaterhouse Coopers: A Leadership Challenge," at http://www.pwc.com/extweb/home.nsf/docid/6E4B7AC62BA3EE0985257364006A43AD.

66. In 2003, "approximately 16 percent of the brokers and 12 percent of the branch managers were women." Ibid., 6.

67. Ibid., 7–8.

68. Ibid., 9–12.

69. Ibid., 7–12. Merrill Lynch pledged to hire more women for a period of five years, but did not meet these goals, without consequence. Ibid., 9.

70. Ibid., 10.

71. Ibid., 8–10.

72. Joan C. Williams and Elizabeth S. Westfall, "Deconstructing the Maternal Wall: Strategies for Vindicating the Civil Rights of 'Careers' in the Workplace," *Duke Journal of Gender Law and Policy* 13 (2006): 31.

73. Michelle A. Travis, Arthur S. Leonard, Joan Chalmers Williams, and Miriam A. Cherry, "Gender Stereotyping: Expanding the Boundaries of Title VII: Proceedings of the 2006 Annual Meeting, Association of American Law Schools, Section on Employment Discrimination Law," *Employee Rights and Employment Policy Journal* 10 (2006): 285–94 (remarks by Joan C. Williams).

74. Ibid., 289–92.

75. Selmi, "Sex Discrimination in the Nineties," 15; Vicki Schultz, "Telling Stories about Women in Title VII Cases: Raising the Lack of Interest Argument." *Harvard Law Review* 103 (1990): 1749.

76. *Dukes v. Wal-Mart Stores, Inc.*, 222 F.R.D. 137 (2004), affirmed, 2007 U.S. App. LEXIS 28558 (9th Cir. 2007) (certifying the class for: "All women employed at any Wal-Mart domestic retail store at any time since December 26, 1998, who have been or may be subjected to Wal-Mart's challenged pay and management track promotions policies and practices"). Also see Bloomberg News, "Court Again Upholds Class-Action Sex-Bias Lawsuit," *Chicago Tribune*, December 12, 2007, 2.

77. Winnie Chau, "Something Old, Something New, Something Borrowed, Something Blue and a Silver Sixpence for her Shoe: *Dukes v. Wal-Mart* & Sex Discrimination Class Actions," *Cardozo Journal of Law and Gender* 12 (2006): 986.

78. *Dukes v. Wal-Mart Stores, Inc.*

79. Ibid.

80. See Selmi, "Sex Discrimination in the Nineties," 2 n. 3 (citing a Wal-Mart official quoted in the *New York Times* that "women's lack of interest in managerial jobs helped explain the lower percentage of women managers"). See Steven Greenhouse, "Wal-Mart Faces Lawsuit Over Sex Discrimination," *New York Times*, February 16, 2003, A22. Wal-Mart also contends that it has instituted diversity programs to increase the number of women managers.

81. Schultz, "Telling Stories About Women in Title VII Cases: Raising the Lack of Interest Argument," 1776–77.

82. Plaintiffs "prevailed on the interest issue in 57.4% of the claims" where the employer asserted this defense. Ibid.

83. Chester S. Chuang, "Assigning the Burden of Proof in Contractual Jury Waiver Challenges: How Valuable is Your Right to a Jury Trial?" *Employee Rights and Employment Policy Journal* 10 (2006): 207 nn. 1–2 (discussing a U.S. Department of Justice survey showing that median damage awards by juries in state and federal courts in 2001, including

employment discrimination cases, are higher than median awards by judges in bench trials). See Thomas H. Cohen and Steven K. Smith, *Civil Trial Cases and Verdicts in Large Counties, 2001*, U.S. Department of Justice, Bureau of Justice Statistics Bulletin, Civil Justice Survey of State Courts, 2001, April 2004, http://www.ojp.usdoj.gov/bjs/pub/pdf/ctcvlc01.pdf.

84. Chau, "Something Old, Something New," 994.

85. See Wendy W. Williams, "Equality's Riddle: Pregnancy and the Equal Treatment/Special Treatment Debate," *New York University Review of Law and Social Change* 13 (1985): 325.

86. Katharine T. Bartlett, "Gender Law," *Duke Journal of Gender Law and Policy* 1 (1994): 2–3.

87. See Arlie Russell Hochschild with Anne Machung, *The Second Shift: Working Parents and the Revolution at Home* (New York: Penguin Books, 2003); Catharine A. MacKinnon, *Feminism Unmodified: Discourses on Life and Law* (Cambridge, MA: Harvard University Press, 1987), 32–45.

88. See Bartlett, "Gender Law," 3–6; Christine Littleton, "Reconstructing Sexual Equality," *California Law Review* 75 (1987): 1279; Martha Albertson Fineman, *The Autonomy Myth: A Theory of Dependency* (New York: New Press, 2004).

89. See Joan C. Williams, "Deconstructing Gender," *Michigan Law Review* 87 (1989): 801, 822.

90. See Katherine M. Franke, "The Central Mistake of Sex Discrimination Law: The Disaggregation of Sex from Gender," *University of Pennsylvania Law Review* 144 (1995): 1; Vicki Schultz, "Reconceptualizing Sexual Harassment," *Yale Law Journal* 107 (1998): 1683.

91. *Employment Non-Discrimination Act of 2001*, HR 2015, 110th Cong. (2007) See Ian Ayres and Jennifer Gerarda Brown, "New Frontiers in Private Ordering: Privatizing Employment Protections," *Arizona Law Review* 49 (2007): 587. After three decades of legislative campaigns, on November 7, 2007, the U.S. House of Representatives passed the bill. The bill, as passed, prohibited discrimination against gays, lesbians, and bisexuals, but did not prohibit discrimination against transgender individuals. The bill was not introduced in the Senate. Carolyn Lochhead, "House OKs Contested Rights Bill for Gays," *San Francisco Chronicle*, November 8, 2007, A1.

92. See Lochhead, "House OKs Contested Rights Bill for Gays," A1.

93. See *United Steelworkers of America v. Weber*, 443 U.S. 193 (1979) (upholding the validity of a training program that reserved 50% of the spaces for blacks); *Johnson v. Transportation Agency*, 480 U.S. 616 (1987) (upholding the validity of the employer's implementation of an affirmative action plan to promote a woman to a job as road dispatcher).

94. See Anna M. Archer, "Shopping for a Collective Voice When Unionization Is Unattainable: 1.6 Million Women Speak Up in *Dukes v. Wal-Mart Stores, Inc.*," *Houston Law Review* 42 (2005): 841, 863.

95. Ibid., 862–63; Michael Barbaro, "Wal-Mart Says Inquiry Names Ousted Official," *Washington Post*, April 23, 2005, E1; Liza Featherstone, "Will Labor Take the Wal-Mart Challenge," *The Nation*, June 28, 2004, http://www.thenation.com/doc/20040628/featherstone.

96. Anthony Bianco, "No Union Please, We're Wal-Mart," *Business Week Online*, February 13, 2006, http://www.businessweek.com/magazine/content/06_07/b3971115.htm.

97. Archer, "Shopping for a Collective Voice," 862–63 nn. 155, 156.

98. Bureau of Labor Statistics, "Union Members Summary," http://www.bls.gov/news.release/union2.nr0.htm (including public-sector employees, unionization rate was at 12% in 2006).

99. See Vicky Lovell, Xue Song, and April Shaw, "The Benefits of Unionization for Workers in the Retail Food Industry," Institute for Women's Policy Research, Washington, DC, 2002, 1, http://www.iwpr.org/pdf/c352.pdf.

100. See Lea Grundy and Netsy Firestein, "Changing Work in America Series: Work, Family, and the Labor Movement" (Berkeley, CA: Labor Project for Working Families, 1997), http://www.working-families.org/organize/pdf/workfamily_labormovement.pdf; Robert Drago and Jennifer Fazioli, "Unions and Work and Family Integration," in *Work-Family Encyclopedia*, ed. Steven Sweet and Judi Casey, Sloan Work and Family Research Network

(Chestnut Hill, MA: Boston College), http://wfnetwork.bc.edu/encyclopedia_entry.php?id=
259&area=All (entry for on-line encyclopedia, written March 27, 2003).

12. Sexual Harassment

1. *Meritor Savings Bank v. Vinson*, 477 U.S. 57 (1986). *Williams v. Saxbe*, 413 F.
Supp. 654 (1976), was the first federal district court to hold that sex discrimination included
claims of sexual harassment. See Catharine A. MacKinnon, *Sex Equality* (New York: Foundation Press, 2001), 909, 924.
2. See *Corne v. Bausch & Lomb, Inc.*, 390 F. Supp. 161, 163 (1975), *vacated and remanded*, 562 F.2d 55 (1977) (early federal district court decision dismissing sexual harassment charge as "nothing more than a personal proclivity, peculiarity, or mannerism,"
reversed on appeal to the 9th Circuit); *Tompkins v. Public Service Elec. & Gas Co.*, 422 F.
Supp. 553 (1976), *reversed*, 568 F.2d 1044 (1977).
3. Catharine MacKinnon, *Sexual Harassment of Working Women: A Case of Sex
Discrimination* (New Haven, CT: Yale University Press, 1979). MacKinnon was also one of
the attorneys representing Mechelle Vinson in the first sexual harassment case before the
Supreme Court. *Meritor Savings Bank v. Vinson*, Brief of Respondent Mechelle Vinson,
February 11, 1986.
4. MacKinnon, Sexual Harassment of Working Women, 180.
5. As MacKinnon observes, "[I]t is the social reality of sexual relations, as expressed
in sexual harassment, that 'normally' and every day sexually oppresses women in order to
affirm male sexual identity, as socially defined." Ibid.
6. Racial harassment had already been found by the lower federal courts to violate
Title VII. See *Meritor*, 477 U.S. 57 (1986), at 65–66.
7. Susan K. Hippensteele, "Mediation Ideology: Navigating Space from Myth to Reality in Sexual Harassment Dispute Resolution," *American University Journal of Gender,
Social Policy and the Law* 15 (2006): 43 n.14 (citing Equal Employment Opportunity Commission [EEOC], "Sexual Harassment Charges and EEOC and FEPAs Combined: FY
1992–2001", http://www.eeoc.gov/stats/harass.html); Mary Coombs, "Title VII and Homosexual Harassment After *Oncale*: Was It a Victory?" *Duke Journal of Gender Law and
Policy* 6 (1999): 113 n. 216 (citing EEOC, "Sexual Harassment Charges, EEOC & FEPAs
Combined: FY 1992—FY 1998"); MacKinnon cites estimates that "90 percent of sexual
harassment cases involve men harassing women, 9 percent involve same-sex harassment, and
1 percent involve women harassing men." MacKinnon, *Sex Equality*, 915 (citing Ellen Bravo
and Ellen Cassedy, *The 9 to 5 Guide to Combating Sexual Harassment* [Milwaukee, WI: 9
to 5 Working Women Education Fund, 1999], 64.) EEOC statistics show that the percentage
of men filing charges has increased from 11.6% in 1997 to 15.4% in 2006, as the rate of
charge filing overall has dropped from over 15,000 in 1997 to about 12,000 in 2006.
EEOC, "Sexual Harassment Charges, EEOC & FEPAs Combined: FY 1997—FY 2006,"
http://www.eeoc.gov/stats/harass.html.
8. For fiscal year 2006, the EEOC reports that 45,785 of the total 75,768 discrimination charges against private-sector employers were Title VII charges. EEOC, "Job Bias
Charges Edged Up in 2006, EEOC Reports," http://www.eeoc.gov/press/2-1-07.html.
9. Coombs, "Title VII and Homosexual Harassment After *Oncale*," n. 216, cites studies concluding that the self-reported incidence rate of sexual harassment ranges from 30% to
90%. See Richard C. Sorenson et al., "Solving the Chronic Problem of Sexual Harassment in
the Workplace: An Empirical Study of Factors Affecting Employee Perceptions and Consequences of Sexual Harassment," *California Western Law Review* 34 (1998): 458. MacKinnon, *Sex Equality*, 915, cites research findings that 40% to 68% of female employees report
experiencing sexual harassment at work (citing United States Merit Systems Protection
Board, *Sexual Harassment of Federal Workers: Is It a Problem?* [1981]; United States Merit
Systems Protection Board, *Sexual Harassment in the Federal Government: An Update*

[1988], 11; and Kimberly T. Schneider et al., "Job-Related and Psychological Effects of Sexual Harassment in the Workplace: Empirical Evidence from Two Organizations," *Journal of Applied Psychology* 82 [1997]: 406).

10. For critiques of this paradigm as creating an overly narrow vision of sexual harassment, see Judith J. Johnson, "License To Harass Women: Requiring Hostile Environment Sexual Harassment To Be 'Severe or Pervasive' Discriminates Among 'Terms and Conditions' of Employment," *Maryland Law Review* 62 (2003): 125–30; Vicki Schultz, "The Sanitized Workplace," *Yale Law Journal* 112 (2003): 2061.

11. *Meritor Savings Bank v. Vinson*, 477 U.S. 57 (1986), at 64.

12. Ibid., 61–62.

13. Ibid., 68.

14. Ibid., 65 (quoting *EEOC Guidelines on Discrimination Because of Sex*, 29 CFR sec. 1604.11(a)(1985).

15. Ibid., 65.

16. *Harris v. Forklift Systems, Inc.*, 510 U.S. 17 (1993), 21. *Faragher v. City of Boca Raton*, 524 U.S. 775 (1998), 788 (quoting Barbara Lindemann and David D. Kadue, *Sexual Harassment in Employment Law* [Washington, DC: Bureau of National Affairs, 1992], 175).

17. *Oncale v. Sundowner Offshore Services*, 523 U.S. 75 (1998), 80. Also see Frank S. Ravitch, "Hostile Work Environment and the Objective Reasonableness Conundrum: Deriving a Workable Framework from Tort Law for Addressing Knowing Harassment of Hypersensitive Employees," *Boston College Law Review* 36 (1995): 259, 262 (discussing the EEOC's view of the reasonableness standard as protecting employers from claims for "petty slights suffered by the hypersensitive" from EEOC, "Policy Guidance on Sexual Harassment," *Fair Employment Practice Manual* 405 [BNA, issued March 19, 1990], 6689). See also *Ellison v. Brady*, 924 F.2d 872 (1991), 879 (using a reasonable woman standard "to shield employers from having to accommodate the idiosyncratic concerns of the rare hyper-sensitive employee").

18. *Harris*, 510 U.S. 17 (1993), 22.

19. *Oncale*, 523 U.S. 75 (1998), 80.

20. In *Faragher v. City of Boca Raton*, 788, the Supreme Court stated: "We have made it clear that conduct must be extreme to amount to a change in the terms and conditions of employment, and the Courts of Appeals have heeded this view."

21. Johnson, "License To Harass Women," 111.

22. *DeAngelis v. El Paso Mun. Police Officers Assn.*, 51 F.3d 591, 593 (5th Cir. 1995) (finding that ten articles in the police association newsletter with derogatory comments about women over a period of thirty months was insufficiently severe or pervasive). The court further explained its approach as showing respect to women, stating that "a less onerous standard of liability would attempt to insulate women from everyday insults as if they remained models of Victorian reticence." See Johnson, "License to Harass Women," 141–42.

23. *Hannigan-Haas v. Bankers Life & Casualty Co.*, No. 95 C 7408, 1996 U.S. Dist. LEXIS 16416 (1996). See Johnson, "License to Harass Women," 112–13; Evan D. H. White, "Hostile Environment: How the 'Severe or Pervasive' Requirement and the Employer's Affirmative Defense Trap Sexual Harassment Plaintiffs in a Catch-22," *Boston College Law Review* 47 (2006): 865.

24. *Kenyon v. Western Extrusions Corp.*, No. Civ. A. 3:98CV2431L, 2000 U.S. Dist. LEXIS 391 (2000), 17 n. 6. See Johnson, "License To Harass Women," 115–16.

25. *Kenyon v. Western Extrusions Corp.*, 15–16. See Johnson, "License To Harass Women," 115–16.

26. *Harris v. Forklift Systems*, 510 U.S. 17 (1993), 5 (Ginsburg, concurring).

27. Johnson, "License to Harass Women," 10 n. 156 (citing federal circuit court decisions).

28. Theresa M. Beiner, "The Misuse of Summary Judgment in Hostile Environment Cases," *Wake Forest Law Review* 34 (1999): 101, table 2. Between 1987 and 1998, employers were granted summary judgment in 175 out of 302 cases (58%), meaning that the court

concluded that there was insufficient evidence of sexual harassment to take the case to trial. Also see Anne Lawton, "Tipping the Scale of Justice in Sexual Harassment Law," *Ohio Northern University Law Review* 27 (2001): 533.

29. EEOC, "Enforcement Guidance on *Harris v. Forklift Sys., Inc.* (1994)," http://www .eeoc.gov/policy/docs/harris.html.

30. *Harris*, 510 U.S. 17 (1993), 23.

31. Kathryn Abrams, "The New Jurisprudence of Sexual Harassment," *Cornell Law Review* 83 (1998): 1224.

32. *Harris*, 510 U.S. 17 (1993), 25–26 (Justice Ginsburg, concurring), quoted in *Oncale*, 523 U.S. 75 (1998), 80.

33. For a critique of this defense, as applied in *Holman v. Indiana*, 211 F.3d 399 (2000), see Michelle A. Travis, Arthur S. Leonard, Joan Chalmers Williams, and Miriam A. Cherry, "Gender Stereotyping: Expanding The Boundaries of Title VII: Proceedings of the 2006 Annual Meeting, Association of American Law Schools, Section on Employment Discrimination Law," *Employee Rights and Employment Policy Journal* 10 (2006): 278 (remarks by Arthur Leonard).

34. *Oncale*, 523 U.S. 75 (1998), 80.

35. Ibid.

36. Travis, Leonard, Williams, and Cherry, "Gender Stereotyping: Expanding the Boundaries of Title VII," 278 (remarks by Arthur Leonard), discussing *Rene v. MGM Grand Hotel*, 305 F.3d 1061 (2002) (en banc), *cert. denied*, 538 U.S. 922 (2003). As Leonard notes, "judges walk a fine line between acknowledging that gay employees may be subjected to sex discrimination, not sexual orientation discrimination, when it is their appearance and behavior and not necessarily their sexual identity that is the focus of unfavorable attention." Ibid., 279. Also see Arthur S. Leonard, "Twenty-First Annual Carl Warns Labour & Employment Institute: Sexual Minority Rights in the Workplace," *Brandeis Law Journal* 43 (2004/2005): 152–58.

37. See *Hicks v. Gates Rubber Co.*, 833 F.2d 1406 (1991), 1416–17, expressing agreement with the intersectional theory approved in *Jefferies v. Harris Co. Community Action Assn.*, 615 F.2d 1025, 1032 (1980), and disagreeing with the rejection of the intersectional theory in *Degraffenreid v. General Motors Corp.*, 413 F. Supp. 142 (1976), *affirmed in part, reversed in part on other grounds*, 558 F.2d 480 (1977). Also see Tanya Kateri Hernandez, "A Critical Race Feminism Empirical Research Project: Sexual Harassment and the Internal Complaints Black Box," *University of California Davis Law Review* 39 (2006): 1269 (noting the "scarcity of intersectional analyses of sexual harassment issues"); Kimberlé Williams Crenshaw, "Demarginalizing the Intersection of Race and Sex: A Black Feminist Critique of Antidiscrimination Doctrine, Feminist Theory, and Antiracist Politics," *University of Chicago Legal Forum* 1989 (1989): 139.

38. See Coombs, "Title VII and Homosexual Harassment After *Oncale*," 126 (quoting the court in *Doe v. City of Belleville*, 119 F.3d 563, 586 [1997], which was vacated and remanded by *Oncale*).

39. Vicki Schultz, "Reconceptualizing Sexual Harassment," *Yale Law Journal* 107 (1998): 16871–91.

40. Katherine M. Franke, *Stanford Law Review* 49 (1997): 696 693–96, 762–72.

41. Abrams, "The New Jurisprudence of Sexual Harassment," 1172, 1215.

42. Ibid.

43. A documentary was made about Brenda Berkman's efforts, with other women, to become firefighters. Bann Roy, "Taking the Heat: The First Women Firefighters of New York City," http://www.pbs.org/independentlens/takingtheheat/film.html.

44. See *Jensen v. Eveleth Taconite Co.*, 130 F.3d 1287, 1304 (1997), stating that "the callous pattern and practice of sexual harassment engaged in by Eveleth Mines inevitably destroyed the self-esteem of the working women exposed to it." As the court explained, "This case has a long, tortured, and unfortunate history." After the class action suit was first filed in 1988 and the plaintiffs won the trial in 1993, the case continued in litigation over the issue of evidence relevant to determining damages.

45. Also see Clara Bingham and Laura Leedy Gansler, *Class Action: The Story of Lois*

Jensen and the Landmark Case that Changed Sexual Harassment Law (New York: Double-day, 2002).

46. Susan Antilla, *Tales from the Boom-Boom Room: Women vs. Wall Street* (Princeton, NJ: Bloomberg Press, 2002). Also see Susan Antilla, "Money Talks, Women Don't," *New York Times*, July 21, 2004, A19 (describing women's status at Smith Barney, where they "made up 36 percent of its investment banking division, but took away only 11 percent of the division's payroll . . . Twenty-five percent of the male sales assistants moved on to become brokers from 1994 to 1998. Only 3 percent of the women did"). Antilla describes the firm of Merrill Lynch, which, in 2004, had women in 15 percent of its stockbroker positions, the same as in 1997, when the female brokers sued for sex discrimination. Ibid.

47. *Meritor Savings Bank v. Vinson*, 477 U.S. at 68–69.

48. Schultz, "The Sanitized Workplace," 2063–72.

49. *Miller v. Department of Corrections*, 115 P.3d 77, 30 Cal. Rptr. 3d 797 (2005).

50. See Jonathan A. Segal, "Dangerous Liaisons: Romantic Relationships between Supervisors and Subordinates Can Involve Thorny Legal and Employee Relations Problems," *HR Magazine* 50, December 1, 2005, 104; Karen Ertel, "Warden's Consensual Affairs Created Hostile Prison Workplace; California," *Trial* 41, October 1, 2005, 78; Mireya Navarro, "Love the Job? What About Your Boss?" *New York Times*, July 24, 2005, sec. 9, p. 1. The California court was influenced by the EEOC's policy guidelines that a hostile environment would result from widespread sexual favoritism. *Miller v. Department of Corrections*, 463–66.

51. Joanna Grossman, "Can Consensual Workplace Sex Create a Hostile Environment?" http://www.cnn.com/2005/LAW/07/29/grossman.workplace/index.html; Ertel, "Warden's Consensual Affairs Created Hostile Prison Workplace;" Navarro, "Love the Job? What About Your Boss?"

52. *Faragher v. City of Boca Raton*, 524 U.S. 775 (1998). The Court reached a similar holding in a second case, *Burlington Industries v. Ellerth*, 524 U.S. 742 (1998).

53. *Burlington Industries v. Ellerth*, 765.

54. *Pennsylvania State Police v. Suders*, 542 U.S. 129 (2004).

55. Anne Lawton, "Operating in an Empirical Vacuum: The Ellerth and Faragher Affirmative Defense," *Columbia Journal of Gender and Law* 13 (2004): 235–42, 260–66; Joanna L. Grossman, "The First Bite Is Free: Employer Liability for Sexual Harassment," *University of Pittsburgh Law Review* 61 (2000): 671; Hernandez, "A Critical Race Feminism Empirical Research Project: Sexual Harassment and the Internal Complaints Black Box"; Theresa M. Beiner, "Using Evidence of Women's Stories in Sexual Harassment Cases," *University of Arkansas Little Rock Law Review* 24 (2001): 117.

56. Lawton, "Operating in an Empirical Vacuum," 213–16.

57. Anne Lawton, "The Bad Apple Theory in Sexual Harassment Law," *George Mason Law Review* 13 (2006): 817 nn. 165–66 (discussing decisions that demonstrate the scope of judicial deference to employers' procedures, including the form of complaints required, penalties to employees who fail to complain within a week of an incident, requiring employees to submit their written complaints to the company president).

58. Lawton, "Operating in an Empirical Vacuum," 235–42, 260–66 (discussing the similarities of the *Faragher* affirmative defense and the standard for proving employer responsibility for coworker harassment).

59. *Circuit City v. Adams*, 532 U.S. 105 (2001). The Court interpreted the *Federal Arbitration Act*, U.S. Code 9, sec. 1–16, to permit employers to condition employment on employees' agreement to arbitrate employment disputes and, thereby, waive their rights to arbitrate. Also see *Gilmer v. Interstate/Johnson Lane Corp.*, 500 U.S. 20 (1991) (enforcing agreements in the securities industry requiring investment brokers to arbitrate employment disputes as a substitute for litigation).

60. In *EEOC v. Waffle House, Inc.*, 534 U.S. 279 (2002), the Supreme Court held that the EEOC, as a government enforcement agency, has the independent power to sue an employer for violations of the ADA, regardless of an employee's agreement to resolve all employment-related disputes through private arbitration.

61. Beth E. Sullivan, "The High Cost of Efficiency: Mandatory Arbitration in the Securities Industry," *Fordham Urban Law Journal* 26 (1999): 343.

62. Lawton, "The Bad Apple Theory in Sexual Harassment Law," 847–48, 865–68.

63. Sullivan, "The High Cost of Efficiency: Mandatory Arbitration in the Securities Industry," 343–44.

64. Ibid.

65. Dennis R. Nolan, "Employment Arbitration After Circuit City," *Brandeis Law Journal* 41 (2003): 867–80.

66. Ibid., 874–75. See *Cole v. Burns International Security Services*, 105 F.3d 1465 (1997).

67. See Dianne LaRocca, "The Bench Trial: A More Beneficial Alternative to Arbitration of Title VII Claims," *Chicago-Kent Law Review* 80 (2005): 945–50; Chester S. Chuang, "Assigning the Burden of Proof in Contractual Jury Waiver Challenges: How Valuable is Your Right to a Jury Trial?" *Employee Rights and Employment Policy Journal* 10 (2006): 211–23. The few courts that have examined the validity of such pre-dispute jury waivers have evaluated whether they were entered with "knowing and voluntary consent."

68. Schultz, "The Sanitized Workplace," 2173–93.

69. Marion Crain, "Strategies for Union Relevance in a Post-Industrial World: Reconceiving Antidiscrimination Rights as Collective Rights," *Labor Law Journal* (fall 2006): 158. Also see Ann C. Hodges, "Strategies for Combating Sexual Harassment: The Role of Labor Unions," *Texas Journal of Women and the Law* 15 (2006): 183.

16. It's All in the Numbers

1. Disparate impact cases are brought under section 703(a)(2) of Title VII, which makes it unlawful for employers: "to limit, segregate, or classify his employees in any way which would deprive or tend to deprive any individual of employment opportunities or otherwise adversely affect his status as an employee, because of such individual's race, color, religion, sex, or national origin."

2. *Griggs v. Duke Power Co.*, 401 U.S. 424 (1971), 432.

3. Ibid. This was only the Supreme Court's second decision interpreting Title VII. Michael Selmi, "Was the Disparate Impact Theory a Mistake?" *UCLA Law Review* 53 (2006): 707–16 (discussing the lower court decisions, legal scholarship, and EEOC positions that influenced the *Griggs* Court). See also, Michael Evan Gold, "*Griggs*' Folly: An Essay on the Theory, Problems, and Origin of the Adverse Impact Definition of Employment Discrimination and a Recommendation for Reform," *Industrial Relations Law Journal* 7 (1985): 429 (taking the position that the *Griggs* Court went beyond congressional intent by creating disparate impact theory).

4. Neither the district court nor the circuit court of appeals found that Duke Power had a discriminatory intent in adopting the high school and testing requirements. 401 U.S. at 428–29. Given the employer's long history of discrimination and the fact that it instituted these requirements at the moment of the effective date of Title VII, though, the Supreme Court could have reversed the lower court's conclusions on the presence of unlawful intent.

5. Ibid., 427–28.

6. Ibid., 430.

7. Ibid., 430 n.6.

8. Ibid., 432.

9. See Mack A. Player, *Federal Law of Employment Discrimination in a Nutshell*, 4th ed. (St. Paul, MN: Thomson/West, 2004), 110–18; *EEOC Guidelines*, 29 CFR 1607.3D.

10. *Griggs v. Duke Power Co.*, 431–32.

11. Ibid., 431.

12. Ibid.

13. Ibid., 431–32.

14. *Albemarle Paper Co. v. Moody,* 422 U.S. 405 (1975), 425. The Civil Rights Act of 1991 explicitly includes this standard. *U.S. Code* 42, sec. 2000e-2(k)(1)(A)(ii).

15. See Selmi, "Was the Disparate Impact Theory a Mistake?" 704–5, n.12 (discussing the broad range of issues proposed for disparate impact analysis).

16. *Dothard v. Rawlinson,* 433 U.S. 321 (1977).

17. Ibid., 331–32.

18. *Berkman v. City of New York,* 536 F. Supp. 177 (1982), *affirmed,* 705 F.2d 584 (1982).

19. Ibid.

20. See "Taking the Heat: The First Women Firefighters of New York City," http://www .pbs.org/independentlens/takingtheheat/film.html.

21. *Berkman v. City of New York,* 812 F.2d 52 (1987).

22. Susan T. Epstein, "Women in the Firehouse: The Second Circuit Upholds a Gender-Based Firefighters' Examination," *Brooklyn Law Review* 54 (summer 1998): 523–27.

23. David E. Hollar, "Physical Ability Tests and Title VII," *University of Chicago Law Review* 67 (summer 2000): 785–93 (describing the types of job-relatedness approaches, from most to least deferential, applied by federal courts in disparate impact cases dealing with physical tests).

24. *Lanning v. Southeastern Pennsylvania Transportation Authority,* 181 F.3d 478 (1999). One judge dissented. See Hollar, "Physical Ability Tests and Title VII," 791–93.

25. *U.S. Code* 29 (1993), sec. 2601–2654.

26. See EEOC, "Enforcement Guidance: Unlawful Disparate Treatment of Workers with Caregiving Responsibilities," http://www.eeoc.gov/policy/docs/caregiving.html.

27. Selmi, "Was the Disparate Impact Theory a Mistake?" 750.

28. See Mary Joe Frug, "Securing Job Equality for Women: Labor Market Hostility to Working Mothers," *Boston University Law Review* 59 (1979): 55; Joan C. Williams, "Deconstructing Gender," *Michigan Law Review* 87 (1989): 797; Lara M. Gardner, "A Step Toward True Equality in the Workplace: Requiring Employer Accommodation for Breastfeeding Women," *Wisconsin Women's Law Journal* 17 (2002): 259.

29. Selmi, "Was the Disparate Impact Theory a Mistake?" 751.

30. Section 703(h) of Title VII provides, in relevant part: "[I]t shall not be an unlawful employment practice for an employer to apply different standards of compensation, or different terms, conditions, or privileges of employment pursuant to a bona fide seniority . . . system, provided that such differences are not the result of an intention to discriminate because of race, color, religion, sex, or national origin." *U.S. Code* 42, sec. 2000e-2(h).

31. See *International Bhd. of Teamsters v. United States,* 431 U.S. 324 (1977), 353–54. ("[A]n otherwise neutral, legitimate seniority system does not become unlawful under Title VII simply because it may perpetuate pre-Act discrimination.").

32. Selmi analyzed 130 federal circuit court of appeals and 171 federal district court disparate impact cases in six years during the period from 1983–2002. As Selmi notes, even these low success rates could be exaggerated, since they include remands and employees' survivals of employer summary judgment motions. Selmi, "Was the Disparate Impact Theory a Mistake?" 735–39.

33. Ibid., 738–39.

34. Ibid., 773–82.

35. In an early case that involved required written standardized tests, the Court detailed the employer's burden of proof. First, the employer must use objectively recognized methods to prove that a test is job related, which often requires a professional job evaluation study. Second, such a study must evaluate the duties that are actually important to the job at issue. Third, the employer must demonstrate that an employee's success on the test correlates with his or her success on the job. *Albermarle Paper Co. v. Moody,* 431–33.

36. *Watson v. Fort Worth Bank and Trust,* 487 U.S. 977 (1988).

37. A plurality of the Court took this position. The plurality consisted of Justice O'Connor, Chief Justice Rehnquist, and Justices White and Scalia. Ibid.

38. Ibid. The Civil Rights Act of 1991 identifies the employee's burden to identify a specific employment practice and show that it caused the disproportionate impact on a protected group. The employee charging discrimination can avoid the specificity requirement only by proving that "the elements of [an employer's] decisionmaking process are not capable of separation for analysis." *U.S. Code* 42 (1991), sec. 2000e(k)(1)(B)(i).

39. See *Wards Cove Packing Co., Inc. v. Atonio*, 490 U.S. 642 (1989), where employees alleged that their employer's hiring practices resulted in a racially segregated workforce in an Alaskan salmon cannery. Caucasians held the better-paid skilled jobs, whereas Filipinos and Alaskan Native workers had the lower-paid unskilled jobs. The Court concluded that these employees had failed to identify a specific employment practice that had caused these highly segregated results. Justice John Paul Stevens, dissenting, drew an analogy between "the segregation of housing and dining facilities and the stratification of jobs along racial and ethnic lines" and "aspects of a plantation economy." Ibid., 663 n. 4 (Stevens, dissenting). Justice Stevens was joined by Justices Brennan, Marshall, and Blackmun. See Linda Lye, "Title VII's Tangled Tale: The Erosion and Confusion of Disparate Impact and the Business Necessity Defense," *Berkeley Journal of Employment and Labor Law* 19 (1998): 332–34.

40. Nicole J. DeSario, "Reconceptualizing Meritocracy: The Decline of Disparate Impact Discrimination Law," *Harvard Civil Rights-Civil Liberties Law Review* 38 (2003): 506.

41. *EEOC v. Joe's Stone Crab*, 220 F.3d 1263 (2000), 1268.

42. Ibid., 1278–80.

43. Ibid.

44. Ibid., 1279. Legal scholar Nicole DeSario argues that the claimants would have been more likely to win under the early Supreme Court approaches to disparate impact. DeSario, "Reconceptualizing Meritocracy," 506. Michael Selmi argues that *Joe's Stone Crab* should have been tried as a case of intentional discrimination. Selmi, "Was the Disparate Impact Theory a Mistake?" 777–78. After the federal appeals court rejected the disparate impact claim, it instructed the federal trial court to analyze the case under disparate treatment. The trial court found for the plaintiff EEOC. The appeals court affirmed in part and reversed in part. *EEOC v. Joe's Stone Crab*, 296 F.3d 1265 (2002).

45. Selmi, "Was the Disparate Impact Theory a Mistake?" 742–44.

46. Ibid., 735.

47. *U.S. Code* 42, sec. 2000e(k)(1).

48. Selmi, "Was the Disparate Impact Theory a Mistake?" 779–80.

49. See Anne Lawton, "The Meritocracy Myth and the Illusion of Equal Employment Opportunity," *Minnesota Law Review* 85 (2000): 594–612; DeSario, "Reconceptualizing Meritocracy," 485–93.

50. *Dothard v. Rawlinson*, 433 U.S. 321 (1977).

51. Selmi, "Was the Disparate Impact Theory a Mistake?" 773–82.

52. See Katharine T. Bartlett, "Gender Law," *Duke Journal of Gender Law & Policy* 1 (1994): 4–6; Mary Becker, "Patriarchy and Inequality: Towards a Substantive Feminism," *University of Chicago Legal Forum* 1999 (1999): 52–59; Martha Albertson Fineman, *The Autonomy Myth: A Theory of Dependency* (New York: New Press, 2004) 36–37, 46–47, 178–79, 256–62.

Contributors

C. G. K. Atkins is a recipient of a Fulbright Award, has published articles on sexuality and disability rights, and was a contributor to *Voices from the Edge: Narratives about the Americans with Disabilities Act*, edited by Ruth O'Brien.

Bebe Moore Campbell is the author of the autobiography *Sweet Summer: Growing Up With and Without My Dad* and four novels, *Your Blues Ain't Like Mine*, *Brothers and Sisters*, *Singing in the Comeback Choir*, and *What You Owe Me*.

Ellen Dannin wrote *Taking Back the Workers' Law: How to Fight the Assault on Labor Rights* (also from Cornell) and *Working Free. The Origins and Impact of New Zealand's Employment Contracts Act*. She is the author of over sixty articles and book chapters on labor law and privatization as well as commentaries on the Torah for the Jewish Reconstructionist Federation. She is the Fannie Weiss Distinguished Faculty Scholar and Professor of Law at Penn State Dickinson School of Law.

Alice Elliott Dark is the author of the novel, *Think of England*, and two collections of short stories, *In The Gloaming* and *Naked to the Waist*. Her work has appeared in, among others, *The New Yorker*, *Harper's*, *Redbook*, *DoubleTake*, *Best American Short Stories*, *Prize Stories: The O. Henry Awards* and has been translated into many languages. The story "In the Gloaming" was chosen by John Updike for inclusion in *The Best American Stories of The Century* and was made into films by HBO and Trinity Playhouse. She has received a National Endowment for the Arts Fellowship. She is writer-in-residence on the faculty of the MFA program at Rutgers-Newark.

Kristen Iversen is the author of the best-selling *Molly Brown: Unraveling the Myth*, winner of the Colorado Book Award and the Barbara Sudler Award for Nonfiction, and a textbook, *Shadow Boxing: Art and Craft in Creative Nonfiction*. She has worked extensively with A & E Biography and the History Channel, and her fiction and essays have appeared in numerous literary journals. Her forthcoming memoir, *Full Body Burden*, chronicles her experiences with Rocky Flats, a government facility that secretly produced the heart of every U.S. nuclear bomb. Iversen teaches at the University of Memphis, where she is also editor-in-chief of *The Pinch*.

Harriet Kriegel's work has appeared in *The Nation* and *Commonweal*. She edited *Women in Drama: New American Library*, and was an editor of *Vim and Vigor*, a healthcare magazine. She also wrote, directed, and edited the film *Domestic Tranquility*, which is included in the MOMA collection.

Stephen Kuusisto is the author of *Planet of the Blind: A Memoir*, which was a *New York Times* Notable Book, and *Only Bread, Only Light*. His work has appeared in *Antioch Review*, *Partisan Review*, *Poetry*, *The New York Times Magazine*, *Harper's*, and *Seneca Review*, among other places. He also wrote a short story for *Voices from the Edge: Narratives about the Americans with Disabilities Act*, edited by Ruth O'Brien. He is a professor of creative nonfiction at the University of Iowa.

Catherine Lewis is the author of two novels, *Dry Fire* and *Postcards to Father Abraham*. Her third book, nonfiction, is forthcoming. Shorter works have appeared in *Inkwell*, *Pleiades*, and *California Quarterly*. She is an associate professor of creative writing at Purchase College SUNY.

Risa L. Lieberwitz is a professor in the Cornell University School of Industrial and Labor Relations. She is the author of articles on labor and constitutional law, and academic freedom in the *Cornell Law Review*, *Indiana Journal of Global Legal Studies*, the *Cornell Journal of Law and Public Policy*, *U.C. Davis Law Review*, *Boston College Law Review*, and the *Boston University Public Interest Law Journal*. She coauthored (with Mack A. Player and Elaine W. Shoben) two editions of *Employment Discrimination Law: Cases and Materials*.

Achim Nowak is the founder and president of Influens, an international training and coaching firm based in South Florida that develops resonant business leaders. His book *Power Speaking: The Art of the Exceptional Public Speaker*, is in its third printing and has become an essential leadership development tool in Fortune 500 companies around the world. Achim's nonfiction writing has been published in numerous anthologies including *Voices from the Edge: Narratives about the Americans with Disabilities Act*, edited by Ruth O'Brien. His essay "Deutsche Welle" was recognized with a PEN Syndicated Fiction Award.

Ruth O'Brien wrote the books *Bodies in Revolt: Gender, Disability, and a Workplace Ethic of Care*; *Crippled Justice: The History of Modern Disability Policy in the Workplace*; and *Workers' Paradox: The Republican Origins of the New Deal Labor Policy, 1886–1935*. She also edited and contributed to *Voices from the Edge: Narratives about the Americans with Disabilities Act* and edits the Public Square book series for Princeton University. She is an adjunct affiliated scholar for the Center for American Progress.

Eileen Pollack is the author of *Women Walking Ahead: In Search of Catherine Weldon and Sitting Bull*; *Paradise, New York*; *The Rabbi in the Attic and Other Stories*; and, most recently, *In the Mouth, Stories and Novellas*. She has had stories and essays in such journals and anthologies as *Ploughshares*, *New England Review*, *Agni*, *Pushcart Prize* XVI and XX. She has also written for the *Boston Globe* and the *Washington Post*, among other publications.

Aurelie Sheehan is the author of two novels, *History Lesson for Girls* and *The Anxiety of Everyday Objects*, as well as a short story collection, *Jack Kerouac Is Pregnant*. She is an associate professor of fiction and the director of the creative writing program at the University of Arizona in Tucson.

Sharon Oard Warner has published three books: *Learning to Dance and Other Stories*; *The Way We Write Now: Short Stories from the AIDS Crisis*; and *Deep in the Heart*. Her essays and stories have appeared in *Sonora Review*, *Green Mountains Review*, *Other Voices*, and *The Year's Best Writing on Writing*, among other publications. She also reviews books for the *Kansas City Star*, *The Dallas Morning News*, *The New York Times*, and the *Des Moines Register*.

INDEX